DISCOVER
AUSTRALIA
AND
NEW ZEALAND

Reader's
Digest

PUBLISHED BY THE READER'S DIGEST ASSOCIATION LIMITED

LONDON   NEW YORK   MONTREAL   SYDNEY

Discover the World: AUSTRALIA AND NEW ZEALAND

Translated and edited by Toucan Books Limited, London
for Reader's Digest, London

Translated and adapted from the French
by Richard Walker

For Reader's Digest
Series Editor: Christine Noble
Editorial Assistant: Caroline Boucher
Production Controller: Byron Johnson

Reader's Digest General Books
Editorial Director: Cortina Butler
Art Director: Nick Clark

ISBN 0 276 42444 1

Discover the World: AUSTRALIA AND NEW ZEALAND
was created and produced by AMDS, Paris, for Selection du
Reader's Digest S.A., Paris, and first published in 1998 as
Regards sur le Monde: L'AUSTRALIE, LA NOUVELLE-ZÉLANDE

© 1998 Selection Reader's Digest, S.A.
212 boulevard Saint-Germain, 75007, Paris

CONTENTS

INTRODUCING
AUSTRALIA
AND
NEW ZEALAND

Australia and New Zealand are often spoken
of in the same breath – both were colonies
of Britain in its imperial heyday, and both share a
remote location at the farthest reaches of the Indian
and Pacific oceans. Yet they are a study in contrasts,
divided by almost 1000 miles (1600 km) of sea and
80 million years of separate geological development.
In Australia, an ancient people lived in spiritual and
physical harmony with their surroundings, while New
Zealand became the domain of Polynesian warriors.
Then came a race of pale men in tall ships, and the
old ways of life ended for ever.

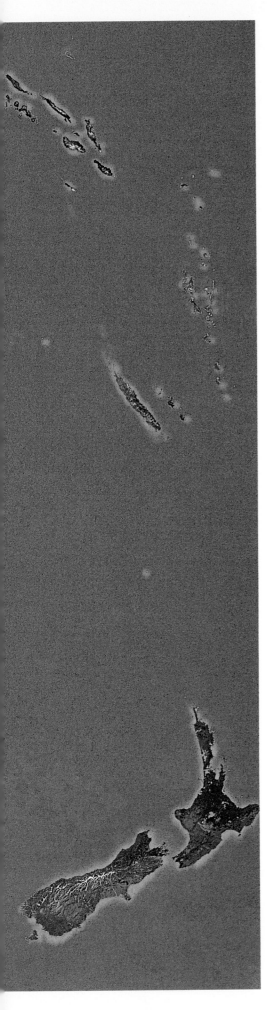

Ancient lands

The history of Australia 'does not read like history, but like the most beautiful lies,' wrote the American author Mark Twain. 'But they are all true, and they happened.' Since Twain's day, the history of Australia has been shown to be even more amazing. Science has pushed the story back to 4000 million years ago, that being the age calculated for rock crystals found in the Pilbara, in Western Australia. In this same corner of Australia, fossils of the world's earliest known life forms have been discovered: single-cell organisms some 3400 million years old.

A thousand million years ago, mountain ranges rose and eventually became the vast, flat Australian outback of today. Some 350 million years ago, when life was just emerging from the seas, proto-Australia was bound into a supercontinent, along with the future Africa, India and South America, all wrapped around Antarctica at the core. Geologists call this landmass Gondwana. Two hundred million years ago, a series of convulsions began to raise the Great Dividing Range.

About 150 million years ago, under the heave of thermal forces deep within the Earth, the supercontinent began to break up. At that time it was laden with steamy forests of tree ferns that were browsed by large sauropods. By 100 million years ago, Africa had sheared off and a shallow sea divided eastern Australia from the western side; giant marine reptiles swam where today there is desert and salt pan.

Around 45 million years ago, Australia snapped its last link with Antarctica and began a northward drift, becoming a time capsule: a Noah's Ark loaded with flora and fauna from a stage in evolution when flowering plants were just emerging and mammals beginning to flourish. Advancing at 2 in (5 cm) a year, the Australian ark drifted into tropical latitudes

All-seeing eye   This satellite image shows a stark contrast between Australia's scorched red interior and the rugged lush landscape of the continent's neighbour, New Zealand.

about 15 million years ago; the fossil record reveals lush abundance and a marsupial menagerie developing in isolation. Now it began to nudge the outer rim of the enormous plate bearing the Asian continent. The bump pushed up mountainous New Guinea, which in turn caused ocean currents to divert and wind patterns to alter, bringing less rain. The Australian interior began to dry out.

In the last 4 million years, humans evolved and spread across the world, aided by periodic ice ages, when the sea level dropped sharply, creating land bridges between islands and even continents. In such a period, 60 000 years ago, the first people reached Australia. Then the sea rose again, cutting them off.

New Zealand: the last Eden

Riding the bow wave of Australia's advance is a small wedge of the old supercontinent. Until between 100 and 150 million years ago, New Zealand lay at the edge of Gondwana, nestled against Australia. Then it split from the supercontinent, opening up the Tasman Sea, and now sits astride the Australian-Pacific plate boundary. Its southwestern tip, Fiordland, is a remnant of Gondwana, while much of the rest of South Island consists of layers of marine sediment that were crushed and hoisted vertically by the head-on collision of the plates. Beneath the North Island, the Pacific plate is sinking under the Australian plate, causing volcanoes to belch and the ground to quake. The result is an archipelago in dynamic flux between forces of creation and destruction, with some of the world's youngest and most spectacular landscapes to show for it.

New Zealand was once canopied by dense forests that would have delighted a dinosaur. Cast adrift from Gondwana before mammals evolved, it was a land of birds – many flightless because there were no mammalian predators. When the first Polynesian voyagers stepped ashore around 1200 years ago, they took possession of the last Eden.

Little monster
Australia's *Thorny devil*
looks as fierce as its Latin
name, Moloch horridus,
but it is threatening only to
ants. From a lineage older than
the dinosaurs, this 8 in (20 cm)
dragon lizard uses the grooves
of its spiky protective armour
to trap precious morning dew.

Rock rainbows   *In the Rainbow Valley (right) of central Australia, 500*
million years of wind and rain, and the gouging of ancient seas, have left
broken sandstone ridges that give off bands of colour when touched by the
rising or setting sun. The effect is caused by iron oxides that were dissolved by
seeping water which percolated to the surface to form a fragile reflective crust.

Against the odds   *Defying the fierce heat of the Gibson Desert (inset), acacia*
bushes send down deep roots to tap buried moisture. Their existence makes life
possible for lizards, tiny mammals and thousands of species of ants.

Drying up   *As water evaporates from a shallow salt lake in the intense heat in*
the interior of Australia, a once-submerged tree becomes encrusted with salt.
The lake is a remnant of tidal seas that lapped here in a faraway time.

Surviving the drought *Aboriginal lore declares that the frog was created by Ancestral Spirits of the Dreamtime. The spirits allowed for drought by creating frogs able to bloat themselves with enough water to survive for years between drinks.*

Dinosaur territory *Mauve mist veils the MacDonnell Ranges (inset), which contain chasms with shaded water holes that nurture some of the world's oldest plant species – primitive ferns and palms that survive from the age of the dinosaurs.*

Wild beauty *Tormented rock formations of the Kimberley Plateau (above), on Western Australia's northern flank, are the petrified wreckage of a coral reef that lost its sea 350 million years ago. The Kimberley is Australia at its most untamed.*

Off limits *The invisible Aboriginal Dreaming tracks crisscross the landscape on the approach to Haast Bluff (opposite) 130 miles (210 km) west of Alice Springs. This is Aboriginal land, and tourists need a permit to enter.*

Cuddly bear
The koala, a cute marsupial pin-up, took to the trees quite recently in evolutionary terms, and has preferred ever since to sit tight and snooze.

Ancient forests
The Australian rain forest (right) survives in wet pockets along the continent's eastern edge, a retreating relic of a system far older than the jungles of the Amazon.

Coastal splendour Constant scouring by two oceans, the Indian and the Pacific, ensures that Australia's coasts are lined with spectacular beaches, such as this stretch of Crowdy Bay National Park (inset) on the New South Wales coast.

Winter wonderland The Snowy Mountains (below) are just high enough and just far enough south to provide Australia with a region of winter snow. The Snowies reach to 7310 ft (2228 m) at Mount Kosciusko, and above 5600 ft (1700 m) the blanket of snow lasts most of the winter. The spring melt feeds a river system that drains more than 625 000 sq miles (1.6 million km²) of south-eastern Australia, and leaves the mountains decked in wild flowers of many colours and scents.

Occasional lake   Once in a lifetime, the 3700 sq miles (9300 km^2) of salt pan known as Lake Eyre becomes a lake (above). Fifty feet (15 m) below sea level, it is fed by rivers that normally run dry long before they reach here. The salt crust is 92 in (233 cm) thick and flat enough for Donald Campbell to set the then world land speed record of 403.1 mph (648.7 km/h) in a jet-powered car in 1964.

Shifting sands   The giant dunes of Mungo in the outback of New South Wales shift with the wind, uncovering hearths and human remains dating back 30 000 years. This was once a lakeside habitat teeming with fish and game, and is now an archaeological site of world significance.

Well adapted   The river red gum tree (Eucalyptus camaldulensis) evolved during Australia's passage across the Southern Ocean, and adapted to the drying conditions without compromising on its great thirst for water. The trees follow the course of rivers that are frequently just ribbons of sand, yet individual trees are able to draw up as much as a ton of water a day. The secret is a root system far larger than the tree above ground, which taps deep reservoirs underground. The heat-reflecting white bark protects the red heartwood.

15

Mighty monolith   Uluru (above) is one of the world's natural wonders – a cathedral of the Aboriginal Dreamtime. It sticks up like the head of a huge rusty bolt hammered into Australia's heart, and with a height of 1142 ft (348 m) and a girth of 5¹/₂ miles (9 km), it takes a place in the record books as the world's largest monolith. Formerly known as Ayers Rock, the name given to it by explorer William Gosse in 1873, the site was restored to its traditional Aboriginal owners in 1985. The many Dreaming tracks that intersect here bear witness to a rich mythological past.

Man-made wonder   Natural forces have sculpted a weird landscape of exposed bedrock strata in the Pilbara (left), a hot and dry upland separated from the Kimberley by the Great Sandy Desert. The erratically flowing Fortescue River hugs an escarpment cut by 300 ft (90 m) gorges containing sparkling pools, where cycads, palms and ghost gums grow. In recent years, people have taken over from nature and gouged the Pilbara with strip mines to remove rich deposits of iron ore. The Pilbara's wonders now include one of the biggest man-made pits in the world.

Many Heads   The mysterious domes of Kata Tjuta (inset) are a huddle of more than 30 sandstone monoliths to the west of Uluru. Formerly known as the Olgas, they are now known by their Aboriginal name, which means 'many heads'. Likened to sleeping dinosaurs, they were laid down 600 million years ago as sea sediment and then compressed, twisted, tilted and sculpted by weathering. Like Uluru, they are at their most mystical when caught by the first or last rays of the sun.

Struggle for survival   The bearded dragon is one of more than 200 Australian lizards engaged in a constant struggle for survival. It has a spiky fold of skin around its head, which it is able to lift up. When danger threatens, the lizard unfolds its ruff and mimics the menacing stance of a predator. In Aboriginal mythology it is associated with Kudnu, the valiant Lizard-man.

17

Ancient forest Rampant forests of giant ferns and pines (inset, left) thrive in the warm, humid climate of the North Island of New Zealand. There are more than 80 fern species here, including the 60 ft (20 m) mamaku (Cyathea medullaris) and the ponga or silver tree fern, whose 12 ft (4 m) fronds are a national emblem. After a few hundred years of human occupation, little of this original forest cover remains.

Majestic volcanoes Mount Ngauruhoe is the youngest of three volcanoes that lord over the heart of the North Island. All lie within the Tongariro National Park, which is equipped with an early warning system of volcano sensors.

A land of waterfalls High rainfall and tumbling terrain make New Zealand a land of waterfalls. This cascade is in the thermal hot zone of Rotorua on the North Island.

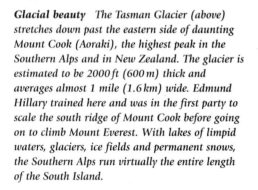

Glacial beauty *The Tasman Glacier (above)
stretches down past the eastern side of daunting
Mount Cook (Aoraki), the highest peak in the
Southern Alps and in New Zealand. The glacier is
estimated to be 2000 ft (600 m) thick and
averages almost 1 mile (1.6 km) wide. Edmund
Hillary trained here and was in the first party to
scale the south ridge of Mount Cook before going
on to climb Mount Everest. With lakes of limpid
waters, glaciers, ice fields and permanent snows,
the Southern Alps run virtually the entire length
of the South Island.*

National emblem *The Kiwi is a freak of
evolutionary isolation, 70 million years in
the making. It cannot fly, can hardly see,
and spends much of its time asleep. Its
feathers are hairy and it has nostrils
at the tip of its long beak. There are
three main kinds of kiwi: the
brown, the great spotted and the
little spotted, and several
subspecies. But extinction looms
unless a rescue programme can
save them from alien predators –
possums, weasels, cats and dogs –
and the destruction of their forest habitat.*

Wide open spaces *Mackenzie Country (above) is a vast arena of
high grassland watered by the snow-melt from the Tasman Glacier. It
is named after a legendary Scots drover who is said to have run stolen
flocks of sheep here. In this unpeopled fastness, so-called 'boundary
dogs' were once tethered for days on end at strategic points to keep
some control over the millions of meandering sheep.*

Glacial debris *The landscape along the precipitous west coast of the South Island moves quickly from sheltered, palm-fringed beaches touched by currents from warmer seas, to the debris fields of glaciers (inset, in Westland National Park) with spectacular deep-cut fiords bordered by peaks rising as much as 5560 ft (1695 m) straight out of the water.*

A brief history

Noble savage and kangaroo An 18th-century perception of the wonders of Terra Australis.

For 3000 generations, and perhaps for thousands more, the people now called the Aborigines made their home in the land we know as Australia. To put this in perspective, there have been 100 or so generations since the time of Christ, and 250 generations since the dawn of civilisation in the Middle East. In that time, the Aborigines perfected a way of life well suited to the land, with which they lived in intimate communion.

A clash of cultures

By the 18th century, the Aborigines numbered about 500 000, split into hundreds of tribal groups, each one subtly different in its ways, according to the needs and circumstances of its particular territory. In 1770, a party of Britons arrived in the territory of one such group, the Eora, who shouted defiantly and threw spears, only to be met with musket fire. Eighteen years later, a much larger group of Britons arrived, most of them convicts, and within a single generation the Eora and their world were no more.

In theory, the Eora could have easily wiped out the ill-equipped invaders. An Eora could throw four spears with deadly accuracy in the time it took a redcoat Marine to reload his clumsy musket, and within months the strangers were weakening, since they had so little notion of how to fend for themselves in this strange environment. But nothing had prepared the Aborigines for this collision with thrusting 18th-century Europe.

Bennelong, a tragic figure

The fate of generations of Aborigines was foreshadowed by that of Bennelong, the first Aborigine to learn English and acquire European manners. Captured by Governor Phillip in 1789, he was taught to speak English so that he could act as a go-between with his people, who kept their distance from the newcomers. A shrewd and curious young man, he was given a hut near the governor's residence, and dined at Phillip's table. In 1792, Phillip took him and another Aborigine to London, where they were apparently presented to King George III. Three years later, he returned home a tragic misfit. He felt superior to his own people, but now belonged in neither society. Little is known of his later years other than that he died in 1813, apparently an alcoholic. The Sydney Opera House was built on the site of his hut.

Ancestral clans

Like all early people, the Aborigines were hunters and gatherers. When their ancestors reached Australia, giant marsupials

Side arms An Aboriginal hunter carries a rifle ... without discarding his boomerang.

The Western attitude towards societies that had not developed agriculture but followed the ancient path of hunting and gathering was for a long time one of contempt, tinged with pity. Nowadays, most prehistorians and anthropologists recognise that hunting and gathering was a way of life of surprising ease and sufficiency – a view supported by studies of traditional Aboriginal societies. In terrain where many white pioneers starved to death, the disdained 'savages' thrived.

A race of hunter-gatherers

Periods of prolonged drought sometimes posed problems, but in normal conditions a band of 10 to 40 people could meet its daily needs in three to four hours of cooperative activity, which served also to bind the community together. Each band ranged over its own territory, which it knew intimately; detailed knowledge of local resources was the key to survival.

The men hunted kangaroos, wallabies, emus and lizards. They were superb trackers and stalkers, able to read the message of every trail and disturbed twig. Their hunting had its own laws, which forbade the killing of any animal that was not required for food. The women and children gathered fruit, seeds and tubers. Varying with the season, scores of plants and succulent grubs formed part of their diet. Much of this 'bush tucker' is still gathered and eaten today.

In bone-dry conditions, Aborigines know where water can be found – not only beneath dusty creekbeds, but in certain plants and even in animals such as the water-holding frog, which can be dug up and squeezed for a thirst-quenching drink. As a source of protein, the witchetty grub, the larva of certain moths and beetles, is nourishing and tasty, while honey ants mixed with grass seeds make an inviting sweetcake.

roamed the land, including kangaroos standing 10 ft (3 m) high and lumbering wombats the size of cattle. These provided plentiful prey until driven to extinction over thousands of years. Fire was the Aborigines' favoured land management tool. They used it to create favourable conditions for grazing animals which were attracted to the burned areas once tender new shoots and grasses had sprung up. Over time, this practice altered the landscape, thinning the forest and promoting grassy woodlands rich in game.

Generation after generation built up knowledge of the terrain and the ways of its flora and fauna. Over time, this knowledge became a set of rules for survival – a stock of wisdom transformed into ritual and taboo. This in turn locked clans into the particular stretch of territory they occupied, each with landmarks that became associated with powerful, unpredictable spirits who had to be appeased in order to ensure the clan's well-being.

Rifles versus spears Many settlers were ruthless when they set about clearing pastoral land of its age-old inhabitants.

The Dreamtime

Binding everything together across the whole continent was a body of oral tradition and vibrant imagery now referred to as the Dreamtime. This harked back to the dawn of creation, when Ancestral Spirits roamed the Earth and conjured everything into existence. These spirits became incorporated into features in the landscape, and so remained a constant presence. Individuals had their own 'dreaming', a personal totem in the form of a plant or animal, and each clan had its own 'dreaming track' – an oral map that defined its territorial range and was handed down in song.

In this way, Australia was crisscrossed with invisible tracks linking clan with clan in mystical kinship with nature, and making every person the effective guardian of a little bit of creation. There were no leaders, no priests, no armies, no sense of property, since anything

Joint venture Hunting is traditionally a male activity, except when landing a big catch (inset).

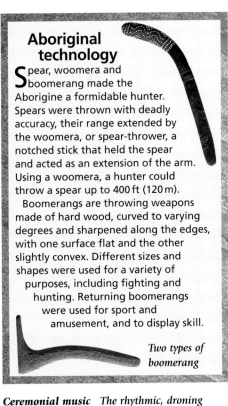

Aboriginal technology

Spear, woomera and boomerang made the Aborigine a formidable hunter. Spears were thrown with deadly accuracy, their range extended by the woomera, or spear-thrower, a notched stick that held the spear and acted as an extension of the arm. Using a woomera, a hunter could throw a spear up to 400 ft (120 m).

Boomerangs are throwing weapons made of hard wood, curved to varying degrees and sharpened along the edges, with one surface flat and the other slightly convex. Different sizes and shapes were used for a variety of purposes, including fighting and hunting. Returning boomerangs were used for sport and amusement, and to display skill.

Two types of boomerang

Ceremonial music The rhythmic, droning sounds of the didgeridoo formed part of corroborees or ritual ceremonies. This 3-7 ft (1-2 m) long instrument made of hollow wood takes much skill to master.

which could not easily be carried from campfire to campfire was an encumbrance. As the modern Aborigine poet Oodgeroo put it: 'We don't own the land. The land owns us.'

Disease and decimation

Within a year of the creation of Britain's convict colony, alien diseases such as influenza were cutting a swathe through local tribes. Pushing into the interior, the settlers found large areas of grassy woodland created by tens of thousands of years

Cultural contrast Television reaches everywhere today, but traditional Aboriginal crafts such as the making of boomerangs (right) have not been lost.

A great prehistoric migration

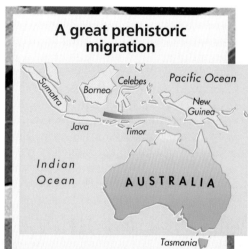

Australia's earliest inhabitants arrived from South-east Asia some 60 000 years ago, and possibly even earlier. Very low sea levels meant that New Guinea was joined to Australia by a land bridge. Much of the Indonesian archipelago was dry land, yet stretches of open water more than 50 miles (80 km) across had to be navigated, making this the first ocean migration in the history of humankind.

The Aborigines share some of their so-called 'Australoid' features with the Vedda people of Sri Lanka and certain populations in southern India, which points to an ancient Asian origin. The evidence indicates successive waves of colonisation by different groups, who merged and adapted to their vast new homeland to become the Aborigines of today. By 25 000 BC, all of Australia and Tasmania – which was part of the mainland until 10 000 BC – was inhabited.

Cave painting

Aboriginal rock art is the oldest known form of human creative expression; in terms of continuity, it outranks any other artistic tradition by tens of thousands of years. Australian landscapes are dappled with rock paintings and carvings, some extraordinarily ancient. Archaeologists argue over the earliest work, but some maintain that paintings were being made more than 50 000 years ago. In comparison, the famous Lascaux cave paintings in France are a mere 15 000 years old.

Painting was an integral part of Aboriginal life, as essential to ritual as song and dance. A palette of red, yellow, white and black was created from ochres, clays, charcoal and sometimes blood. Styles and techniques varied between regions and altered over the millennia, with sites being constantly reworked. Some sites are kept secret by their Aboriginal owners because they are held sacred, or are believed to harbour dangerous spirits.

Rock of ages This painting at Kakadu shows mythic figures of the Dreamtime.

of Aboriginal fire management. To clear these pastures of 'troublesome' natives, some settlers organised shooting parties. 'No wild beast of the forest was ever hunted down with such unsparing perseverance', wrote one observer in 1839.

The worst incidents were in Tasmania, which had some of the strongest resistance by Aborigines, and the most hardened population of ex-convicts. In 1830, the settlers tried to round up remnants of the island's population, but they only captured one woman and a boy. Shortly after, an attempt was made to resettle the Aborigines on Flinders Island; the 70 or so living there by 1835 were half of the surviving population. The last tribal Tasmanian Aborigine is thought to be a woman named Truganini. Two years after her death in 1876, her skeleton was exhumed and displayed in the Tasmanian Museum.

In search of Terra Australis

Belief in Terra Australis Incognita ('Unknown Southern Land') can be traced to the Ancient Greeks, who reasoned that a huge southern continent had to exist to counterbalance the northern landmass of the known world of their day. Ptolemy of Alexandria backed up this argument with a map, Marco Polo heard of a rich land to the south of Java, and from the Middle Ages the

Sea of hands   In 1997 these hands were planted in front of Parliament House in Canberra as a symbol of racial harmony.

idea of a fabulous southern continent was firmly fixed in the popular imagination.

Australia, which originally presented its parched western aspect to European explorers, did not seem to fit the bill, and this delayed its 'discovery' by 250 years. In 1601 the Portuguese were first to sight the continent, and ignored it, but the Dutch were persistent in snubbing it: through much of the 17th century Dutch East Indiamen bound for the Spice Islands caught the Roaring Forties to scud across the southern Indian Ocean before steering north. It required only a slight miscalculation for a ship to bump into Australia, as numerous wrecks along the western Australian coast affirm. The first documented sighting of the Australian mainland by a European was by Dutch skipper Willem Jansz in 1606, who reported that the land was 'for the greater part desert, with wild, cruel black savages'. To make certain, the East India Company twice dispatched Abel Tasman, who became the first European to sight New Zealand and the island off mainland Australia that now bears his name, Tasmania, but with these voyages Dutch interest virtually ceased.

Forced labour   A convict work gang sets forth to clear the bush near Sydney in the 1830s.

Raising the flag   Captain Cook takes possession of New South Wales in 1770.

Captain James Cook, the complete explorer

This superb sailor was born in 1728, the son of a Yorkshire farm labourer. He made his reputation charting the North Atlantic coastline and the Gulf of St Lawrence before setting out on his three great voyages of discovery, from 1768 to 1779. Cook was unique among explorers of the time for his compassionate interest in the peoples he encountered, and in his concern for his crew's welfare. He was the first ship's commander to find a solution to scurvy, a disease caused by a deficiency of vitamin C, which had long been the curse of sailors on long voyages.

Apart from securing Australia and New Zealand for Britain, Cook put Hawaii and numerous other Pacific islands on the map. In 1779 he was killed, at the age of 51, in a confrontation with Hawaiian islanders.

The voyage of Captain Cook

The first Briton to set foot on Australian soil, in 1688, was no more enthused. William Dampier, a pirate-explorer, described the natives as 'the miserablest People in the world'. This was enough to secure Australia another century of Dreamtime, broken finally by the navigational skills of Captain James Cook.

In 1768 Captain Cook was dispatched in the *Endeavour*, a small but stout craft, to make a scientific survey in the South Seas, including the task of observing the transit of Venus across the Sun. He visited Tahiti and spent four months charting the coasts of New Zealand. Sailing west, he was nudged north by a gale, and suddenly encountered what others had missed – Australia's more promising eastern flank. He named his first anchorage Botany Bay for its profusion of new plant species, then followed the coast north, almost coming to grief on the Great Barrier Reef. Having charted the entire eastern coast, he claimed it for Britain on August 20, 1770, naming it New South Wales.

Cook was the first of a very few Europeans to look favourably on the Aborigines, perceiving them as romantic, noble savages in line with the latest philosophical thinking. 'In reality, they are far more happier than we European', he wrote, somewhat ungrammatically.

Captain Cook's voyage might have been the end of British interest, had the American colonies not won their War of Independence in 1783. Britain had been accustomed to transporting its criminals to the American colonies, and suddenly found itself with its jails full and an overflow of criminals crammed into

rotting hulks moored on the river Thames. Somewhere had to be found to dump these undesirables before matters got out of hand.

The first settlers

After Gibraltar and corners of Africa had been considered and rejected, it was decided to found a penal colony at Botany Bay, largely on the strength of a report botanist Joseph Banks had given to the House of Commons committee in 1779. Two navy ships and nine transports under the command of Captain Arthur Phillip sailed from Portsmouth with 19 staff and officials, 210 crewmen, 233 merchant seamen, 206 Marines (in four companies) with 27 wives and 19 children, and 770 convicts including 13 children. Some of their crimes were trivial indeed: in one case the theft of a handkerchief.

Toehold *Sydney in 1795, two decades before the push into the interior (inset).*

The voyage of more than 15 000 miles (24 000 km) via Rio de Janeiro and Cape Town took eight months and cost the lives of 23 convicts and two children – surprisingly few considering the length of the journey. Six children were born during the voyage. Arriving at Botany Bay, Captain Phillip found the location unpromising, so he sailed farther up the coast and found what he described as 'the finest harbour in the world'. At sunset on January 26, 1788, he raised the Union Jack beside a deepwater inlet on the southern shore of Port Jackson, which he named Sydney Cove after the British home secretary, Lord Sydney.

Marooned between an uncharted ocean and a seemingly impenetrable mountain range, the convict colony struggled to survive its first years, only to fall victim to a cartel of military officers who gained a hold over its economy through their control of rum shipped from Bengal. In 1808, they went too far when they deposed Governor William

On the edge *A wall of giant trees dwarfs this early Tasmanian encampment (right). The prison barracks at Port Arthur (below) have been restored as a tourist attraction.*

Bligh, who had earlier suffered a mutiny while commanding HMS *Bounty*. To the rescue came Lt-Col Lachlan Macquarie, who arrived with his own regiment.

Free settlers, a trickle at first, were joined by emancipists – convicts released after serving their time. In 1813, the Blue Mountains were crossed, opening up the interior for farmers and explorers. Rivers flowing westward encouraged visions of an inland sea and lush lands beyond. It took decades of exploration to prove this an illusion, one expedition after another floundering in bone-dry seas of sand, stone or salt. Some explorers were speared to death, others perished from privation. Some simply disappeared. Ludwig Leichhardt was hailed as a hero in 1845 when he staggered out of the bush after a 14 month, 3000 mile (4800 km) trek from Brisbane to Port Essington near modern-day Darwin. He set out again in 1848 with seven men and 77 pack animals, and the entire party vanished.

Port Arthur, an Australian gulag

A major problem in any convict colony was what to do with those who kept offending. An initial answer was found in so-called penal settlements such as Norfolk Island, a speck of land far out in the Pacific. From the 1820s, however, Tasmania became the prime dumping ground for persistent offenders, with the entire island run as a virtual prison by a disciplinarian governor, George Arthur, whose massive, leather-bound 'Black Books' recorded every lash administered under his regime of 'enlightened rigour'. Escape into the surrounding wilderness was so impractical that the only man to do so became a cannibal, eating his companions in flight. In 1830 the governor established Port Arthur on the Tasman Peninsula as a 'natural penitentiary', its only access being along a thin neck of land, across which he chained a line of ferocious dogs.

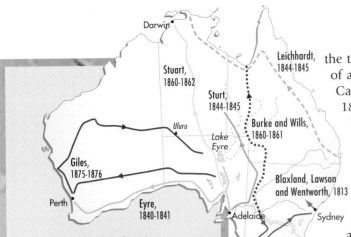

Australian exploration
in the 19th century

The first crossing

In 1860, an expedition led by Robert Burke and William John Wills set out from Melbourne to cross the continent from south to north. Burke and Wills reached the Gulf of Carpentaria in February 1861. On the return journey, they arrived at their base camp at Coopers Creek only hours after it had been vacated and failed to locate the supplies that had been left for them. All but one of their party starved to death.

John McDouall Stuart set out from Adelaide in 1860 on the same quest. He reached the centre of the continent and planted a Union Jack, but was driven back by scurvy and hostile Aborigines. Another attempt in 1861 also failed. Third time lucky, he finally reached the northern coast on July 25, 1862, and returned by stretcher to a hero's welcome.

A growing city Sydney in 1855 (right).
Ships of the desert *Camels were imported from Afghanistan by early explorers (below).*

the threat now being a loss of able-bodied men to the California gold rush. In 1851, Edward Hargraves, back from two years of unsuccessful panning in California and lured by a reward the government was offering for gold finds, began prospecting in an area around Bathurst, on the western slopes of the Great Dividing Range. His two companions found gold at nearby Ophir, and Hargraves returned to Sydney to establish the claim, walking off with the recognition and reward. Australia's gold rushes had begun.

The same year, businesses in the newly proclaimed colony of Victoria offered a prize to lure prospectors their way, and within weeks gold had been found near Ballarat, 70 miles (110 km) from Melbourne. Finds followed at Bendigo and Castlemaine. It was California all over again: towns deserted, ships abandoned by their crews, business at a standstill, lucky diggers squandering their gains. Over the next decade, Victoria produced more than a third of the world's gold.

Gold transformed the colonies' prospects. From 400 000 in 1850, the population jumped to over 1.7 million in 1871. Most were British, but thousands of Chinese flocked to the goldfields. In 1859, no less than 20 per cent of Victoria's male population was Chinese.

The quest for gold

By the 1870s, when Ernest Giles was exploring the western deserts, interest had waned in the face of a more compelling quest – for gold. The presence of gold in the colony had been known from the 1820s, but fears of inciting unrest in the convict population caused the authorities to discourage interest until 1850, when transportation was being phased out and fears were reversed,

The legend of Lasseter's reef

Along with the bones of lost explorers, the outback holds the secret of a vanished prospector and a legendary reef of gold. Harry Lasseter claimed to anyone who would listen that in 1897, aged 17, he had stumbled upon a 'vast reef' of gold on the edge of the Gibson Desert. Finally, in 1930, a well-financed expedition was mounted with Lasseter to guide it.

The hunt went badly, and Lasseter struck out on his own with two camels, never to be seen again. In 1931, his diary was unearthed

at one of his last camp sites. In it, he claimed to have rediscovered the reef, only for his camels to bolt, leaving him stranded without water. Periodic searches for Lasseter's reef continue.

The way it was *A reconstruction of a gold-digger's shanty in Western Australia.*

A new sense of confidence found dramatic expression in a conflict between gold diggers and the authorities over official corruption, licences and the right to vote. In November 1854, diggers at Ballarat hoisted a rebel Southern Cross flag and burned their licences; then they built a stockade at nearby Eureka. Though soon overwhelmed, at the cost of some 30 lives, their stand roused such popular support that juries refused to convict the rebels and the hated licence fees were replaced by a miner's right, effectively giving the diggers the vote. This mood of rebellion extended to an admiration for some of the bushrangers who held up stage coaches and bullion wagons. The most celebrated was Ned Kelly, who made his last stand against the police in 1880 in a suit of homemade armour. His last words, just before he was hanged, were 'Such is life'.

Sporadic gold strikes continued, each stimulating a new area of growth, and culminating in a big rush to Western Australia in the 1890s. By then there were six colonies, often at loggerheads, which were united as one nation on January 1, 1901, by an act of the British Parliament. One of the first acts of the new Australian Parliament was to introduce the so-called 'White Australia' policy, with laws designed to keep out non-Europeans.

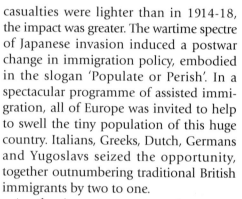

Gold rush Prospectors lured from around the world (right) gave Australia a major economic boost. Today's visitors can still pan for gold at a re-created 1860s mining township in Ballarat (inset).

Wartime heroes

Australians marched onto the world stage in uniform. Some 16 000 'Diggers' went to South Africa to fight alongside the British against the Boers, and less than a generation later 330 000 (out of a population of 5 million) sailed off to fight in the trenches of Europe; their 65 per cent casualty rate was the highest of Commonwealth forces in the First World War.

Over half a million Australians served in the Second World War, and while casualties were lighter than in 1914-18, the impact was greater. The wartime spectre of Japanese invasion induced a postwar change in immigration policy, embodied in the slogan 'Populate or Perish'. In a spectacular programme of assisted immigration, all of Europe was invited to help to swell the tiny population of this huge country. Italians, Greeks, Dutch, Germans and Yugoslavs seized the opportunity, together outnumbering traditional British immigrants by two to one.

Another important postwar change was that the USA replaced Britain as Australia's key ally and source of influence. More than 50 000 Australian soldiers, many of them conscripts, were sent to fight in Vietnam,

Uncommon harmony Relations between gold diggers and Aborigines were not always this cordial. This carefully arranged group portrait was taken in Western Australia.

Changing faces Immigrants in the 1950s were strictly white (above). Today's generation of schoolchildren reflects a multi-ethnic Australia (right).

sparking an anti-war reaction that found broader expression in the questioning of old values. The White Australia policy was modified until it was totally abolished in 1972; by the 1990s, a third of new immigrants were from Asia.

The changing face of Australia

At the end of the century the British monarch remained head of state, but for how long was uncertain as polls indicated that public sentiment was leaning towards cutting this last colonial tie.

After more than a century of persecution and denial, the rights of Aborigines were also taken up. Viewed as a 'dying race' when Australia achieved nationhood in 1901, they had had their movements restricted and had not been counted as Australians. This changed when a referendum in 1967 granted them citizenship and the vote. A Department of Aboriginal Affairs was set up in 1972. Soon, 'land rights' became an issue, with Aborigines claiming large stretches of land on the basis of traditional ownership. In 1992, the High Court overturned the long-held legal assumption that Australia, when it

was occupied by Europeans, had been *terra nullius* – that is, land having no legal owners. For 200 years this assumption had sanctioned settlement without treaty or compensation. In 1993, a tribunal was set up to deal with Aboriginal claims, with large tracts of land passing back to 'traditional owners'.

The militancy of young Aborigines translated into a flowering of traditional arts and music. Many entered mainstream society on their own terms. In the 1996 census, 350 000 Australians identified themselves as Aborigines, a significant increase that reflected a new willingness to claim indigenous roots.

Pioneer spirit Those who choose to live in the outback are often regarded as the 'real' Australians by the urban majority.

A strong identity

Every nation is shaped by its past, and few British colonies had a less promising beginning than Australia, whose founding fathers and mothers included many petty criminals dragged from the prisons of England, Scotland and Ireland – or, as an Australian wit would have it, 'selected by the best judges in Britain'.

From among these convicts would be drawn Australia's first builder, its first architect, first artists, even its first lawyers. 'Bolters', or runaways, were its first reluctant explorers; and it was a convict's son, William Charles Wentworth, born on a transport ship, who opened up the interior by pioneering a route over the Blue Mountains with Gregory Blaxland and William Lawson.

In the first generation to be born free in a penal colony, a recognisable Australian personality emerged, already complete with a high twang accent, that owed something to Cockney and an Irish brogue. They were known as 'currency lads and lasses', after the colony's local coinage (in contrast to 'sterling lads and lasses born in England), and they displayed common traits born of their unusual circumstances – a fierce loyalty to 'mates', only grudging acceptance of authority, suspicion of

snobbish pretensions, and a love of the outdoors. 'You cannot imagine such a beautiful Race as the rising generation,' a colonial administrator wrote in 1831. 'There is a degree of Liberty here which you can hardly imagine at your side of the Equator.'

Twenty years later, gold re-made Australia's image, quickening immigration, putting an end to transportation – which totalled over 150 000 from 1788 to 1867 – and stimulating a sense of national pride. Convicts made bad folklore, but not bushrangers, who robbed settlers and travellers and held up gold wagons, occasionally pretending to be Robin Hoods. And when there was no more gold, only drought and depression, itinerant workers were romanticised in the folksong figure of the 'jolly swagman'. Finally, the 20th century's wars cast the bronzed Australians in a heroic light: 'they walked and looked like the kings in an old poem', wrote poet laureate John Masefield of 'those smiling and glorious young giants'.

*Aussie spirit
An Australian soldier marches through Paris in 1915.*

Land of the Long White Cloud

According to Maori lore, a Polynesian navigator named Kupe discovered Aotearoa, the 'Land of the Long White Cloud', or New Zealand, as the first visitors from Europe decided to call it.

In a tale reminiscent of a Viking saga, Kupe and his crew set out from 'Hawaiki' following a giant octopus. Far beyond the setting sun, they came upon a 'great southern land with mountains covered with mist, inhabited only by birds'. Kupe explored the coast and paddled up the Whanganui River in the North Island, then he sailed home with the news. Calculated on the basis of counting back generations in the oral

And Maui created Aotearoa

The god Maui went fishing with his brothers. When they had gone a long way, Maui dropped anchor and with a magic hook made from the jaw of his grandmother he caught a gigantic fish. So it is to this day. The North Island is Te-Ika-a-Maui ('the fish of Maui'), the South Island is Te-Waka-a-Maui ('the canoe of Maui') and Stewart Island in the south is Te-Puka-o-te-waka-a-Maui ('the anchor of Maui').

record, Kupe's voyage of discovery would perhaps have taken place in the 10th century, which is when the sagas say that Erik the Red discovered America.

One Maori tradition holds that a migration from Hawaiki took place, possibly in the 14th century. The names of several ocean-going canoes, their occupants and where each canoe landed have come down by word of mouth, though no hard proof exists. Nor can the location of Hawaiki be determined, other than that it was certainly not Hawaii. Stories and opinions vary, with some traditions favouring the sacred island of Raiatea, near Tahiti, while some anthropologists lean towards the Marquesas, also part of French Polynesia, but more distant.

The evidence, supported by archaeology, points to a succession of voyages, each a formidable undertaking across thousands of miles of open ocean against prevailing winds. The migrants brought with them plants and seeds, together with dogs and rats – the first mammals other than a few wind-blown bats ever to reach here.

The waters teemed with fish and the forests were a fabulous bounty for a

Grace and beauty *Reports of the beauty of Maori women and the stunningly rich landscape fed European perceptions of New Zealand.*

people to whom wood was very precious. Strutting in the clearings were flocks of enormous flightless birds that the Maori called moa – their word for 'chicken' – with drumsticks taller than a man. But the temperate climate proved a problem. Many of the plants the voyagers brought, such as coconut, breadfruit and plantain, did not survive, and even their staple kumara, the sweet potato, could not be grown successfully in the colder, frostier parts of the country. They found a substitute in a fern root,

The Treaty of Waitangi   Amid the ceremonial pomp of 1840 (above) the Maori chiefs did not appreciate that they were signing away their country. Like the land, lineage is sacred in Maori culture, and this endures even among those of mixed descent (inset).

which had to be pounded heavily before eating; they slashed and burned tracts of forest to encourage its growth and were profligate in other ways – they had hunted the moa to extinction by the time Captain Cook arrived.

Cook's first visit

A Maori eyewitness account survives of Cook's first visit in 1769. Horeta Te Taniwha was a child at the time. In old age, he described in vivid detail how the sailors in the long boat were taken for *tapua*, 'goblins', who seemed to have eyes at the back of their heads, since they rowed towards the shore facing the other way. Cook was remembered fondly: 'He seldom spoke, but some of the goblins spoke much. He was a very good man, and came to us children and patted our cheeks, and gently touched our heads. His language was a hissing sound.'

The Maori had by Cook's time developed a complex warrior culture based upon hierarchy and kinship. Each family belonged to a clan, which belonged to a tribe, which was part of a confederation called a *waka* – a word also meaning 'canoe' – with the entire structure of society based upon oral genealogies (*whakapapa*) reaching back to the first voyagers. Communal life revolved around the *marae*, a gathering place with a meeting house that functioned as a social and spiritual centre, as well as a hostel for visiting outsiders. Most communities, especially in the more heavily populated North Island, were within easy reach of a strategic *pa*, a heavily fortified hill village.

Feuds simmered down the generations. Warfare was fearless and was conducted with war clubs (*mere*) made from jade found in the South Island. Losers were enslaved, or might even be eaten with their heads preserved as trophies. Victors gained *mana*, 'status' or 'prestige'.

Settlers and colonisers

Once Cook had put the islands of Kupe on the map, sealers and whalers steered a course for them, with the inevitable introduction of diseases to which the Maori had no immunity. Metal

The Haka   The Maori war chant is delivered with shouts and gestures, and much stamping of feet. Today, it is world famous as the pre-match challenge of New Zealand's rugby team, the All-Blacks.

technology proved an equal menace, as chiefs bartered flax (in demand for ships' canvas) for firearms in order to settle old scores. In 1820, a North Island chief, Hongi Hika, visited Britain, where he was presented to King George IV and helped to compile a Maori dictionary. On his voyage home he exchanged his many gifts for 300 guns, with which he launched a devastating campaign against his enemies.

Moa hunters, turnips and 'South Seas Poms'

Among the first Polynesian voyagers to arrive in New Zealand waters were, according to some experts, a distinct group known as the Moriori, or 'moa hunters', who lived on the remote Chatham Islands. The Maori began calling themselves Maori, 'normal people', to distinguish themselves from Pakeha, the name for Europeans. The origin of the word Pakeha is uncertain, but it could derive from the Maori word for a variety of white turnip. Europeans chose to refer to themselves as Kiwis, after New Zealand's unique and somewhat comical flightless bird.

In more than a decade of internecine war, between 20 000 and 80 000 Maoris died, leaving them ill-prepared to cope with land speculators seeking to open up the country for settlement. Under the leadership of Edward Wakefield, founder of Adelaide in Australia, colonising enthusiasts planned to obtain land from the Maori as cheaply as possible, work it using immigrant British labour, who would in turn work hard for the landowners, until they had saved enough money to buy their own landholding and employ newly arrived immigrant labourers.

Wakefield's plan, together with complaints from missionary groups and the belief that the French were about to establish large settlements, persuaded the British Government to intervene. In 1840, with Wakefield's scheme already under way, and a boatload of prospective French

Finely decorated
Wood carving occupies an important place in Maori art, producing lively artefacts such as this.

colonists at sea, Captain William Hobson arrived in the Bay of Islands with orders to persuade the Maori to accept British sovereignty over the region. Less than a week later, on February 6, 1840, 45 chiefs signed the Treaty of Waitangi accepting British protection and citizenship rights for their people. Missionaries took the treaty on tour and obtained another 500 signatures over the next few months.

Under the Treaty of Waitangi, Britain proclaimed sovereignty over New Zealand while agreeing to respect the land ownership rights of the Maori. Though remarkable for its day, the treaty proved of little worth in the face of land-hungry settlers. By 1843, when the first violence erupted, Wakefield's New Zealand Company had dispatched 57 ships with more than 18 000 immigrants, and it was not alone. Hone Heke, a chief who had been one of the first to sign the

Cultural revival *Action songs and war dances are a popular feature of concerts staged by the Maori of Rotorua.*

treaty, took to chopping down the flagstaff of the British governor at Kororareka (now the quiet little port of Russell). He did so three times, then sacked the settlement. When the governor offered a £100 reward for Hone Heke's head, the chief returned the compliment. Chiefs would sometimes sell land

Sheep: foundation of the economy

Sheep farming began in the mid 19th century but was not significant until the development of refrigeration gave New Zealand access to world markets. The first cargo of lamb carcasses reached England in 1882 aboard the *Dunedin*, after a voyage in which the captain almost froze to death repairing the cold storage unit. A century later, the country's sheep population reached 70 million. Although this subsequently fell, there are still 12.8 sheep for each human New Zealander.

against the wishes of their tribe, or even try to sell the land of a rival tribe. To eradicate such irregularities and form a united front against exploitation, several North Island chiefs banded together in 1858 to elect a paramount chief, or king. But in 1860, fighting broke out in Taranaki over a land dispute and Imperial troops were brought in from Sydney.

The Maori fought bravely and might have prevailed in what became known as the Maori, or Land, Wars, had they not been riven by rivalries that led some tribes to fight on the British side. Peace was restored in 1872, though skirmishes continued for nine more years until the formal surrender of the Maori king. The rebel tribes suffered land confiscation, but when the government abandoned attempts to control land dealing all tribes endured heavy losses.

Utopian ideals

Wakefield's vision of idyllic British communities in the Antipodes had been taken up by others, including the

From tattoos to false teeth

The amber resin of the kauri pine, known as kauri gum, was a significant export in the 1890s. The Maori used it as chewing gum and as fuel for torches. They also mixed its ash with shark oil to pigment their tattoos. Amber resin was exported for use by makers of varnish, linoleum and even false teeth.

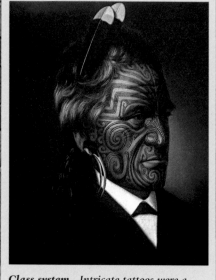

Class system *Intricate tattoos were a mark of nobility in Maori society.*

French presence *A French atmosphere still prevails in the South Island port of Akaroa where Captain Jean Langlois landed a party of settlers in 1840 (left).*

time, however, the numbers recovered and Maori politicians began to assert themselves. Maori forces fought with distinction in the Second World War and a postwar economic boom brought many to the cities.

A cultural revival

The late 1960s saw a renewed interest in all aspects of Maori culture (Maoritanga), with activists taking to the streets to protest against old wrongs. Agitation prompted the New Zealand government

Modern Aucklander   This woman hails from Tonga, 1150 miles (1850 km) away.

Auckland, capital of the South Pacific

Wellington might be the capital of New Zealand, but Auckland can claim to be the capital of Polynesia. More than 100 000 Pacific islanders have flocked to New Zealand's biggest city, many from Samoa, but also from the Cook islands, Tonga, Niue and tiny dots in the ocean such as Tokelau. The migration began after the Second World War, when the New Zealand economy boomed and the government needed to supplement its labour force. By the 1960s, it found an eager response from islands with little opportunities of their own, and to this day individuals continue to provide for entire families who stayed behind. Their presence has given Auckland a cultural lift, filling the air with poetic Polynesian tongues that flow easily together in a similarity born out of a single origin. As a result, this self-styled 'hub of the Pacific' has become a melting pot, out of which has emerged a cultural fusion dubbed 'urban Pacific chic'.

Southern pipes   Scottish immigration made a profound impact on the South Island. Here the pipes skirl in Dunedin. Artefacts from colonial life are preserved at the Matakohe Museum in the North Island (inset).

Free Church of Scotland, which founded the town of Dunedin in 1848, and the Canterbury Association, an Anglican body that founded Christchurch in 1850. While ongoing fighting retarded development in the North Island, the South Island was flourishing, its economy stimulated by gold strikes and by the agricultural expansion that would earn New Zealand the epithet of being Britain's 'offshore farm'.

The utopian ideals of some of the European settlers manifested themselves in a phase of radical innovation. Large land-holdings were broken up and small farmers encouraged. Beginning with free compulsory education in 1877, New Zealand became the first country in the world to extend the vote to women (1893). It also established court procedures for the arbitration of labour disputes in 1894, and granted an old age pension in 1898. By 1938 it had a comprehensive health care and social security system.

The Maori had the vote, but seemed too few to matter. By the end of the 19th century, the Maori population was estimated at just 42 000, mostly concentrated on poor land in remote areas. In

to set up the Waitangi Tribunal in 1975 to investigate land claims.

The work of the tribunal was later extended to look into grievances dating back to 1840. Hundreds of claims were lodged, but few were settled as the

Stepping back in time   Tauranga on the North Island's Bay of Plenty boasts a restored 19th-century 'Main Street'. The red-feathered headdress (right) accords with ancient Polynesian tradition.

authorities struggled with resentment and protracted battles of litigation; Maori activists countered with sit-ins on the annual Waitangi Day.

The Maori cultural revival had a more immediate impact on New Zealand society as it flowered into a renaissance and began to draw in the Pakeha (non-Maori) community, numbers of whom started to learn to speak Maori, which is New Zealand's second official language.

A JOURNEY THROUGH
AUSTRALIA
AND
NEW ZEALAND

Most people thinking of Australia conjure visions of kangaroos and koalas, bronzed surfers and lean stockmen, the lonely outback and rollicking Sydney. But these are mere cartoon images of a nation-continent that is never quite what it seems. New Zealand can also be something of an illusion: a setting of volcanoes and primeval forests that the British determined to turn into an idealised version of home. For almost two centuries, these lands were deemed too far away to matter, but today their cultures are influencing the rest of the world as much as it is impacting upon them.

CHAPTER 1

THE MAJESTY OF THE LANDSCAPE

Say the name slowly, as Australians do – 'Awe-streye-lia' – and you will catch a hint of the power of this enormous land to inspire and to daunt. It is a land of immense distances and baking heat; of blue-vault skies that become awesome planetariums by night; of glaring red deserts and the interminable grey-green bush that covers so much of the interior. This is the driest of all inhabited continents, yet it has lush rain forests, snowy mountains, coral wonderlands and beaches apparently stretching towards infinity. The physical challenge of New Zealand is no less for being quite different. It is as volatile a landscape as Australia is brooding. If the fires that created Australia died down aeons ago, New Zealand is still flaming, spewing smoke and steam, and heaving up mountains from the sea. Its combination of volcanoes, geysers, fiords, glaciers, forests, and alpine and lowland meadows makes it a world-spectacle in microcosm.

The domes of Kata Tjuta, Australia.

The island continent

Australia is the only nation in the world to have a continent to itself. To walk the long way round from North Head to South Head of Sydney Harbour would involve a hike of around 22000 miles (35000km), taking in mangrove swamps, coastal bushland and some of the world's most magnificent beaches and cliffs.

Modern Australia began at Sydney, where Captain Arthur Phillip's First Fleet of soldiers and convicts dropped anchor. Two world-famous beaches now flank the approaches to Sydney Harbour – Bondi and Manly, the latter so-called because here Phillip encountered a group of Aborigines whom he considered to be very 'manly' in their appearance and demeanour.

For modern city-dwellers, going 'up the coast' from here involves joining a four-lane stream of vehicles heading for the sea and golden sands. Route One, the Pacific Highway, sometimes begins with bumper-to-bumper traffic, a demonstration of the fact that 90 per cent of Australians live along the coast, and a very large proportion of them along this coast. Yet nature still generally prevails beside the highway, and along the breathtaking beaches, even where challenged by theme parks and the jostling high-rise apartment blocks of the Gold Coast – named originally for the colour of its sands, not its neon lights.

Ancient forests

Scattered along the Queensland and northern New South Wales coasts are fragments of the rain forest that 60 million years ago covered large parts of the continent. The biggest fragment, almost half of all that remains, forms a large patch where the northern extremity of the Great Dividing Range dips down to the sea, near the exquisite beaches of Cape Tribulation, the name a permanent reminder of Captain Cook's mood after he nearly came to grief on a nearby coral reef.

Under a thick canopy of trees, some more than 1000 years old, enormous butterflies flutter across narrow shafts of sunlight, while the calls of brightly plumed parrots echo through the forest.

The cassowary, a large, flightless bird that grunts and has a lethal kick, crashes head-first through the forest undergrowth while tree kangaroos climb adeptly in the branches overhead.

Calm before the storm The wild and ragged coastline of north-west Australia is subject to massive tidal surges and periodic cyclones.

Survivor Once hunted almost to extinction, the southern right whale has now returned to its old haunts.

The Bight's bite Extensive dunes around the Great Australian Bight testify to the grinding power of the Southern Ocean.

Whale resort

Asmall stretch of Australia's south-eastern coast around Warrnambool, Victoria, is a holiday home and nursery for the southern right whale which journeys here from Antarctica to give birth, mate and relax through the winter. Hunting drove the whales away, and by the 1930s they faced extinction. Now protected, they have returned to a warm welcome. At Logan's Beach there is a viewing platform, from which visitors can observe these magnificent 60 ton leviathans as they dive and play for hours on end.

Mud flats and mangroves

In the far north, where the Cape York peninsula points like an outstretched finger at New Guinea, the forest fringe gives way to mud flats and mangroves, and the hot silence is broken only by the sounds of birds and insects. Offshore, the heads of giant turtles bob in the eddies of contesting currents. This topmost point of Australia is known simply as the Tip, to distinguish it from the Top End – the country's northern bulge west of the Gulf of Carpentaria. Here, in the north, life is subject to two seasons of violent extremes, aptly called the Wet and the Dry. This is the lair of 23 ft (7 m) 'salties', dangerous saltwater crocodiles, which will take a full-grown man if given the chance. Another being here is the Rainbow Serpent, one of the most important of Aboriginal ancestral spirits, variously said to have carved out the landscape with its writhing body or to have created everything, including people.

Splendours of the coast

Over on the west coast, the continental plateau extends to the edge of the Indian Ocean. In some places, the desert dunes march right into the sea; in others, the plateau snaps off at the water's edge, a serrated red slice dropping vertically into a royal-blue sea. This is Australia's least-populated coastline.

Once around the south-west corner, and into the stormy Great Australian Bight, the arid nothingness of the Nullarbor

A clear blue paradise

The charming port of Narooma in New South Wales nestles at the mouth of the River Wagonga on a stretch of sandy coast with a reputation for good fishing – ranging from simply dropping a hook and line into the water to chasing game fish in the open sea. It is from Narooma's waters that Sydney gets much of its fish.

Narooma takes its name from an Aborigine word, *Noorooma*, meaning 'blue and clear water'. Off Montague Island, about 5 miles (8 km) away and close to deep water, record catches of tuna, shark and kingfish have been made; while along the coast at Batemans Bay, an 880 lb (400 kg) swordfish was caught in January 1998.

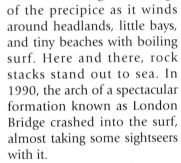

Montague Island is now a restricted wildlife sanctuary with colonies of seals and Little Penguins – the smallest member of the penguin family and the only one to breed in Australia. It is also a breeding ground and migratory resting place for many other sea birds. The National Parks and Wildlife Service run tours to the island to see the flora and fauna, as well as its 19th-century lighthouse.

Plain ends abruptly in sea cliffs and immense beaches. Beyond the Bight, where seas pile up to crash into Bass Strait, steep, forested hillsides and extreme cliff erosion combine to form one of the world's most stirring stretches of coastline. For some 200 miles (320 km), the Great Ocean Road clings to the edge of the precipice as it winds around headlands, little bays, and tiny beaches with boiling surf. Here and there, rock stacks stand out to sea. In 1990, the arch of a spectacular formation known as London Bridge crashed into the surf, almost taking some sightseers with it.

Across Bass Strait, the coast of Tasmania emerges as a black wall in the face of the spray. Off its southern tip, pillars of black rock march into the sea, to rise again, identical in geological formation to those found in Antarctica, due south across the southern ocean. This is no chance connection, for at one time these coasts were part of the same land mass.

Sea sculpture *The Twelve Apostles stand offshore, near the entrance to Bass Strait, as evidence of the power of ocean breakers to penetrate a cliff face.*

39

The living reef

Coral formation *This fan coral has created a delicate tracery set against the deep blue of the ocean.*

The Great Barrier Reef has been called the world's largest living thing. More accurately, it is billions of living things, the largest biomass on Earth, sustaining in turn the most diverse ecosystem on the planet. It extends over thousands of square miles, shimmering under luminous waters that are inset with gem-like coral islands.

In 1770 Captain James Cook was sailing peacefully up the Australian coast – so peacefully that he began to wonder why the Pacific Ocean was so calm. Then a jagged edge of coral reef ripped into the *Endeavour's* hull, all but sinking the ship, an event that could have changed the course of history. The great navigator had come up against one of the great natural wonders of the world.

A great barricade

From north of Fraser Island, off the coast of Queensland, to the Torres Strait, the Great Barrier Reef shields the coast from the full force of the ocean. It is not one reef, but more than 2500 reefs that form an interlocking underwater maze 1400 miles (2300km) long. It must be seen from the air for its magnitude and magnificence to be appreciated.

The outer ramparts of this great living barricade rise abruptly from the abyss at the edge of shallow water. This occurs some 180 miles (290 km) offshore in the south, but only a few miles from shore in the north. The reef therefore narrows like a funnel towards the north, and this is what trapped Cook. Between reef and shore, the warm, protected waters form a lagoon-like channel dappled with islands. Some are the exposed tops of old reefs, low 'cays' formed from accumulated sand and dead coral; others are continental, encircled by their own little coral reefs.

Viewed from above, the reef is a picture-postcard paradise of emerald-green isles fringed by white sandy beaches and swaying coconut palms. Looked at under water, what appears to be a colourful wonderland is an aquatic jungle, whose inhabitants are engaged in a perpetual life-and-death struggle. In raw

Over and underview *Only by flying over the reef (above) and then entering the water (left) is it possible to appreciate the reef's immensity, diversity, complexity and beauty.*

statistics, they include 1500 species of fish, 4000 species of clam, snail and other molluscs, 400 species of sponge, 350 members of the star fish, sea urchin and sea cucumber family, and innumerable kinds of crab, shrimp, worm and other creepy-crawlies. The reef also provides a livelihood for 250 species of bird.

A world in danger ?

Damage to the reef by a plague of coral-eating starfish and unexplained 'bleaching' episodes, with the loss of essential algae, have dramatised its fragile nature and raised fears of further degradation as a result of commercial fishing and pollutants. Now that the threat of oil exploration has diminished, the greatest direct danger may lie in tourism. The reef draws more than a million tourists a year, and each new development carries a price in damage to the coral from dynamiting, dredging, silting and sewage.

Water purifier *The giant clam acts as a water filter, maintaining the purity of a lagoon.*

The coral polyp

The creator of this universe is a tiny, primitive marine animal that evolved from the sea anemone and is related to jellyfish: the coral polyp. A polyp is no more than a soft, hollow tube with a ring of feeding tentacles at one end. However, it seals itself into a limestone casing, from which, after dark, it extends its pretty tentacles like a flower in bloom to stun and grab minute plankton carried by the current. When daylight returns, the tentacles retreat to safety. When a generation of polyps dies, another generation builds its limestone cases on the foundations of the old; and so a reef grows, generation upon generation.

Polyps are fussy. They require the water to be warm and salty, and they need sunlight to reach

One of the many remarkable partnerships to be found in reef waters is that between little fish and the larger fish for which they provide a cleaning service. Shoals of striped wrasse set up 'cleaning stations', swimming in spirals to advertise themselves to customers that range from parrot fish to moray eels and giant manta rays. The customers hang in the water, almost motionless, with gills open, while the cleaners pick off their parasites – even swimming into mouths that in other circumstances would gobble them up.

Clownfish shelter from their enemies within the poisonous tentacles of anemones, which are in turn protected from their predators by the clownfish. The partnership is most marked in the case of some gobies and shrimps, who set up home together. The shrimp digs a shared burrow and the gobie does guard duty. When the fish senses danger it signals the shrimp, and they then disappear together into their burrow.

No opportunity is missed in the underwater jungle. The sabre-toothed blenny, a species of fish striped like a wrasse, has learned to imitate the cleaners. When a big fish presents itself, the little predator takes a quick bite out of it, then darts away.

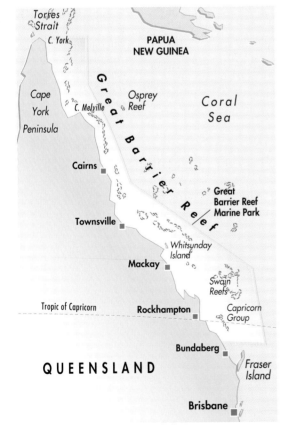

Plant propagators *Coral islands are nesting sanctuaries for birds, which return the favour by depositing plant seeds in their droppings.*

Development danger *Human activities are regulated along the Great Barrier Reef, and 160 islands have been declared national parks.*

Aquatic garden
Fragile coral formations rise towards the light. Most types of coral prefer to live within 30 ft (10 m) of the surface, though a few can tolerate greater depths. The polyps are easily damaged: they can die when brushed by a snorkeller and a yacht anchor causes severe damage.

down to them; they cannot endure fresh water, or long exposure to the air. Sunlight is a crucial ingredient, being converted into energy by minute algae that live within the polyp casing. In their quest for light, each species of coral has its own growth pattern, some forming boulder shapes, some thin sheets, some branching out to resemble shrubs. There are more than 350 species in all.

Continental drift

Australia harboured coral reefs hundreds of millions of years ago, but the origin of today's reefs – including a smaller 'twin' barrier off the north-west coast – goes back only 15 million years, to the period when the northern edge of the continent drifted into warm waters. As the drift continued, the reef system was able to extend southward, and in this way the foundations of the Great Barrier Reef were complete about 2 million years ago. At that point, the ocean level came into play. Each time the seas rose, the reef rose with them; each time the seas fell, the reef died from exposure, leaving limestone ramparts to be recolonised by a future age of drifting polyp spawn once the seas returned. The present reef dates from about 6000 BC, when the sea level rose after the last great ice age.

The struggle for survival

The reef itself, like all the life forms it sustains, is engaged in a perpetual struggle for survival against many agents of destruction, storms being the least of them. It is even at war with itself, since coral species attack one another with poisons and tissue-digesting chemicals. Some fish feed exclusively on the polyps, having evolved immunity to the sting carried by the polyp tentacles. More insidious are the

How coral reefs are created

A coral reef is formed by the mass effort of generation upon generation of tiny soft polyps, which extract calcium carbonate from the sea to build little cups of limestone – protective external skeletons. When the polyps die, the cups fill with debris and become encrusted with algae which cement them together to form hard reef rock, on which further generations can build their cups. Over long periods of time, the little creatures can build whole islands and even reconfigure oceans.

Cloned colonies can be created by a storm smashing off a section of reef, which then resumes construction elsewhere. Polyps also propagate over long distances, reproducing once a year in a spectacular manner. At different times along the Great Barrier Reef, on moonlit nights, whole colonies erupt, as if triggered by some secret signal, simultaneously releasing clouds of spawn that fill the sea with colour.

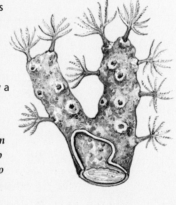

Night blossoms
Coral blooms when the colourful polyp tentacles emerge to find food at night.

various worms, mussels and sponges that bore into the coral, dissolving it with acid secretions. The crown-of-thorns starfish (*Acanthaster planci*) is the most voracious foe of all. It clamps onto a coral and dissolves the polyps with its digestive juices. A survey in 1988 found that a third of the Barrier Reef was damaged in this way.

For unwary human visitors, there are many dangers. Tales of giant clams trapping the legs of divers may be fanciful, but there are sharks, which can be dangerous. The venom of the little blue-ringed octopus and the box jellyfish, or 'sea wasp', can be fatal, while the sharp, poisonous dorsal spines of the stonefish make it as menacing as it is ugly. The stonefish is one of many species that use camouflage for protection, or as a device for ambushing prey, but most reef fish are of the opposite persuasion, advertising themselves in bright colours and bold patterns. Fish have excellent colour vision, and in the clear, crowded waters of the reef, distinctive colours and patterns are the best means of sending a signal, either to defend a territory or to find the right mate.

Alien invasion Tourists pose an ecological threat to islands like Heron (right) and Whitsunday (below).

Blue horizon

The Blue Mountains, just visible on Sydney's western horizon, seemed an impregnable barrier to the first colonists, who for an entire generation failed to find a way across them. Now lying within the city's commuter belt, they have not lost their magic and mystery, and can still spring astounding surprises.

The Blue Mountains are not truly mountains, but rather the rim of a sandstone plateau that has been fractured and eroded to form a ragged, infinitely contorted precipice guarding the interior of Australia. They are called 'blue' because of the blue haze that hangs over them. This is made up of microscopic droplets of eucalyptus oil rising in the air from the gum forests below. The eucalyptus 'dew' increases the refraction of sunlight, and so produces an intense blue aura.

Whenever it rains, the plateau's rivers and streams cascade over the precipice, causing tumbling, smoking water vapour to refract the sunlight into little rainbows rendered doubly vibrant by the unreal blue of the air around them. Sandstone crags glimmer through these light games, standing sentinel over the mass of silvery trunked trees and exotic ferns. The illusion of an enchanted forest is complete when a small wallaby bounds onto the scene, as if from nowhere.

But to early settlers intent on farming, these magical crags sometimes seemed more like symbols of a hostile, unyielding continent. When eventually a route was found over the mountains, the colonial governor commissioned an ode to the conquest of 'yon Blue Mountains, with tremendous brow'.

The Great Western Highway out of Sydney follows the ridge found by the pathfinding expedition. On either side, the land plunges into precipitous valleys, notably the Grose Valley and the Jamison Valley, whose panoramic features include the famous Three Sisters rock formation and a 'Giant Stairway'. Just 40 miles (65 km) from the heart of Sydney, the Blue Mountains are threatened by increasing pollution and development. Despite their modest height – they average 2300 ft (700 m) – the Blue Mountains are so steep and rugged that vehicles cannot enter many areas, and much forested wilderness remains, including 2849 sq miles (7379 km²) of national park. In one of these parks, a ranger came upon a pine tree that turned out to be an entirely new species. Named the Wollemi, its origins go back 160 million years to the heyday of the dinosaurs.

A difficult barrier to cross

For 25 years, the little colony around Sydney was restrained by the mountain wall that even Aborigines said was impassable. Disoriented convicts, desperate for freedom and believing somehow that China lay on the other side, were the first to try to scale it, only to perish in the attempt. Official expeditions also failed.

In 1813, after three weeks' struggle against ravines and torrents, William Wentworth, Gregory Blaxland and Lt William Lawson followed the line of a geological fault and discovered a way to the top of the escarpment, sighting kangaroo pastures beyond. Governor Macquarie offered pardons to 30 convicts if they could cut a road up the mountain face in six months, as against the three years it would otherwise take. They did it, and those that survived were set free.

The Three Sisters *These sandstone pinnacles striding into the Jamison Valley have become a signature image of the Blue Mountains.*

43

Five hundred national parks

The Australians began creating national parks in 1879, before they had fully explored their enormous land. However, when mining enterprises set about extracting minerals in the mountain ranges, and oil companies prepared to drill the Great Barrier Reef, and property speculators began to carve residential plots out of the rain forest, people realised that something more had to be done to protect their natural wonders.

The Blue Mountains are still blue thanks to an incident in 1932, when a group of bush-walkers chanced upon a party of men about to start cutting down a forest of giant blue gums in the Grose Valley. Efforts to stop the destruction were the first steps in a conservation campaign that led to the designation of the Blue Mountains National Park and several other parks in the same mountain belt.

Conserving Australia's natural wonders has not often been so straightforward. To early settlers, it was a 'rude, peculiar country' that needed to be tamed before it could be admired, even though they were often stunned by its magnificence. As his ship sailed into Sydney cove in January 1788, a surgeon with the First Fleet was reporting in his journal 'the stupendous rocks from the summit of the hills', and describing the kaleidoscopic birdlife as 'an enchantment'. He was already prepared for the kangaroo. Years before, an animal had been shot, shipped to England and stuffed, to sit for its portrait by the eminent painter George Stubbs. The fact that it was a wallaby was too fine a distinction for those times.

Along with explorers and gold diggers came geographers and naturalists, often accompanied by artists. In 1872, before the first east-west crossing of the interior had been accomplished,

Australia's world heritage

A dozen areas in Australia are inscribed in UNESCO's World Heritage list, a register of the Earth's natural and cultural treasures. Australia's heritage sites are: the **Great Barrier Reef** with its corals; the **Wet Tropics and the Daintree National Park** of northern Queensland; **Kakadu National Park** with its flora and fauna; **Uluru-Kata Tjuta National Park**, the heart of Aboriginal culture in The Northern Territory; the subtropical and temperate **Rainforest Reserves** of the central east coast; **Fraser Island**, the largest sand island in the world; **Shark Bay** in Western Australia, with its islands, bays and peninsulas; the **Willandra Dry Lakes** of western New South Wales with their fossils; the **Fossil Mammal sites of Riversleigh** in north-western Queensland and **Naracoorte** in South Australia; the **Tasmanian Wilderness**; and the spectacular **Lord Howe volcanic islands**, 300 miles (480 km) off the New South Wales coast.

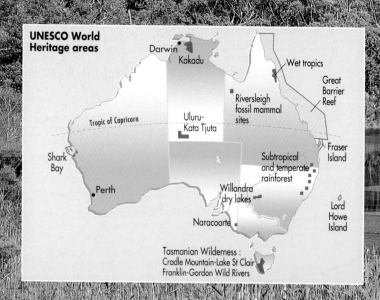

UNESCO World Heritage areas

Darwin
Kakadu
Wet tropics
Great Barrier Reef
Riversleigh fossil mammal sites
Tropic of Capricorn
Uluru-Kata Tjuta
Fraser Island
Shark Bay
Subtropical and temperate rainforest
Perth
Willandra dry lakes
Lord Howe Island
Naracoorte
Tasmanian Wilderness :
Cradle Mountain-Lake St Clair
Franklin-Gordon Wild Rivers

Kakadu National Park   Yellow Water Billabong is a dry season retreat for tall Jabiru storks, graceful brolga cranes and water birds of every description. Its crocodiles have become accustomed to the sight of tourists.

the Western Australians demarcated for preservation an expanse of virgin bush on a rise overlooking their little colonial capital, Perth. This was the year in which the Congress of the United States established Yellowstone Park in the Rocky Mountains as 'a public park or pleasuring ground', thereby creating the world's first national park. There are Western Australians who still argue that the honour of being first rightly belongs to their Kings Park, 1000 acres (405 ha) of which are still largely untouched bush.

The first national parks

No one, however, will deny the historic status of Australia's Royal National Park, gazetted in 1879, as a true progenitor of the world national parks movement. Just down the coast from Botany Bay, it remains a major attraction, with 12 miles (19 km) of rugged cliffs and secluded coves, eucalypt forest, rain forest and abundant wildlife – even the occasional passing whale. Victoria responded to the initiative taken by New South Wales, its rival, by creating three national parks in the 1880s, including Wilsons Promontory, Australia's southernmost peninsula,

Croajingolong National Park   A quiet inlet filled with birdsong belies the savage grandeur of the 60 miles (100 km) of cliffs and headlands fronting this magnificently preserved eastern wedge of Victoria. Dales Gorge (inset) in Karijini National Park, in the Pilbara region of Western Australia, has sheer rock walls typical of the deeply incised Hamersley Range, and a surprise bonus of permanent water.

affectionately known as 'the Prom' by the thousands who now wander its tracks and beaches.

Australia now has more than 500 national parks, many more than the United States. But numbers can deceive. Though 'national', the parks are run individually by the states in which they are situated, and their management varies, although in principle, conservation and the protection of the environment are priorities. In reality, these noble principles constantly clash with economic interests, which until recently almost always prevailed.

Earth Sanctuaries

Apart from the country's national parks, private nature reserves are beginning to contribute to the Australian conservation movement. One promoter, Dr John Wamsley, launched his 'Earth Sanctuaries' programme in 1969 with the object of buying and enclosing tracts of land, restoring them to their original state by eradicating alien flora and fauna, and breeding rare and endangered species. By the late 1990s, five Earth Sanctuaries had been established in South Australia and New South Wales, and on the York Peninsula. They are promoted through the international eco-tourist movement. Australians themselves can be hard to entice. In many ways, they are spoilt for choice, and distances within the country are so great that travel is both time-consuming and costly.

Protecting the environment

Despite Australia's sparse population and the extent of its open spaces, there has been serious depredation. The 200 years of European occupation have seen the loss of 40 per cent of the forest cover, and 75 per cent of what remained of the ancient rain forest; furthermore, 70 per cent of all vegetation has been modified by human activity, and some of the continent's thousands of unique plants and animals have been lost.

In 1972, a generally complacent attitude ended amid a struggle over the fate of the Tasmanian wilderness, which the state had begun to dam and flood in order to harness its energy. This coincided with a surge in worldwide concern for the environment and with diplomatic moves by the United Nations Educational, Scientific and Cultural Organization (UNESCO) to identify for protection 'World Heritage' areas of exceptional value. Some of Australia's natural wonders were on the UNESCO list, giving the national government in Canberra leverage over state authorities in ensuring their conservation.

The Australian ecosystem

A geologically stable island, worn down by sheer age, Australia is flatter than any other continental mass, and also the driest after Antarctica. The one significant elevation, the Great Dividing Range, divides it north to south, obliging the winds coming off the Pacific to dump their moisture on its eastern flanks. Beyond the divide, the land slopes gently towards the interior, through an intermediate region of uncertain rains where grazing animals outnumber people by hundreds to one. There are a number of arid mountain ranges, but finally, the land levels into the Western Plateau, the desiccated tableland that is two-thirds of Australia: the limitless 'Never-Never'.

But such simplicity obscures much that is unique. Australia straddles the Earth's tropic and temperate zones, and around its margins many weather systems come into play. The humid wetlands of the far north are at the mercy of a monsoon cycle of seasons: the Wet and the Dry. In the south-east, the landscape bears the scars of glaciers,

Watarrka National Park Sunk beneath weathered sandstone domes in the arid heart of Australia (right) is spectacular Kings Canyon and a sunken valley with palm-fringed rock pools named the Garden of Eden. The galah (left) is a typical Australian parrot. It ranges widely over the continent in large, raucous flocks.

Uluru National Park At the northern extremity of the park, savagely beautiful Lake Amadeus is a dry salt lake which occasionally fills with water. As the water evaporates, salts form in rings around the islands, starting with the paler, least soluble salts.

Shark Bay Marine Park Almost landlocked, the warm, salty waters of Shark Bay sustain mysterious, 3.5 billion-year-old life forms that are revealed at low tide. The bay is also a playground for whales and dolphins.

and snow covers the highest ground in winter. The far west, isolated by broad deserts, has seen the development of its own unique species. As for the Never-Never – it was not always so, as the fossils in its rocks and the deposits of salt in its dry lakebeds testify. In a few clefts and crannies, where the consuming glare of the sun cannot reach, patches of a lush past

Hinchinbrook, where rain forest meets reef

In places along Queensland's tropical north-eastern coast, rain forests and the waters enclosed by the Great Barrier Reef meet to create in unison what UNESCO has described as the world's greatest storehouse of biological material. Where Hinchinbrook Island nudges close to the mainland, the sea is squeezed into a narrow passage that snakes like a jungle river between a tumble of coastal rain forest and mangrove swamps on the one side, and the island's own precipitous peaks on the other. Hinchinbrook is the largest of 160 islands on the reef to have been designated as national parks. Its 156 sq miles (400 km²) consist largely of unexplored forest choked with vines, with acacia and bright-flowered banksia covering the high interior. As well as a profusion of bird life, there are gorgeous butterflies, pretty wallabies, and an aquatic population headed by crocodiles and dugongs.

The World Heritage sites of Fraser Island and Shark Bay share approximately the same latitude, but lying on opposite sides of the continent they offer an interesting study in Australia's contrasts. On the west, Shark Bay is set in a semi-arid region of scrub and desert grasses. Its hyper-salty tidal shallows are home to living fossils known as stromatolites – hard, squat lumps formed by microbial algae which are the oldest form of life on Earth. It is also a playground for dolphins. Fraser Island, in the east, is a subtropical paradise with an ecology like no other island on Earth. This giant sandbar is 76 miles (122 km) long, and 15 miles (25 km) wide, making it the largest on the planet. Its dunes were built up over 700 000 years and are now laden with dense rain forest, reedy swamps shaded by 200 ft (60 m) satinay trees, and limpid blue lakes.

Battleground *The summit of Mount Anne overlooks the scene of Tasmania's most bitter environmental battle, in Wild Rivers National Park.*

Water world *The 131 ft (40 m) Russell Falls are one of many cascades in Mount Field National Park, Tasmania. Glacier-carved Lake St Clair (inset) is Australia's deepest lake. It lies at the heart of the Tasmanian wilderness park system.*

Fraser Island suffered greatly from logging and mining (the sand contains minerals) before being protected. The Aboriginal inhabitants, the Butchulla, suffered even more. Many were 'resettled' far from home, and by the beginning of this century only a handful were left on the island they knew as K'gari.

Birth of the Greens

The 'green' movement owes its origin to disquiet over the fate of a Tasmanian lake. In 1972, environmental activists formed the United Tasmania Group (UTG) to fight in state elections a plan to dam the Gordon River and flood Lake Pedder, one of the jewels of the Tasmanian wilderness, as part of a hydroelectric scheme.

The concept was taken up in New Zealand, where the world's first national green party, called 'Values', was founded that year. A British 'ecology party' was formed in 1973. In Germany Die Grünen, 'The Greens', was the first party to adopt the name officially in the early 1980s. By the late 1990s, there were 70 green parties around the world.

survive against the odds, each sustaining its own tiny, unique ecosystem. In fact, the entire Australian ecosystem is a triumph of isolated adaptation to a slow process of drying-up, spread over millions of years. The flora and fauna that have thrived, no matter the conditions, have ancestral roots in a time when Australia was mostly rain forest. The mutations are impressive: 144 species of marsupial and more than 500 species of eucalyptus.

World Heritage sites

Precious rain forest remnants have been protectively included within a pair of World Heritage areas, which together incorporate dozens of national parks, state forests and some private land, in tracts scattered down the east coast from the far north to within an afternoon's drive of Sydney. Their diversity is astounding: they include six distinct types of rain forest, and each tract is unique.

Southern fiords
Milford Sound is the most famous of the 14 fiords of Fiordland, in the South Island. Mitre Peak rises 5550 ft (1695 m) sheer from the waterline. An annual rainfall of 215 in (5500 mm) feeds the waterfalls.

The sacred gift

New Zealand was too perfect and too fragile to endure in its virgin state, but the inspired gift of a Maori chief paved the way for the protection of sanctuaries of nature guarded by snow-capped peaks and rumbling volcanoes.

New Zealand, even more than Australia, is a land apart. While continental drift brought Australia within range of chance colonisation by plant seeds and creatures cast ashore on driftwood from South-east Asia, New Zealand's course kept it locked in oceanic seclusion for 80 million years. Walking through some of its virgin forests, under giant tree ferns and towering, lichen-covered podocarp trees, is to discover Gondwana, the supercontinent of 200 million years ago. New Zealand severed from Gondwana before the appearance of mammals, and therefore has few ground predators. As a result, birds colonised the land as well as the air. They included many flightless species, among them the colossal 12 ft (4 m) moa.

The arrival of humans
No vulnerable Eden can endure the appearance of man. The Maori brought many aspects of Polynesia with them: plants and seeds stowed aboard their ocean-going canoes, together with dogs and rats – the Polynesian rat, the kiore, being a delicacy. They set about clearing forests, slashing and burning millions of acres, and hunting the giant birds, which they drove to extinction.

The British settlers were seized by a desire to transform the spectacular landscape into one that looked like home, and the mellow climate, with its lack of extremes and year-round rainfall, was cooperative. They mowed down much of the remaining forest and created pastures for their imported farm stock. Yearning for the sounds of the British countryside, they formed 'acclimatisation societies' to import the blackbird and skylark, starling, thrush and dozens more, along with pheasants, partridges and other game birds. These birds flourished, and the humble sparrow was soon a proscribed pest.

Yellow-eyed penguin *This shy bird is now rare. It was once hunted for its oily meat.*

Preserving New Zealand

New Zealand has two areas on UNESCO's World Heritage list – **Tongariro** in the North Island, and **Te Wahipounamu**, which incorporates all the south-west of the South Island. Together they represent 10 per cent of the entire country. The country's national parks are: **Tongariro**, volcanic mountains (1887); **Egmont**, Mount Taranaki (1900); **Arthur's Pass**, forests and alps (1929); **Abel Tasman**, beaches and forests (1943); **Fiordland**, mountains and fiords (1953); **Aoraki Mount Cook**, mountain and glacier (1953); **Te Urewera**, natural forest reserve (1954); **Nelson Lakes**, glacial lakes Rotoiti and Rotoroa (1956); **Westland**, mountain seascapes (1960); **Mount Aspiring** (1964); **Whanganui**, river route of the first Maori explorers (1986); **Paparoa** (1987) and **Kahurangi** (1996), both prime landscapes with rich fauna and flora. New Zealand also has three marine parks and scores of forest and other nature reserves.

Mount Cook
New Zealand's highest peak at 12 316 ft (3 754 m) also shoulders the country's largest glacier. The mountain is still growing.

Stocking with wildlife

The first cat had come with Captain Cook, who also dropped off the first sheep and goat. Now came ferrets and weasels, stoats and hedgehogs, intended to check the rampant spread of other introduced fauna. Further alien wildlife was introduced from Australia and the Americas. Only snakes, and the fox, were banned in this wholesale stocking operation. 'The islands of birds' became a menagerie, especially of mammals.

Insidiously, the native vegetation was gnawed back by a plague of possums from Australia, together with rabbits, deer, goats and other browsing strangers; it was also attacked by alien insects that arrived as unintended supercargo. The ground-dwelling native birds, bereft of their forest cover, fell easy prey to stoats, cats, dogs and ferrets.

The struggle for preservation

Fortunately, some bastions of Eden remained, on smaller islands, and in the fastness of New Zealand's mountains. The first step in what has become a valiant preservation struggle was taken by a Maori paramount chief, Te Heuheu IV, who in a far-sighted gesture gave as a gift to the nation the mountain region of Tongariro, at the centre of the North Island. Tongariro, with its three active volcanoes, was for the Maori a place of great spiritual significance, and a focus for heroic myth and legend. The gift ensured that the area would remain sacred, rather than be sold off and used for other purposes. Towards the end of the 19th century, at the height of a process that was transforming the land around it into an idealised version of England, Tongariro became New Zealand's first, and the world's fourth, national park. Later Te Wahipounamu, which incorporates all of the south-west of the South Island, also became a protected area.

Waiotapu *The name of this geyser near Rotorua on the North Island means 'sacred waters'. It spouts every day at 10.15 am.*

Nature sanctuaries in the sea

Six small and remote island groups are used by New Zealand as sanctuaries for some of its more than 50 species of endangered birds. The wild, volcanic Chatham Islands, with a human population of 750, is the only inhabited group among them. Here the black robin was rescued from extinction after being reduced to five individuals by 1980. The population now numbers 300. The Chathams are also a human sanctuary, being home to descendants of the mysterious Moriori. The islands lie 480 miles (770 km) east of the South Island.

Constant heat *At Rotorua, ꞏ ꞏfrom geysers veil a ꞏꞏꞏ village. 'Whaka', as it is know ꞏs New Zealand's most popular natural attraction.*

Tasmanian paradox

The story of Tasmania is one of beauty and beastliness. The island's past was so laden with cruelty that its name was changed from Van Diemen's Land in 1855. In its landscape the gentle and savage contrast dramatically, but nowhere else in Australia is there such a luxuriance of green.

Tasmania, or 'Tassie', as Australians fondly call it, is everything that the mainland is not. Heart-shaped, and half the size of England, the moist, green island enjoys a temperate climate, four distinct seasons and comparatively long twilights. Although joined to the mainland in the past, the two have been separated by the turbulent Bass Strait for the past 10 000 years, which has been long enough to make Tasmania a world apart.

In the north, in the central midlands and on the east coast, where the land is fertile and most of the 450 000 Tasmanians live, what once was eucalyptus forest is now a domesticated patchwork of rolling meadows, farmlands, orchards and vineyards, dappled with trees from the English countryside. Along the coast, sailboats bob against a green landscape dotted with sheep. A relaxed, old-time charm pervades even the southern Tasman Peninsula: this 19th-century gulag with its penal settlement of Port Arthur is now a tourist attraction.

Verdant sanctuary   This valley lies in Cradle Mountain-Lake St Clair National Park, a prime part of Tasmania's World Heritage area. The Tasmanian devil (left) howls, growls and shrieks, pretending to be more fierce than it really is.

A beautiful wilderness

To the west, Tasmania seems to revert to its original fearsome nature, when it was known as Van Diemen's Land. Jagged mountains poke above tangled forest and lakes, creating a beautiful but forbidding wilderness that was not penetrated by a single road until the 1930s. The landscape, large parts of

The fight to save the wilderness

little merit in untamed nature, and dreamed of solving the state's unemployment problem by harnessing the rushing waters to generate cheap electricity and attract new industries.

Supported by the Tasmanian government, the state Hydro-Electric Commission pressed forward with dam construction, which would have transformed the heart of the wilderness by flooding the Franklin and Lower Gordon rivers and the surrounding rain forest. Protesters blocked the site and hundreds were arrested before construction was halted by the intervention, in 1983, of the federal government in Canberra.

Tasmania gained an increase in tourism to offset the loss of power, but the 'Greenies' continued to campaign for the restoration of Lake Pedder by opening the sluices of the dam that destroyed it. An official enquiry in 1995 determined that this was feasible.

Lake Pedder was unique in having gently sloping shores of white quartz sand, but its beaches were lost beneath the silted bottom of artificial reservoirs containing 27 times the volume of water in Sydney Harbour. The destruction of Lake Pedder was decried as an ecological tragedy. Many in Tasmania, however, saw

The oldest living things

The temperate rain forest of south-west Tasmania is one of the last of its kind in the world. In its depths are to be found some of the most ancient forms of life, and possibly the oldest living organisms, including lichens and mosses.

The huon pine (*Lagarostrobus franklinii*) can grow to 130 ft (40 m) in height, and has a circumference of 15 ft (4.5 m). Its kind has existed for an estimated 135 million years, and individual trees can live for more than 2000 years. A stand of huon pines was recently estimated to be 10 000 years old – making it older than Bass Strait, which separates Tasmania from the Australian mainland. Unfortunately, the huon pines made perfect ships' timber and they were the prime target of loggers until no more were to be found. The survivors are now protected.

River idyll *The Derwent River rises in the sparkling lake country of Tasmania's central plateau. Seen here below New Norfolk, it widens before reaching the sea at Hobart.*

Ocean hazards *Dangerous shoals and currents near Strahan (below) make this only anchorage on the west coast too dangerous for most shipping. Across the island, at the same latitude, the 1000 ft (300 m) granite mass of the Hazards (inset) rises abruptly from the Tasman Sea.*

which are unlike anywhere else in Australia, is a result of geological upheaval and a succession of ice ages in which the mountains were chiselled by glaciers to leave deep ravines and troughs, which filled to become hundreds of lakes and tarns.

Throughout the 19th century, access to the west was possible only by sea. Sailing ships had to beat around the coast against the prevailing gale-force winds of the Roaring Forties, then thread through a narrow passage, aptly named Hell's Gate, to reach the only safe anchorage on the west coast. The worst of Tasmania's convicts were assigned to this 'Place of Ultra Banishment and Punishment', where they were forced by strokes of the lash to fell valuable stands of timber for up to 16 hours a day. The conditions were so harsh that many prisoners considered death to be preferable.

Prospectors braved the wilderness later in the century, and there were pockets of fevered activity where gold, silver, copper and tin were discovered. But the boom was short-lived and most of the mining camps were soon reclaimed by the forest. In 1912, an Austrian named Gustav Weindorfer built himself a pine chalet in the woods and was largely responsible for the

area around it being proclaimed a scenic reserve in 1922. He proposed 'a national park for all time'. Five national parks were mapped out and now fall within a UNESCO World Heritage zone that incorporates more than 20 per cent of Tasmania.

The primordial rain forests

Mists swirl through the wilderness rain forests, with ferns and mosses in the damp gulleys and proteas growing on drier ground. Rain-laden clouds break across the windswept highlands, drenching alpine rock gardens set amid green carpets of cushion plants and clumped buttongrass. Here and there, a palm-like pandanus, reaching up to 40 ft (12 m), makes a surprise statement. Slightly lower down is the domain of the giant King Billy pine and the smaller pencil pine, as well as the hunting ground of the fierce, spotted quoll, or native cat, and the Tasmanian devil – the world's largest carnivorous marsupial.

Canopied forest engulfs the lower slopes; mosses and lichens hang from the branches of myrtle beech and sassafras, cloaking a moist understorey of tree ferns. Out of the dank valleys soar huon pines, some of which were growing before the birth of Christ. Life swarms on the forest floor in the

Underworld *Lichen-draped rain forest with a damp, green undergrowth of ferns thrives at lower altitudes in Tasmania's western mountains. Environmentalists vow to protect these areas, which make up only part of Tasmania's forests.*

Wild heritage *The Tasmanian Wilderness zone on UNESCO's World Heritage List includes five national parks and more than a dozen reserves and conservation areas. Mount Ossa (left) and the King William Range (below) lie at its heart. The preservation fight is far from over. Grazing, some mining, and electricity generation continue to be permitted in many areas.*

The first Tasmanians

Tasmanian Aborigines had a distinct culture from those on the mainland. Cut off for 8000 years by the flooding of Bass Strait, they lacked the boomerang and woomera, and their stone, flint and shell tools differed in design. By making a comparative study of island and mainland lifestyles, beliefs and legends, anthropologists and social scientists might have had a unique opportunity to make an analysis of human cultural evolution over a vast span of time.

Unfortunately it was not to be. One early 'anthropological' activity was a gruesome one. Shortly after the first settlers landed in 1804, a cannon was turned on a group of Aborigines, and the bones of those killed were packed in casks and shipped to Sydney for study. When the Aborigines tried to fight back they were hunted down. The last tribal indigenous Tasmanian died in 1876.

form of insects, lizards and frogs, while tiny marsupials wait for the night hidden in nests dug into rotting logs. In places, the undergrowth is so thick that it is hard to progress more than a mile a day.

Disregarded when not abused, the region has now become a mecca for hikers, white-water rafters, naturalists and 'ecotourists' drawn by its primordial delights. Trails lead through some of the world's last remaining temperate rain forest, and possibly the last lair of a striped thylacine, the Tasmanian tiger which was assumed to have become extinct in 1936, but is still the subject of unconfirmed sightings. A favourite trail is the 53 mile (85 km) Overland Track from Cradle Valley to Cynthia Bay, at the foot of Lake St Clair; it takes five to seven days to traverse.

Yet these wonders very nearly did not survive. Many Tasmanians in the early 1980s seemed to agree with their premier, who saw the wild rivers as 'brown and leech-ridden' eyesores that needed to be harnessed as an energy source. Part of the Gordon River was dammed and beautiful Lake Pedder flooded before the scheme was halted amid a bitter Australia-wide debate. Even now, the issue is not dead.

Mythical landscapes

Australia has no Stonehenge or other ancient man-made monument, but it doesn't need them. Nature has sculpted fabulous rock formations that stir profound feelings of wonder and awe. Uluru (Ayers Rock) is the most famous of these monoliths.

Uluru sunrise   *The rock emerges from the night in an astonishing fiery glow.*

The massive sandstone rock known as Uluru is perhaps the best known image of Australia. Close to the centre of the continent itself, Uluru's reddish-brown mass rises from a vast plain of ochre sand. In Aboriginal culture, it's an important meeting point of the 'dreaming tracks', the crisscrossing mythical and sacred tracks that mark the journeys their ancestors made as they moulded the landscape – and even the most jaded tourist is seized by a sense of the sacred in nature when, at sunset, the mountain-sized rock is transfigured from vermilion to purple, to mauve, to violet, to midnight blue and, in a magical instant, to deepest black.

Wave Rock

The forces of wind and water have combined to produce this extraordinary formation in Western Australia: a granite outcrop that looks like a petrified ocean breaker 50 ft (15 m) high. Even before it was exposed to the elements, Wave Rock was being formed underground as water combined with acids in the soil to scoop away the rock by dissolving it. Many visitors make the 430 mile (700 km) round trip from Perth to see it with their own eyes.

Ocean breaker   *This freak of nature has achieved fame as a surfer's dream turned to stone.*

A half-hour's drive away are the 36 reddish-brown domes of Kata Tjuta. The highest was named Mount Olga by the explorer Ernest Giles in 1872, in honour of a German queen, and the whole became known as The Olgas. They are now called by their Aboriginal name, which means many heads. They once were joined to Uluru, but separated some 65 million years ago.

The powers of erosion

Geologists explain how Uluru and the Kata Tjuta are the residue of mountains that weathered and washed into a sea hundreds of millions of years ago, there to be laid down as seabed, then compressed, uplifted and tilted almost vertically. Like the ancient mountains from whose sands they are made, the monoliths are not immutable. The elements eat away at the corners, rounding off the edges, while sand in the wind scours and polishes them. The sculpting never ceases. Iron particles in the rock combine with moisture to form rust, which expands to produce flaking in a process called 'exfoliation'. It is this process that has created the Devil's Marbles, a jumble of smooth granite boulders, like monster bowling balls, that litter the roadside 245 miles (390 km) north of Alice Springs. Various Aboriginal legends are associated with them.

In the far west, the Pinnacles Desert is another strange site. The first explorers to reach the area found an eerie landscape of rough-hewn stone columns and spires of every size, from 16 ft (4.8 m) monoliths to spikes no taller than a finger. Scientists eventually established that these were the remains of an ancient forest, which had been turned into limestone.

Pinnacles Desert   *An 'ancient city' turned out to be a petrified forest.*

CHAPTER 2

EXTREMES OF NATURE

Three-quarters of Australia is desert or arid steppe that loses more moisture to evaporation than it receives in rainfall, yet the continent also lies in the path of the tropical monsoon. It contains the largest expanse of sand-ridge deserts in the world, yet in their midst are moist pockets where exotic life flourishes. Being so large and flat, without mountain ranges to interrupt the build-up of menacing weather patterns, it is subject to hot tropical winds and to cool air from the Antarctic, producing cyclones, sand storms and racing bush fires. Across the Tasman Sea, the Roaring Forties howl around the Southern Ocean, to crash into the South Island of New Zealand, whose peaks are being thrust up by forces within the Earth and ground down again by glaciers. The North Island wobbles as a result of one plate sliding beneath another on the Earth's crust, causing lava and volcanic ash to spew and jetting geysers into the air. New Zealand has been called 'the Shaky Isles'.

The MacDonnell Ranges, Australia.

Deserts of many colours

To those on the ground, the Australian interior is a vast arid expanse under a fierce blue sky. But seen from the air, it is a spectacle of incredible beauty and diversity, like an immense work of abstract art. Seas of sand give way to stone, salt and scrub, patterned and coloured in multiple tones, and dissected by the huge white veins of dried-up riverbeds.

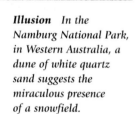

Illusion *In the Namburg National Park, in Western Australia, a dune of white quartz sand suggests the miraculous presence of a snowfield.*

Nineteenth-century explorers had a name for the enormous inner core of the Australian outback that repeatedly drove them back, blinded by its glare and turned into tottering scarecrows by its lack of sustenance. They called it the 'Ghastly Blank'.

Deluded by westward-flowing rivers, they searched for a bountiful inland sea, only to find that the rivers petered out in deserts, each one more hostile than the last. This was not the desert of Arabian romance, but a succession of blighted zones of incredible perversity. The explorers tore their legs to shreds on the aptly named spear grass, only to confront interminable lines of compacted sand dunes, ruler-straight and stretching from horizon to horizon; or they would hobble onto rock deserts of gibbers – wind-polished stones, bright as gems and like a bed of hot coals when heated by the sun. Exhausted, and with their water run out, they would then fall upon a desert of dried-up salt lakes.

The termites of Tanami

The Tanami Desert, in the Northern Territory, is the kingdom of the termite. Brick-red mounds are scattered 300 to the acre (800 per ha) over a wide plain of spinifex. Each mound is a citadel-city, linked to others by subterranean highways. Spinifex, which is too tough for grazing animals, makes a perfect pasture for chomping termites. These industrious little insects make a nourishing meal for lizards and small marsupials, who in turn provide a bounty for birds. What seems like an arid emptiness is in fact thronged with life.

Australia has about 350 species of termite, sometimes called the white ant, and they have a tremendous capacity for construction. The mounds can be 20 ft (6 m) high, and the shape varies according to the species. Some species design in an east-west alignment to minimise the impact of the hot afternoon sun. The walls are made of sand or soil particles cemented with saliva and baked rock-hard by the sun. Inside are chambers and galleries interconnected by a maze of passageways. The structure is ventilated and drained and the temperature is maintained at a constant 30°C (86°F). Each mound has royalty – a queen and king who are mother and father to the entire colony. Egg production can reach 30 000 per day.

Desert wildlife *Life thrives despite the extreme aridity.*

56

Sand and salt   The Painted Desert of the Arckaringa Hills (left) lies to the north of the Coober Pedi opal field. Above: Lake McLeod owes its colour to mineral salts.

Viewed from the air

Dozens of expeditions established the dimensions of the 'Ghastly Blank', but it took the development of aircraft to reveal its beautiful, patterned complexity, and only from space was it possible to fully discern its dynamics. Satellite views have revealed a series of sand ridges fanning out like the spokes of a cartwheel. The system is the largest of its kind in the world, its present arrangement dating from the last ice age, when a constant, fierce wind swirled around the continent in an anti-clockwise direction, blowing the finest, lightest particles towards the eastern and southern coasts and heaping heavier grains in waves that settled and compacted as the world warmed and the winds died down. This is most marked in the Northern Territory's Simpson Desert, where regimented lines of dunes are up to 200 ft (60 m) high and can stretch in a straight line for 75 miles (120 km). The first pilot to fly over the desert, in 1929, reported 'a pink and gigantic circular gridiron ribbed with close, straight sand ridges from horizon to horizon'. The deep red

Monsters out of Australia's past

Aboriginal rock paintings of giant kangaroos and wombats were presumed to be flights of fantasy until 1892, when massive bones were found scattered over Lake Callabonna, a salt pan in the Cobbler Desert, east of the Eyre basin. Subsequent expeditions retrieved scores of huge skeletons belonging to 2 ton diprotodons, the largest marsupial that ever lived, and a similarly enormous species of kangaroo. The creatures became extinct around 20 000 years ago.

Naming the deserts

Because deserts were all they found, the early Australian explorers did not become world-famous, as some of their contemporaries on other continents did, and their only memorial is their name attached to some stretch of wilderness, or to a desert plant. Sturt's Stony Desert is as forbidding now as it was when Captain Charles Sturt struggled through it in 1845. Sturt lost his second-in-command to scurvy, having hauled a boat over hundreds of miles of spear grass in expectation of setting sail on the fantasy sea. He and his men pressed on, limping over the gibbers and dodging fissures deep enough to engulf a horse, only to be blocked by another desert, the immense, sand-ribbed Simpson.

Sturt escaped with his life, but other explorers did not. The Gibson Desert commemorates one of them, Alfred Gibson, who was lost there in 1874. His companion, Ernest Giles, survived by tramping 35 miles (60 km) to recover two water kegs they had left in a tree as an emergency supply. Much of the water was gone, but he hoisted a 35 lb (16 kg) keg on his shoulder and staggered back to their depot. He beat starvation by chancing upon a dying baby wallaby and eating it raw, including the fur and bones. Giles had had other near escapes, his packhorses once sinking into a quagmire of hot salt mud. His dream was to cross the continent from east to west. He achieved it, after crossing 'a region utterly unknown to man, and as utterly forsaken by God'. On finding a hollow with fresh water, he dedicated the spring and the whole godforsaken tract to his queen, naming it the Great Victoria Desert.

Desolation in stone   This parched expanse of gibber desert fringes the Oodnadatta track, west of the Eyre basin.

to rose-pink colour of the dunes – and the reason that the heart of Australia is called the Red Centre – is the result of a thin coating of iron oxide on each grain of sand; in other words, rust.

Adaptation and survival

The Australian deserts are the product of millions of years of drying out. The continent reached its present arid state about 2.5 million years ago, when a series of swings between the arid

The crossing of the Simpson

The Simpson Desert covers 55 000 sq miles (143 000 km²), more than three times the size of Switzerland. It was a death trap for early explorers and later aerial surveys persuaded people that crossing it was impossible. But in 1936 Edmund Colson, who had waited many years for an unusually wet season, traversed the desert's southern fringe from Oodnadatta to Birdsville, taking with him an Aborigine, five camels and a month's supply of food and water. In 1939 a scientific expedition made the first 300 mile (480 km) crossing of the heart of the desert. Tracks for four-wheel-drive vehicles now cross the desert, parts of which are a national park.

regimes of global ice ages and wetter periods accelerated the process of pulverising sediments and rock fragments. This very gradual transformation from lush plenty to arid wasteland gave Australian plants and animals time to adapt, and helps to explain why even the most forbidding zones of sand or gibber are far from dead.

Spiky hummock grass, a uniquely drought-resistant species of Australian grass, holds much of the desert together with its tangle of roots, driving deep into the sand and spreading near the surface. Its bristling, spear-like clumps provide refuge for a host of small creatures. Where the sand overlies slightly richer gravel soils, mulga scrub takes over. Like hummock grass, this desert wattle can survive in a dormant state through the worst times.

Amid the burning gibber, patches of tiny plants are home to insects, lizards, the tiny hopping mouse and a small marsupial carnivore, the kowari. Uniquely adapted gibberbirds, or desert chats, build their nests among the stones. Even the beds of salt sustain life. Ants harvest microscopic algae that grow between the salt crystals, and they themselves provide salty morsels for specially adapted lizards; a food chain thus exists in seemingly impossible circumstances. Each type of desert has its own types of lizard, all camouflaged and adapted to their particular environment. Most creatures hide in burrows during the day and eliminate the need to drink by ingesting moisture when they eat plants or prey; some hibernate when all moisture is gone.

The desert blooms Downpours of rain are rare, but when they come long-dormant seeds sprout. More than 800 plants have been found in the forbidding Simpson Desert. Left: Australia has 70 venomous snakes, but most are non-aggressive.

River crossing The normally dry Diamantina River traverses the Queensland channel country to the margins of the Sturt and Simpson deserts – a zone that proved fatal to early explorers. Burke and Wills crossed here on their final march.

Waiting for the rains

All life in the interior is geared to the next drop of rain, no matter how long the wait. Annual rainfall averages just 5 in (125 mm) in the driest areas, but is less predictable than in other arid parts of the world: a short season of plenty can be bracketed by many years of no rain at all.

Beneath the desert cloak, an old landscape lies hidden. In deep ravines carved by ancient torrents, permanent rock pools preserve vestiges of a lush past, while beneath the smothered beds of dormant rivers is just enough moisture to sustain stands of coolabah trees, silvery trunked ghost gums and river red gums. These are home to parrots and flocks of squabbling budgerigars, and provide

Desert island This patch of desert is in one of Australia's usually dry salt lakes. The spinifex clumps grow outwards to create rings as old growth dies off.

shade for the red kangaroo. Only the emu can withstand the noonday heat, thanks to its double layer of feathers.

At the centre of the old drainage system into which the continent's ancient rivers flowed are hundreds of salt lakes, which are normally dry. Their beds of mineral salts were leached from rocks and laid down over millions of years by waters that alternately flowed and then evaporated. The largest of these lakes is Lake Eyre in South Australia, a 3600 sq mile (9000 km²) sheet of salt. Three or four times a century, a tropical cyclone over the Coral Sea strays off course sufficiently to flood the area that drains towards Lake Eyre. Then it is reborn. Following phenomenal rains in 1974, the salt flat – on which Donald Campbell had set a world land speed record in 1964 in his car, *Bluebird* – disappeared under 20 ft (6 m) of water. That year, a boat crossed Lake Eyre for the very first time. Such a flood attracts many birds from distant wetlands, including seagulls drawn 400 miles (640 km) from the coast.

Water miraculously transforms this sandy, stony landscape. Seemingly dead scrub turns green and blossoms, while desert peas, daisies and wild hops spatter the plains with their bright colours. As pools form in claypans and dormant rivers run, every living thing is caught up in a frenzy of feeding and reproduction. Fish eggs hatch, desert frogs emerge from their burrows, and within days, dragonflies are mating in flight and desert swifts swoop over the water to snap up insects. In a race against time, birds' courtships are as rapid as their breeding cycles. The gums and coolabahs along the watercourses are rapidly crammed with nests; soon, bright clouds of budgerigars are swirling over the desert.

Then it is over. Much of the water evaporates, but some sinks down to feed into the drainage systems, topping up reservoirs that will sustain ribbons of life through the next period of desiccation.

Hunters and miners

Over thousands of years, the Aborigines learned to contend with all but the harshest parts of the interior. Family groups moved according to the rains and the availability of food. They were superb trackers and hunters, able to blend with their surroundings and bring down prey with boomerangs cut from mulga. Away from waterholes, they drew on generations of accrued knowledge, knowing where to find moisture stored in cracks in the rock, in plants, even in some animals. A number of tribes, such as the Karadjeri and Nygina of the Great Sandy Desert, still live largely by traditional means.

Europeans continued to perish in harrowing circumstances. But one enterprising community of miners 'built' a town called Coober Pedy – from *kupa piti*, an Aboriginal word meaning 'hole in the ground'. Coober Pedy, in the mid-north of South Australia, stands atop the world's greatest lode of opals. The area is subject to blinding sandstorms and temperatures that range from 50°C (122°F) on some summer days to freezing cold on winter nights. Digging for gems, the miners discovered what the desert creatures had always known – that conditions underground are much more tolerable than on the surface. They created subterranean homes in which the temperature stays constant at around 25°C (77°F). Today the town has underground shops, restaurants, churches, and even an underground hotel, with air conditioning.

Evaporated hope   The early explorers looked for an inland sea, but all they found was salt. The mineral deposits in hundreds of salt lakes often form a solid enough crust to serve as a landing strip for aircraft.

A mystery mole in the sand

The marsupial mole (*Notoryctes typhlops*) is a wonder of evolution and the most elusive resident of the

Simpson Desert. Its discovery under a spinifex tussock in 1888 excited naturalists because it supported Darwin's theory of convergent evolution. Although descended from different stock, it had developed the same physical characteristics and habits as its namesake in other continents. Blind and deaf, the marsupial mole has large claws and powerful forelimbs that enable it to 'swim' just below the surface of the sand in search of insects and the occasional small reptile. Its sand-coloured coat renders it virtually invisible, and its metabolism slows down to conserve energy when conditions are most harsh.

Indian
Ocean

Darwin

Tanami
Desert

Great Sandy
Desert

Simpson
Desert

Tropic of Capricorn

Gibson
Desert

Oodnadatta

Cordillo
Downs

Great Victoria
Desert

Lake
Eyre

Nullarbor Plain

Perth

Great Australian
Bight

Sydney

Tasmania

The islands that smoke and tremble

New Zealand's stunning beauty is a product of its instability – the landscape remains in a process of violent flux. Yet its inhabitants are temperamentally disinclined to be disturbed by the islands' numerous eruptions and shocks.

Ice and fire   Locked in ice at the summit of the North Island, the crater lake of Mount Ruapehu is sometimes too hot for swimming. In 1953, the crater lake discharged its watery contents down the mountain, causing many deaths far below.

New Zealand shakes and shudders: 15 000 earth tremors register each year, of which around 200 are strong enough to be felt. When a large shallow earthquake occurs – about once a year – house foundations tremble, road surfaces crack and fissures appear in the ground.

The North Island straddles one of the Earth's great plate boundaries, where one giant plate slides under another, in the process releasing tremendous energy. The South Island is piling up, the Southern Alps rising at more than half an inch (12.7 mm) a year. Were it not for compensating erosion, Mount Cook would be 59 000 ft (18 000 m) high – more than twice the height of Mount Everest. Meanwhile in the North Island, a million Aucklanders are living in an area formed by more than 50 volcanic eruptions, the most recent between 700 and 800 years ago, and thus unlikely to be the last.

New Zealand's Antarctic connection

New Zealand's location has made it a prime launch base for Antarctic exploration, and the country plays an active role in the protection and scientific study of the continent. Sir Edmund Hillary followed his conquest of Everest by taking part in the British Commonwealth Trans-Antarctic Expedition, reaching the South Pole on January 3, 1958.

Belching volcanoes

The North Island's central plateau is commanded by a line of active volcanoes. Ngauruhoe is associated with Ngatoro-i-rangi, a legendary tohunga or high priest, in Maori lore. It is the youngest volcano, a mere 2500 years old and already rising to 7516 ft

Eruption   Mount Ruapehu spat rocks and belched massive clouds of ash that disrupted air traffic in 1995 (left and below). The following year its rumblings ruined the skiing season.

(2291 m) at the tip of its perfect cone. Ngauruhoe has erupted 50 times in the past 150 years, at other times venting gases of up to 1000°C (1800°F). Mount Ruapehu, its elder brother, is more active still. Decked in snow, with ski lifts on its slopes, Ruapehu seems benign, but the skiing is liable to cancellation because of volcanic mudflows, or eruptions of hot rocks and ash, as happened in 1996. The main crater contains a lake that has mood swings as dramatic as its changes of colour – from

Preparing for the next big shake

Despite their outward calm, New Zealanders are concerned about the instability of their land. The country has hosted international seminars on seismic disturbance, and new buildings have incorporated the latest 'shock absorber' technologies. In 1993 the government created an Earthquake Commission, which quickly proved its worth by stabilising a landslip threatening homes on the Banks Peninsula.

grey to yellow to vivid green, depending upon the alchemy beneath it. On Christmas Eve, 1953, it belched a muddy torrent that swept down the mountain and destroyed a railway bridge moments before an express train arrived, killing 151 people.

Earthquakes

Where there is no volcano to threaten the immediate neighbourhood, the ground may be moved by other means.

Sulphur cauldron
The gurgling hot springs of Rotorua (above) give off a sulphurous smell much like that of rotten eggs.

Fiery line *The majestic volcanoes of the North Island form a line of beacons resulting from the movements of two plates colliding near the edges of the Pacific Ocean – the so-called 'Ring of Fire'.*

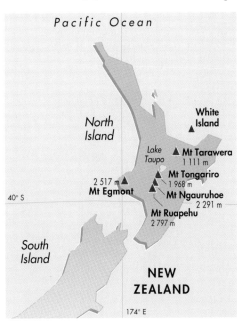

Pacific Ocean

North Island

White Island

Lake Taupo

▲ Mt Tarawera
1 111 m

▲ Mt Tongariro
1 968 m

2 517 m ▲
Mt Egmont

▲▲ Mt Ngauruhoe
2 291 m

40° S

Mt Ruapehu
2 797 m

South Island

NEW ZEALAND

174° E

Mount Tarawera's anger and a lost wonder of the world

The pink and white terraces beneath Mount Tarawera drew 19th-century travellers to what was regarded as one of the wonders of the world. The beautiful stepped terraces were formed over centuries from silica deposited by thermal waters trickling down to Lake Tarawera, a few miles from Rotorua.

On May 31, 1886, tourists on the lake reported seeing a phantom Maori war canoe, a portent of disaster. In Te Wairoa, on the lakeside, an aged sage warned of impending disaster, allegedly because the fire spirit within the mountain was angered by a lack of respect shown in turning the village into a tourist resort – the first in New Zealand.

Ten days later, just before dawn on June 10, the ground shook and the mountain split open along its length. The eruption swallowed up Te Wairoa and two other villages, consumed 147 Maori and six Europeans, and destroyed the famous terraces. The sage was rescued by Europeans after his fellow villagers refused to dig him out. Te Wairoa has been excavated and preserved as a 19th-century Maori village.

Mineral baths *Taking a tip from the Maori, Europeans seized upon the health benefits of New Zealand's geothermal waters. Rotorua's first building was a bathhouse.*

Wellington has experienced a dozen earthquakes in its short history; the first, in 1848, flattened the early settlement; the second, in 1855, raised the shoreline by several feet. Another earthquake in 1942 caused widespread havoc, including damage to 8000 homes.

Napier, on Hawke's Bay, is renowned for the charm of its Art Deco-style buildings, all erected at the same time as a statement of defiance after an earthquake on the morning of February 3, 1931, destroyed the original town with the loss of 256 lives. The Napier earthquake registered 7.9 on the Richter scale, slightly more powerful than the one that flattened the small town of Murchison in the South Island two years earlier.

Hot springs and geysers

The focus of New Zealand's tourism is Rotorua, where the volcanism manifests as playful geysers, gurgling mud pools and hot springs. Between Rotorua and Mount Ngauruhoe lies Lake Taupo, covering 234 sq miles (606 km²), the central portion of the volcanic zone. The lake lies in a crater formed by an eruption so massive it caused skies to darken over China and Rome in AD 186. Still mightier, earlier cataclysms slung debris from Taupo around the world. The lake is peaceful for now, though steam hisses at its margins.

Nature's rages

Drought, fire and flood are part of the natural order in Australia. Flood replenishes and fire encourages new growth, even when the short-term effects appear terrible.

Rampage *Cyclone damage near Cape York.*

The weather in Australia can be a matter of life or death. The first settlers learned this lesson when, in 1806, sudden floods threatened to wash away their little colony; then a drought lasting from 1813 to 1815 drove them to the brink of starvation.

Flooding is seasonal in the north, and a hazard down the populated east coast whenever heavy rainfall hits the Great Dividing Range. In the Big Wet of 1974, every Australian state suffered; in Brisbane, 6700 houses were damaged and 12 people killed. Drought is a greater threat. Australia straddles a zone of high atmospheric pressure that inhibits cloud formation, even as it sucks up moisture. In the Great Drought of 1895 to 1903, almost every settled area was hit; crops failed, millions of sheep and cattle died, and entire communities were ruined.

Wind has also to be reckoned with in the wide, open spaces. Thermal spirals, 'willy-willys', can develop into vicious whirlwinds, and storms in the far north can become deadly cyclones. Cyclones, like the typhoons and hurricanes of the Northern Hemisphere, are caused by winds swirling around a low-pressure pocket, the eye of the storm. They carry the added danger of devastating tidal waves; since 1800, tidal waves have killed more than 1000 people.

Drought and wind combine to foster raging bushfires that regularly obliterate great swathes of the outback, and are a deadly peril when they engulf major settled areas, as happened in 1851, 1939 and 1983 – disasters memorialised as Black Thursday, Black Friday, and Ash Wednesday.

Devilish dust *Often fierce, and common during the Dry, sandstorms sweep over large areas. Sometimes they may be caused by localised disturbances, yet are strong enough to uproot trees, or remove a roof. The clearing of forests, overgrazing, and attempts to farm marginal land have exacerbated the problem; some formerly productive areas have been turned into dust bowls.*

In the eye of Tracy

Darwin, resilient capital of the Northern Territory, was hit by cyclones in 1897 and 1937. On Christmas Eve, 1974, the city's inhabitants ignored radio warnings that a severe monsoon storm was approaching, and prepared to party.

Around midnight, Cyclone Tracy struck, creeping across a 24 mile (40 km) front and subjecting Darwin to the most ferocious and prolonged assault ever suffered by a modern town. The airport windmeter registered 134.5 mph (217 km/h) when it failed at 3.05 am. Gusts up to 175 mph (280 km/h) were estimated. The cyclone demolished public buildings and 70 per cent of the city's houses were left structurally damaged, most of them beyond repair. Sixty-five people were killed.

Darwin's entire population of 45 000 was evacuated while a new city was constructed. Half of the people did not return, resulting in a population shift as marked as the city's drastic change in appearance. The old Darwin, with its elegant homes on stilts, was gone forever. In its place, an architecturally more monotonous, but far safer city, has now grown to almost twice the size of the old.

Ominous signs
Drought combined with overgrazing can have dire results, as seen here near Broken Hill, in the New South Wales outback. Satellite images show that the desert is expanding, leading some experts to question the merit of any grazing in the interior.

The outback – another world

Rains as violent as they are rare, winds sometimes exceeding 125 mph (200 km/h) and temperature swings of as much as 33°C (60°F) between day and night have combined to strip bare a landscape once green and fertile. It is now so daunting that the human population is measured in square miles per person.

Buried treasure
The Hamersley mountains in the Pilbara (above) have a harsh beauty, and hidden riches in the form of massive reserves of iron ore.

Stripy hills *The quaintly named Bungle Bungle massif in the Kimberley (above and left) is one of the extraordinary scenic jewels of the Australian landscape.*

Take off from Sydney and fly over the Blue Mountains. Beyond spreads a rolling plain, which was dotted with eucalyptus trees when the bullock carts of the pioneer home-steaders first lumbered into it, and is now dotted with sheep where it is not under wheat. Here and there, the glint of sun on tin roofs betrays the presence of a small town. This is the 'sun-burnt country' of the Dorothea Mackellar poem that every Australian child learns by heart. The geometric patterns of cul-tivation blur into a smudgy grey-green expanse of eucalyptus scrub, known as mallee. The vegetation thins, exposing bare red earth daubed with prickly spinifex and drought-defiant mulga trees. Ahead lie 2 million sq miles (5 million km²) of scrub and desert, watercourses lacking any water, saltpans, and a dead-straight horizon broken occasionally by the worn outlines of some exceedingly ancient mountain range.

The boundless plains

Captain Charles Sturt, first in a long line of explorers who attempted to conquer the Australian interior, propounded a theory about the 'immense gloomy plains'. He suggested that the stones and sand ridges had been swept together by 'the mighty current' of a vanished ocean. His guess was good: there have been several seas, though it is 60 million years since the last one retreated. Now even the rivers flow only occasionally, mostly soaking into the thirsty earth and trickling their last drops into some inland billabong or salt pan.

Since it receives, on average, less than 10 in (254 mm) of rainfall a year, the entire outback is technically speaking a desert, though it is not so in the classic sense. The land is arid, with

Dragon of the outback *Dragon lizards belie their name, as they are usually timid.*

Season of plenty *In the summer rainy season, cascades add to the beauty and colour of the remote Kimberley region.*

clear skies and starry nights, and it is common for parts to go for years without a drop of rain. But rain does eventually fall, and then the landscape is transformed as dormant vegetation springs to life. In addition, rivers from the watershed of the Great Dividing Range percolate through the eastern outback, so that even when these are reduced to bone-dry tracks, there is enough underground seepage to sustain a line of deep-rooted gum trees.

There is another life-source. Had Sturt been able to drill thousands of feet down, he would have come upon his 'ocean', albeit of fresh water. The Great Artesian Basin, stretching from the Gulf of Carpentaria to northern New South Wales, is a massive reservoir of water trapped deep beneath the world's largest internal drainage system – more than twice as big as the Great Basin of Utah, Nevada and California. In some places, this water rises under pressure to the surface as springs, which can be piping hot. At Dalhousie Springs, on the edge of the Simpson Desert, tiny fish have adapted to live in spring-fed pools with a water temperature of 38°C (100°F). No related species exist elsewhere in Australia; this one's origin is one of the many mysteries of the outback.

Back o'Bourke

There is no line defining precisely where the outback begins; it is 'beyond the Black Stump', a folkloric location as evocative as it is vague. In New South Wales, the outback is colloquially referred to as 'back o'Bourke', Bourke being a small town on the Darling River almost 500 miles (800 km) north-west of Sydney. The Darling River is a tributary of the Murray River, and together with the Murrumbidgee, these rivers were once the outback highways of eastern Australia. The paddle steamers that plied the Darling carried wool from Bourke, though only seasonally – for part of the year, the Darling is reduced to a series of billabongs, or pools.

Beyond Bourke are red dust, flies and the dingo fence. Begun in the 1880s, the fence was once twice the length of the Great Wall of China. Although the original fell into disrepair, dingo fences patrolled by boundary riders are still in operation, in an attempt to keep out the wild dogs.

Souvenirs of a vanished life

It has been said that in the outback you can go farther and see less than anywhere else in the world. In such nothingness, isolated signs of past human endeavour linger into the present – mining debris, lonely memorials to explorers, desolate graves near abandoned homesteads. The Aborigines did not surrender this wilderness gladly. Near the small bush town of Kajabbi, in the cattle country of Queensland's far west, a memorial stands to one such tribe, the Kalkadoon, who in 1884 fought settlers and native mounted police on the slopes of what is now called Battle Mountain. 'Honour their name,' the inscription reads. 'Be brother and sister to their descendants.'

Mining and stock rearing

Prospectors followed the explorers, at first looking for gold and soon finding many other minerals. Mining remains a reason for being in the outback, along with rearing stock. Dotting the plains are clanking wind pumps that draw up artesian water for livestock on stations (ranches) larger than some countries.

Old cattle trail *The Canning Stock Route, along which Kimberley cattle were driven to the goldfields, now challenges amateur adventurers.*

Aborigine stockmen *Aborigines have worked on the cattle stations of the outback since the 19th century. Some now own their own stations.*

Here and there is a settlement with a pub, a store and a few dozen rugged individualists. Eccentricity thrives: one outpost has established the sport of lizard-racing, and another has a 'surf club' though it is many hundreds of miles from the sea. Chance has sometimes determined a location. According to local legend, Tennant Creek, in the Northern Territory, grew up where a miners' beer cart broke down.

The most celebrated spot in the outback is probably Birdsville, once at the junction of a number of stock routes. The main street is still broad enough for a mob of cattle to be driven through it. Residents depend on a borehole whose water reaches the surface almost at boiling point, and the pub is famous throughout Australia. Birdsville's population of 100 swells to thousands in September for the world's most remote horse-race meeting.

The tropical monsoon

Even the outback has an end, and 70 years after the first bullock cart issued from the Blue Mountains, overlanders reached the far side of the continent. There, in the Kimberley region of the far north-west, desert meets the tropical monsoon, whose summer rains drench the northern coastal belt, turning creeks into torrents and driving green gashes deep into the red interior. Even by Australian standards, the landscape is surreal, with dumpy boab trees (relatives of the African baobab); crocodile-infested fiords with tidal races that give the illusion of being 'waterfalls' going backwards; gigantic meteor craters; dry riverbeds that can become dangerous torrents within minutes; mountain ranges consisting of the petrified coral reefs of ancient seas – or tiger-striped in the case of the Bungle Bungles, whose sandstone domes look like gigantic beehives. In the 1880s, from a mustering-point near Birdsville, Queensland, cattlemen drove

Ancient survivor In the Finke Gorge National Park, Palm Valley is home to red cabbage palms, whose ancestors once covered Australia.

8000 animals some 2000 miles (3200 km) through fearsome terrain to new pastures in the north-west. Few others tried until deposits of iron ore were discovered in the Hamersley Range, across the desert to the south-west. Along with the mines, dams were built to conserve the precious summer deluges and boreholes were sunk to tap artesian reserves. In 1979 diamonds were discovered in the irrigated zone, and the Kimberley now has the world's largest diamond mine.

Desert marker Chambers Pillar in central Australia is a natural monument to the powers of erosion that created the outback.

Gardens of Eden in the arid outback

Parts of the Outback defy any settlement – especially the stone, salt and sand deserts at its heart – but even in these regions there are moist pockets that sustain life forms from a distant past. The MacDonnell Ranges are a series of parallel quartzite ridges separated by broad corridors. Once rising to 15 000 ft (4500 m), they have been worn down to stumps, cut through by gorges so narrow and deep that they retain permanent pools of water, one nearly 330 ft (100 m) deep. The pools, which can be icy even at midday in summer, create microclimates that sustain little gardens of Eden.

The most celebrated gorges are those cut by the Finke, a river older than the Nile but now an occasional torrent that dies out in the Simpson Desert. Sheltered by chasm walls and kept moist by permanent seepage are some of the world's oldest plants, relics of ancient rain forests, including ferns, dark green cycads and a unique species of tall, slender palm, the red cabbage palm (*Livistona mariae*). Black-footed rock wallabies sip from pools full of fish, and on the reed-rimmed banks are green tree frogs. In attendance are darting rainbow birds, kingfishers, herons and ground-dwelling spinifex pigeons.

CHAPTER 3

NATURE WITH A DIFFERENCE

Trees that offer no shade, mammals that lay eggs, animals that bound instead of run, birds that cannot fly . . . it was such sights in Australia that first led Charles Darwin to question the Biblical account of creation, and to think in directions that led eventually to the theory of evolution. Snapped off the primeval supercontinent 40 million years apart, Australia and New Zealand became alternative Gardens of Eden, their plant life and animal forms separating at differing stages of mainstream evolution. Australia's dowry included primitive mammal types. New Zealand, departing earliest, had only reptiles and birds. Each became a unique ecosystem, until humans in boats arrived to break these fragile cocoons. Both Aborigines and Maoris hunted the biggest, slowest animals to extinction. But neither could compare with the devastating impact of Europeans.

The eucalyptus-feeding koala has been a protected species since 1936.

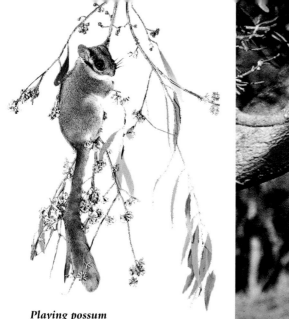

Playing possum
Nocturnal possums are common in parks and gardens.

Mobile nursery
A baby grey kangaroo, or 'joey', inspects the world from the safety of its mother's pouch. Joeys spend several months in the pouch.

Land of the kangaroo

A big red kangaroo bounding across the plain in graceful 30 ft (9 m) leaps, which enable it to reach speeds of 40 mph (65 km/h), represents the apex of the marsupial world. In Australia, there are more than 140 species of marsupials, some as small as a mouse.

Joseph Banks, the naturalist who accompanied Captain Cook, did not know what to make of the odd creature that Australians today familiarly refer to as a 'roo'. It had the head of a hare, but otherwise bore no resemblance to any other animal he had ever seen. Odder still, it hopped. He questioned an Aboriginal hunter about its name, and recorded in his journal that it was called a 'kang-a-rou'. Later explorers discovered that the creature had other names: around Sydney, for example, it was a patagarang.

By then, naturalists' journals were filling up with more and more colourful names as the wonder of Australian wildlife revealed itself: bandicoots, bilbies, koalas, numbats, possums, quolls, wombats – the list seemed endless. Cut adrift from the rest of the world at a very early stage in the evolution of mammals, Australia fostered its own unique animal kingdom. Its mammals are almost all marsupials – creatures that give birth to their young after a very short gestation, then nurse them (usually in a pouch covering the mother's nipples) until they are ready to emerge into the world. Some marsupial species are also found in the Americas, but elsewhere they became extinct, unable to compete with placental mammals whose offspring

Creatures of the night

Wombats have seen better times. These shy cousins of the koala resemble small bears and include in their ancestry lumbering herbivores as big as buffalo. There are now three species of wombat, all of them inoffensive burrowers that come out of their dens at night to munch on roots and tree-bark. Solidly built on stumpy legs, they move slowly. Many are killed by vehicles at night, but many more are legally destroyed by farmers who claim their tunnelling damages crops and fences.

Making an escape In the breeding season, male kangaroos kick each other fiercely until the loser turns tail and flees. The smaller females look on.

Animal or bird?

The platypus is so peculiar that when the first specimen reached the British Museum, experts took it to be a hoax, created by stitching together bits of several animals. In fact, the animal is a living clue as to how mammals evolved from reptiles. It has a streamlined, thickly furred body, like an otter; a tail like a beaver; large webbed forepaws; and a soft, leathery snout like the bill of a duck. However, the platypus does not quack: it growls. A powerful diver and swimmer, it prowls river bottoms, using its sensitive snout to detect worms under the mud. The female digs a burrow under the river bank and builds a leafy nest in which to lay a pair of eggs, clutching these to her belly until they hatch. The hatchlings are naked and blind. After being nursed on their mother's milk for about 3 months, they join her in the stream and learn to hunt.

The platypus and the unrelated echidna (of which there are several species) are the only egg-laying mammals, or monotremes. Their ancestral paths are thought to have separated from the mainstream early in mammal evolution – about 125 million years ago.

develop much more fully in the womb. Spared such competition, the marsupials of Australia diversified to fill every ecological niche.

Their common ancestor was a mouse-sized creature, much like a tiny possum, that fed on insects and fruit in the forests of the Gondwana supercontinent 100 million years ago. Over time, some marsupials began to eat bulkier food and grew larger. Further diversification produced ground-dwellers such as the dasyurids: predatory marsupials now represented by the cat-like quolls, the Tasmanian devil and the little desert kowaris, all fierce nocturnal hunters. The abundant possums, with their long prehensile tails, are still tree-dwellers.

Kangaroos great and small

Joseph Banks's kangaroo could have been any one of a number of species. The kangaroo family – called Macropodidae – contains over 40 species, including small, agile wallabies and stocky wallaroos. There are also kangaroos that live in trees, wallabies that look like rabbits, and potoroos, which are like jumping rats. However, the biggest members of this family are the great grey of the woodlands and the red kangaroo, king of the dry plains. A big red buck can stand over 6 ft (1.8 m) tall when it rears up on its powerful hind legs, and can weigh some 200 lb (90 kg). Yet at birth, it measures less than an inch (1-2 cm) and weighs less than an ounce (28 g).

All sorts of marsupials

In diversifying to fill every ecological niche in Australia, many marsupial species came to behave, and sometimes even to look, like other, unrelated mammal species in the rest of the world. This phenomenon is known to science as convergent evolution. The quokka, a tiny member of the kangaroo family, was mistaken for a rat by early explorers. There are likewise marsupial 'cats', 'monkeys', 'squirrels', 'rabbits', 'badgers' and 'anteaters'. Of course, some marsupials look like no other creature – kangaroos, for example.

Kangaroo curiosity Kangaroos come in all sizes. This quokka sits just 12 in (30 cm) high on its haunches.

The red kangaroo is superbly adapted to arid conditions. It rests under shade in the heat of the day and licks its bare forearms to get rid of excess heat; rather than wasting moisture in sweat, it pants like a dog. Capable of delivering a savage kick, it has few enemies other than man. Paradoxically, the large kangaroos benefited from the arrival of Europeans. The spread of grazing lands and artesian wells in the interior led to a dramatic increase in kangaroo numbers. To the stockman, kangaroos are pests: grass-pirates, good only for processing into meat. Under an official culling policy, up to 3 million are killed annually, but as many again may be shot illegally. Many carcasses are processed into pet food. Increasingly, though, kangaroo meat can be found on the menus of fashionable restaurants. The kangaroo cull is an emotional issue, hotly debated.

Feathered enchantment

Australia's early settlers were as much entranced by the bird life as they were puzzled by the animals and challenged by the landscape. One of them summed up their feelings in one word – enchantment.

Bird blossom *A flock of parrots taking their siesta make a tree appear to be in full bloom. Most parrots form very large flocks, yet pairs can pick each other out in a crowd of thousands. Bonds are maintained by mutual grooming, as in the case of a pair of budgerigars (bottom).*

An elegant black-and-white bird, which the settlers thought was a magpie, and came to be known as the bell-magpie, woke them at dawn with its distinctive warbling song, while an unruly bundle of feathers that the Aborigines called a kookaburra mocked them with such an infectious laugh that it was hard not to smile. There was also the currawong; settlers called it the bellbird for its peeling call. Squabbling parrots added their din and brightened the grey-green bush with their colourful plumage. The growth of cities drove many of these birds away, but they have been enticed back in recent decades as many people have replanted their gardens with native plants instead of European species.

Australia has more than 700 species of birds, of which 200 migrate to other parts of the world. Many are native species of familiar bird families, but even the familiar can be startlingly different: the swans look like their European relatives, only they are black; and some members of the crow family have beautiful songs, unlike anything heard from their European cousins. In the far north, the wetlands are home to the glossy Jabiru stork, and the brolga, a crane with a delicate courtship dance.

Cockatoos, budgerigars and other parrots

Parrots and their kin abound, especially on the east coast, but also deep in the interior, wherever there are trees for nesting holes. Among the most common are the pretty pink-and-grey galah and the noisy sulphur-crested cockatoo. Rosellas and lorikeets dart at astonishing speed between the boughs of eucalyptus trees. The budgerigar of the wild would surprise most owners of its caged kin around the world. This Australian parakeet is

Flightless survivor
The weka of New Zealand (above) is most active at nightfall. It has learned to scavenge for scraps from human refuse.

supremely adapted to desert conditions. In good times, it breeds prodigiously: within a few months, a few thousand become swirling flocks of millions. In bad times, its metabolism slows down to conserve energy.

Cockatoos usually pair for life, often returning to the same nesting hole year after year, whereas certain other birds constantly engage in the toils of romance. In the rain forests, male birds of paradise – like the riflebird – invest everything in finery. Velvet-black with green-tipped plumes, the riflebird lures a mate with wings fanned upwards until they touch, then performs a seductive dance. The lyrebird goes further; the males build mounds to stage spectacular song-and-dance performances while displaying to best advantage their tail plumage. These birds are stunning mimics, repeating perfectly the calls of dozens of other birds and any other sound they happen to pick up – a tractor engine, car alarm, mobile telephone. Male bowerbirds build bowers, intricate structures which

Big foot *The pukeko, a New Zealand swamp bird, is a good swimmer, which enables it to escape predators.*

Centrally heated nests

The malleefowl of southern Australia builds an 'incubator' to hatch its eggs. The work is done by the male bird, who fills a hole with vegetation, which gives off warmth as it ferments – just like a garden compost heap. To check that the temperature remains a constant 32°C (90°F), the bird regularly pokes his thermometer-beak into the mound and makes the necessary adjustment by adding soil to the pile, or scraping some off.

The laughing kookaburra

The loud, cackling call of the laughing kookaburra is one of the signature tunes of the Australian bush. It has also been pressed into service as background 'bush sound' in innumerable movies. The sociable, engaging kookaburra is the biggest member of the kingfisher family, an affiliation obvious from its method of hunting. Perched motionless on a branch, bright eyes alert, it will suddenly plunge down to snatch an insect, lizard or snake. Kookaburras are protected by law, have no fear of humans, and are often seen in parks and gardens. They can become quite tame and will tap on the window panes of obliging households to seek a handout. Their loud cackle has a serious purpose: it announces their territory, and helps them to stay in touch with relatives, who often help in tending eggs and feeding the young.

they decorate with bright objects to dazzle the female. But the big, flightless cassowary has no time for such finesse. He has a horned crown and spiked feet with which to bully rivals.

Curiosity can kill the emu

The nomadic emu of the plains is related to the cassowary and shares a common ancestry with the African ostrich and the extinct moa of New Zealand. Standing up to 6ft (1.8m) tall, it is insatiably curious, a characteristic exploited by Aboriginal hunters, who would hide behind a tree and lure the bird closer by waving a bunch of feathers. The emu's long, strong legs enable it to cover great distances at speed, helping it to get out of trouble. In 1932, a machine-gun detachment of the Royal Australian Artillery was dispatched to wipe out 20 000 emu threatening wheatfields in Western Australia. The birds scattered and the army returned to barracks, mission unaccomplished. The antagonism of farmers can be misplaced. Australia's mightiest bird of prey, the wedge-tailed eagle, was for many years shot on sight, until somebody realised that the bird lived largely on a diet of rabbits – the real pests of the land.

Fatherhood The male emu incubates the eggs, and the chicks stay close to their father for 6-7 months.

New Zealand crisis

New Zealand's bird life includes some of the world's rarest species. The nocturnal kakapo is the world's biggest parrot, but only about 55 survive on offshore islands. The takahe, a large flightless bird with bright blue-and-green plumage, was not seen for a century. It recently reappeared, but only around 200 are known to exist. The kotuku (or white heron) also numbers about 200, while the black stilt, a river wader, is reduced to a population of around 70, with only about 11 breeding pairs. The South Island's high country forests and mountains are home to the kea, the world's only alpine parrot.

The world of tiny creatures

The bush hat with a fringe of corks suspended from its brim has become a humorous Australian icon. There is a serious side to it, however, for the corks were an attempt to ward off bushflies. Most working stockmen do not attach corks to their hats, and end up mechanically brushing their hands past their faces – an action now called 'the Australian salute'.

Clouds of flies, swarming in their millions when sheep are present, are the most exasperating aspect of Australia's teeming insect life. Its 380 species of butterflies are a redeeming feature. There are also around 22 000 species of moths, 30 000 species of beetles, including the shiny-green Christmas beetle, and at least 4000 kinds of ants, including species more primitive than are found anywhere else.

Nibbling, cutting, sucking, burrowing . . . tens of thousands of species shape the environment from coastal rain forests to the deserts of the interior. It is estimated that well over 50 per cent of eucalyptus foliage is consumed by insects, usually in the form of caterpillars and other larvae. This pruning conserves nutrients, which are returned in the form of insect droppings that fertilise the ground around the tree. Australia's deserts are unique in their abundance of ants; by ceaseless foraging, they make the most of meagre resources and support food chains that otherwise could not exist.

Spiders and crickets

Australia's thousands of spider species include large and hairy horrors, but only two that are known to be lethal. The small redback is kin to the American black widow; still more venomous is the larger and more aggressive Sydney funnel-web, which hunts lizards and frogs in leafy glades (including suburban gardens) around Sydney. Fortunately, antitoxins have been developed for both.

New Zealand has only one dangerous spider: the katipo, another member of the black widow family. Fortunately, it is rare. The ubiquitous pest here is a sandfly (*namu* in Maori), whose bite causes a painful itch. The country's largest insects are species of weta, members of the cricket family. The giant weta grows to nearly 4 in (10 cm). It can inflict a painful bite, but it is not dangerous.

Perfect camouflage
A cricket (above, inset) blends into its desert habitat.

Insect fortress *Termite mounds are impervious to storms and enemies. Raiders like the sharp-clawed numbat have to dig into surrounding soil to reach the tunnels that radiate from beyond the mound's concrete-hard walls.*

Witchetty grubs: an Aboriginal delicacy

Insects were important food for Aborigines – but not because the land offered little else. As well as being highly nutritious, they were much prized as a tasty addition to the diet. Bogong moths were considered a great treat, as were mangrove worms and various ants and their larvae. But the most famous Aboriginal insect food is undoubtedly the witchetty grub. This is the name given to the larvae of various moths and beetles found in the stems or trunks, or around the roots, of certain shrubs and trees – especially acacias and eucalypts. Largest of all are the larvae of the giant wood moth.

Rich in protein and fat, witchetty grubs have a nutty taste, thanks to their wood diet. Eaten raw, they can be reminiscent of scalded cream or butter, but they are especially delicious roasted or cooked in the warm ashes of a campfire, when they variously taste like pork rind or sweet almonds.

Scaly and scary

Australia harbours some of the world's most ferocious and deadly reptiles, but the ferocious are not deadly, and the deadly are not ferocious – unless cornered. A notable exception is the saltwater crocodile (Crocodylus porosus), *the one-ton terror of northern estuaries, rivers and billabongs.*

Serpents and lizards abound in Aboriginal legend and ritual for the good reason that they are so abundant in nature. Australia has more than 400 species of lizard, from tiny geckos to 7 ft (2 m) goannas. A big goanna will rise on its hind legs and display sharp claws and forked tongue when cornered, but most lizards rely for protection upon camouflage and bluff.

Striped danger *The tiger snake is both lethal and quick to take offence.*

Common tactics include a menacing hiss with jaws opened wide. To increase the effect, some have deceptive bodywork. When surprised on the ground and unable to dash for cover, the harmless but side-spiked bearded dragon tries to warn off predators by puffing out its throat skin like a 'beard', while the frilled lizard erects a strikingly coloured ruff, sometimes jumping at the potential predator with gaping mouth. With fewer escape routes in its desert home, a fake monster known as the thorny devil has to stand its ground. Despite its fearsome appearance, at 8 in (20 cm) this little dragon is a threat only to ants. When threatened it lowers its head to present a spiky neck lump, trusting in its spike-covered body armour to see it through.

Squeaking frogs

New Zealand's reptile population is sparse, but also peculiar. Its frogs squeak rather than croak, and the 20 in (50 cm) lizard-like tuatara is a living fossil, from the age of the dinosaurs. It has a crest down its back, from large head to sturdy tail, and the vestiges of a third eye.

New Zealand is free of snakes – in contrast with Australia, which harbours over 170 species, more than 100 of them venomous. The inland taipan is among the deadliest, its bite able to cause death within minutes; and the tiger snake is the most likely to strike. Even so, all the snakes would rather avoid humans and are dangerous only if they feel threatened.

Deadly reptile of the north

Warnings posted by inviting pools in northern Australia need to be taken seriously. The saltwater crocodile – or 'saltie' – is the world's largest living reptile, occasionally reaching 30 ft (9 m). Protected since 1972, it has not observed the truce, nor does it limit its operations to reflect its name: it may be found in or near any body of water, salt or fresh. It preys upon anything that moves, including people, and can suddenly surge from the depths to seize a victim on dry land. A smaller relative, the freshwater crocodile, has a narrower snout and is generally considered to be harmless. Intrepid Aborigines consider crocodile eggs a delicacy.

Pure bluff
The menacing appearance of the Australian frilled lizard is an elaborate charade. Pretence is the creature's only defence: in reality, it is timid, does not bite and flees at the first opportunity. Other lizards, like Boyd's forest dragon (above right), depend on camouflage.

Alien invaders

For over 200 years, Europeans have been importing animals to Australia and New Zealand. Some of these strangers have acclimatised themselves all too well, putting unbearable pressure on the native fauna and flora. At times, the ecological impact has verged on the catastrophic.

In Australia, the story begins with mice. They arrived with the First Fleet and multiplied alarmingly to become at times a problem of plague proportions. Rabbits also arrived with the prison ships, but were not a problem until 1859, when a hardy breed was released into the wild. Conditions proved perfect; the invaders displaced small marsupials like bilbies from their burrows and quickly penetrated far inland. By the 1880s, sheep runs were being abandoned where rabbits had consumed all vegetation, and had even gnawed the bark from trees.

Possums: shot on sight in New Zealand

Not content with importing European animals into New Zealand, settlers also introduced the brush-tailed possum from Australia, in the hope of stimulating a trade in its fur. The scheme failed, but not the possum. Now estimated to number 60 million, possums cause incalculable damage to the rata and other native trees.

Alien beasts   Up to 200 000 camels add an exotic touch to Australia's deserts. They are descended from pack animals imported to supply distant settlements, and to assist early explorers. Despite their size, they cause little damage compared with rabbits.

Adapting and thriving

Foxes, originally released for sport, multiplied on a diet of rabbits as well as native fare, as did domestic cats, which were released in a misguided attempt to control the rabbits. The cats have thrived in the wild to the extent that a new subspecies of feral 'super cat' weighing more than 20 lb (10 kg) has begun to appear.

The rabbit has also adapted. After being almost eradicated by the myxomatosis virus in 1950, it developed resistance to the disease and by 1955 was breeding again. Since 1996 a new biological control in the form of the calicivirus disease, specific to rabbits, has reduced their numbers again.

Herds of brumbies

Discharged from duty with the advent of motor transport, abandoned horses, along with donkeys and camels, have multiplied to become a further scourge by competing with native creatures for food and water. Despite much ruthless killing over the years, thousands of wild horses ('brumbies'), donkeys and camels today roam the outback. In the Top End, around Darwin, water buffaloes and wild pigs caused incalculable damage to the wetlands for years, but have recently been brought under control.

The cunning of the dingo

The dingo, a big yellow dog, is Australia's largest carnivore, and its earliest known animal import. It arrived from Southeast Asia within the last 5000 years, probably with a group of Aboriginal latecomers. Some lived a semi-domesticated life with Aborigines, while other dingoes took to the wild, displacing their only competitor, the marsupial wolf. European sheep farmers soon came to loathe the dingo's high-pitched howls – especially at lambing time – but were foiled by its cunning when they tried to hunt it down. The farmers' solution was the dingo-fence to keep the wild dogs out of the sheeplands. It was the longest fence in the world – a continuous wire mesh curtain extending for 3437 miles (5531 km). The original fell into disrepair, but dingo fences are still maintained and patrolled. A similar attempt to halt rabbits with fencing was a total failure.

Big mistake   Introduced to protect the sugar crop from beetles, the poisonous cane toad itself became a pest.

A virgin forest of conifers

The trees of New Zealand, like those of Australia, had many millions of years to develop in splendid isolation. They successfully colonised most of the land, before being forced to give way before rapacious humankind.

Before the arrival of humans, some 70 per cent of New Zealand was covered by towering evergreens of ancient lineage – rimu, kahikatea, totara, kauri and native beech. The Maori cleared some of this virgin forest, but much more has been cut down by Europeans for its fine timber, or to create pasture or farmland. Only about a tenth of the natural forest cover remains. The North Island has subtropical vegetation, the forests mainly evergreen, with an undercover of ferns, flowering creepers and mosses. In the South Island, grassland in the east gives way to belts of dense forest that rise to alpine meadows high on the western mountains.

The strange and the remarkable

The kahikatea, or white pine, is New Zealand's tallest tree, but the pride of its forests is the kauri, restricted to the warm North. The kauri can live over 1200 years and has the grandeur of the American sequoia. Its straight trunk of mottled bark can reach 170 ft (52 m) in height and attain a girth of almost 50 ft (15 m). The soft, fine-grained wood is the colour of honey, sometimes tinted with pink.

New Zealand's 2500 native plants also include giant tree ferns with a 400-million-year ancestry and 23 ft (7 m) fronds; creeping pygmy pines; and the world's largest buttercups. The cabbage tree may look like a palm, but is actually a member of the lily family; Captain Cook's crew thought its shoots tasted like cabbage, hence the name. The beautiful rata clamps itself to a host tree, which it eventually strangles, leaving it to rise to the sky as an empty tower. It has crimson flowers and sometimes bears perfumed Earina orchids. The pohutukawa, the New Zealand Christmas Tree, blooms deep crimson in December.

Deadly cuts
Tapping kauri trees was banned in 1905, but digging for fossilised resin continued.

Green fronds
The tree fern is one of New Zealand's national emblems.

Kauri: the tree that was almost bled to death

Exploitation of the kauri forests of the North Island provided New Zealand with its first major industry, but drove this magnificent tree to the brink of extinction. When not felled for timber, kauri trees were tapped for their resin until they bled to death. At the peak of the trade, 20 000 'gum-diggers' tapped the trees or dug up the forest floor looking for lumps of fossilised resin, used in making varnish and linoleum. The kauri was saved by the development of synthetic resins in the 1930s, but only 200 000 acres (80 000 ha) of mature forest exist today. Fossil resin, a form of amber, is still in demand for jewellery.

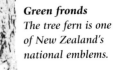

The bounty of Tane

The Maori gave thanks to Tane, god of nature, for filling the land with plants, which they used for many purposes. They believed the giant kauri tree had supernatural powers, being a special bounty of the god, and they carved their war canoes from the totara tree. They ate the pith or *ti* of the cabbage tree, for its high sugar content, and fashioned wild flax into fishing nets and clothing. They also learned to avoid the ongaonga (left), a stinging nettle that is not only very painful, but has caused at least one death.

The flaming flora of Australia

Australian trees and shrubs have adapted to cope with all manner of extreme conditions – heat, drought, flood, and even fire. The last of these is used as an agent of renewal.

Like much else in Australia, the bush fire knows no restraint. A line of roaring flames several miles wide advances at the speed of the wind, and leaves behind nothing but ash and blackened tree skeletons. Yet within weeks, the bush will be green again. The secret lies in the speed of the conflagration. Much of the foliage is impregnated with aromatic oils that catch alight with a sizzling flash at the first instant. The fire quickly moves on, leaving the trees stripped and scorched but with the sapwood primed to put forth fresh buds.

In place of seasons, fire and rain set the rhythm of life in the bush. The fruit of some species will not burst open until roasted by the heat of a fire; while rain following a fire is the trigger required to germinate the seeds of others. This is the signal for large numbers of wattle seedlings to burst through the charred ground.

Evergreen ancestors

The enormous variety of uniquely Australian flora arose out of a few rain forest evergreens, which adapted to changing conditions. Fragments of the primeval forest remain along the east coast, from steamy tropical pockets in the far north to the sombre fastness of the Tasmanian wilderness. In wet forests of the south-east, the

Adaptable eucalypts Varieties of eucalypt, also known as gum trees, thrive throughout Australia, from the frosty slopes of the Snowy Mountains to the scorching plains of the Red Centre. These trees surrounding Lake Mournpall in Victoria's Hattah-Kulkyne National Park are river red gums, Eucalyptus camaldulensis.

Australian diversity Isolated ghost gums (right) share the solitude of the interior plateau with clumps of spiky spinifex grass. Below: Cycads and tree ferns dominate a misty green rain forest in the south-east corner of Victoria.

majestic mountain ash forms a cathedral-like canopy. Its name is deceptive: the mountain ash is really a eucalyptus, or gum tree. Regularly surpassing 330 ft (100 m), it is the tallest flowering plant in the world.

More than 500 types of eucalyptus – slender, with wispy haloes of olive green or silvery leaves – set the character of the Australian bush. A typical eucalyptus has a thick bark to retain moisture, and an oily film seals the leaves. Often, the leaves are turned edge-on to the sun, or are silvery on one side to protect them from the fierce heat of its rays. The

Fire, the friend of Aborigines

Bushfires are a natural phenomenon, caused by a combination of dry plant material, heat and lightning strikes. However, the Aborigines learned to use fires deliberately to flush game, to stimulate nourishing regrowth, and to lessen the danger of uncontrolled fires. Their techniques were not random, but carefully planned to create a patchwork of plants in different stages of recovery from previous fires. Over tens of thousands of years, the practice led to subtle changes in the distribution of plants and animals in many areas. This started to change as soon as Aborigines moved into settlements and no longer managed the land in this way.

The wattle – Australia's national flower

A single wattle in bloom is striking enough; a forest of them is an unforgettable spectacle. For most of the year, the tree – actually an acacia – is a drab, dark green, but in spring it bursts into golden yellow blossoms. This combination of gold and green can be seen in the jersey of the national rugby team, while the flower figures on the nation's coat of arms.

Wattles have been successfully transplanted to many parts of the world. The famed mimosas of the French Riviera are Australian wattles, though proud riviera locals might deny such a suggestion.

eucalyptus is a member of the myrtle family, which relates it to hundreds of other native species, from the pretty paper-bark to the brightly flowered bottlebrush.

Wattles and banksias

The hardy wattle – the name Australians give to acacias – is even more diversified and adaptable. There are around 850 native species, able to cope with conditions ranging from salty bog to sand dune. Many acacias have stalk-like leaves, which are reduced to needles in the case of mulga, a tree that can survive as scrub in the most difficult conditions. In a severe drought, the mulga can discard branches and virtually shut itself down until rains bring new life. The casuarinas, exemplified by the noble desert oak, provide a different solution to water retention: they have scale-like leaves on feathery branches.

Banksias belong to another ubiquitous family. Named after Captain Cook's botanist, Joseph Banks, these bushes take many forms. Some are chandeliered with large flower heads comprising myriad tiny blooms, others have single flowers that look like delicate white spiders. The banksia family is related to proteas, and includes the pink-bouqueted grevillea and the magnificent waratah, whose single blossom resembles a giant red chrysanthemum. The waratah is the symbol of the state of New South Wales, and is protected in the wild. To deter unscrupulous florists, park rangers spray-paint the underside of the flowers so that they can be easily identified as stolen.

Australian jungle In the Queensland rain forest, large ferns grow on the sides of trees; the seeds germinate in tiny hollows in the tree trunks, after being deposited there in the faeces of passing birds.

Painting the desert with flowers

Wild flowers are Australia's secret glory. Their seeds can lie dormant in the desert sand for years, ready to burst forth whenever rain happens to fall. At such a moment, a single species – Sturt's desert pea – turns vast tracts into a carpet of red. In Western Australia, the lechenaultia achieves the same effect in blue: Aborigines call it 'the floor of the sky'. The state's south-western corner is a floral garden walled in by ocean and desert, where species developed in isolation. Many Australian flowers have small petals, or none at all – an adaptation to aid pollination by birds instead of bees.

CHAPTER 4

EXPLOITING NATURAL RESOURCES

Australia and New Zealand were built along classic colonial lines, supplying the motherland with raw materials and foodstuffs, and receiving the products of her factories in return. New Zealand settlement was a model of planning, with farming and artisan families appropriate to the potential of its forests and pastures. In contrast, Australia's founding stock of convicts and marines was a model for anarchy and strong individuality. Yet both proved successful. Australia is second only to the United States in exports of rural produce, and Japan's industries rely on its minerals; New Zealand leads the world in dairy exports. Australia grew into a successful example of a kind of pragmatic socialism, while New Zealand became dedicated to ideals of equal opportunity and social security, secured initially by a guaranteed market in Britain for its produce. The chill effects of Britain's entry into the European Community forced both countries to seek out new trading partners and resources.

Stockmen settle down for a night outdoors in the outback.

The bush: end of a myth

The Australian ethos has always drawn heavily on 'the bush' and the ideal of the heroic bushman – the proud, laconic loner at home with nature. But times change and today's rural Australia presents a new set of challenges.

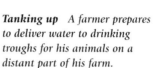

Down the years, the bushman in his broad-brimmed hat, typically an Akubra, personified the Australian virtues of fortitude and self-reliance, belief in the 'fair go', and contempt for any kind of intellectual pretention. Stoical in his approach to hard work and bad times, he had his store of black humour, delivered in a laconic monotone, and the solace of Saturday night in the outback pub.

Today, he feels misunderstood and under threat. Drought has followed drought in recent years, and when his livelihood is not being devastated by lack of water, it might be obliterated by floods – Australia is the flattest land in the world – or plagues of grasshoppers, birds, mice or rabbits. Last, but not least, there are the bankers who, having liberally advanced loans in times of relative plenty, could seize his property when times are hard.

Tanking up   A farmer prepares to deliver water to drinking troughs for his animals on a distant part of his farm.

Changing outback

Life in the bush – the outback, the Never-Never – is very different from how it is widely imagined to be, even by urban Australians, most of whom would never dream of living there, except in their romantic fantasies. Furthermore, although much of the old character of the bush remains, a great deal has changed. Many years have passed since taciturn swagmen (itinerant workers) could be seen 'humping bluey' (carrying a sleeping blanket) on dusty tracks in search of a few days'

Outback station   The isolation is a psychological as well as a geographical reality. Children are educated by radio, and do their homework by post or computer.

Bush carnival   Bushmen at a rodeo. Events include bulldogging, where they jump from a galloping horse and wrestle young cattle to the ground.

work. Likewise, the roving sheepshearer 'on the wallaby track' has been supplanted by 'suburban shearing', in which men work a local area and drive home each night.

Improved roads and a bigger transport network have lessened many of the old hardships. These days, even in the most distant towns, the beer is refrigerated, and the pub itself may even be

Labour relations and the not-so-jolly swagman

The anti-authoritarian bushman, exemplified by the swagman of the song 'Waltzing Matilda', had a profound effect on politics. The 'swaggie' with his swag and billy – sleeping mat and cooking pot – was said to be 'walking Matilda' as he journeyed across the bush. This was corrupted into 'waltzing' by the song, which tells how a jolly swagman steals a jumbuck (sheep), then drowns rather than be caught by the agents of authority. The song's defiant note is in the same

spirit as events in the 1890s when sheepshearers rose against their abject conditions and spurred the formation of the Australian Labor Party along with the world's first socialist government (in Queensland). Australian workers were guaranteed an eight-hour working day long before their counterparts in the Northern Hemisphere. However, conditions did not change much on farms in the bush, where Aboriginal stockmen lived in semi-feudal conditions.

Watering hole The pub is the focus of social life in small outback towns. Tall tales are exchanged and a lot of beer is drunk.

The flying doctors

Injury or illness in the bush was often a death sentence until a missionary, John Flynn, conceived an air-rescue system in the early days of radio. The first base was established in Cloncurry, Queensland – birthplace also of the national airline, QANTAS. The Royal Flying Doctor Service now operates from 19 bases and covers 80 per cent of the continent. Its 40 aircraft evacuated more than 21 000 patients in 1998. The service also handles around 44 000 consultations using a system of radio diagnosis cleverly simplified to rule out error, and keyed to a medical chest supplied to bush homesteads. Inspired by the success of the medical service, the government established a School of the Air for outback children in 1951.

air-conditioned. Against this, the services in a number of small outback towns have declined, increasing the sense of isolation for those that remain.

Farming in Australia is still, by and large, a family affair, but it is now highly mechanised: an agribusiness, in which station managers fly their own aeroplanes and consult their computers. Only the most sophisticated are able to prosper through traditional activities such as raising livestock or growing wheat. Many Australian farmers have turned to the lucrative tourist trade in order to supplement their income.

Environmentalists breathe down the farmer's neck, accusing him of destroying the soil, polluting rivers and eradicating native flora, while in some cases Aboriginal groups want his land – their land – since a 1992 court ruling validated Aborigines' status as prior owners. Restrictive interpretation and the political strength of the farming lobby have severely limited the ruling's impact, but the situation remains uncertain.

The cost of agriculture

The land has paid a heavy price for the agricultural bounty it has provided. The thin, poor soils of an old continent that had never felt the impact of a hoof were suddenly pounded by hundreds of millions of hooves, pressing the soil into a layer too hard to allow roots to penetrate or water to percolate. The sweetest grasses were cropped out. Deforestation worsened natural floods, which washed away the topsoil. Fragile, overworked arable land turned to dust. Some experts claim that for each ton of wheat harvested, at least a ton of soil was lost. Irrigation caused the creeping blight of salinisation. Chemical fertilisers caused acidification.

Soil erosion was not acknowledged as a serious problem until the 1930s, when research in Victoria began. Space satellites monitoring patterns of drought, overgrazing and erosion have found that the deserts are expanding. Two-thirds of the interior is at risk. Since the start of the 1980s, a land rehabilitation movement, Landcare Australia, has promoted involvement through its 5000 community groups in land-care activities such as tree planting.

The Australian cowboy: stockman, drover, jackaroo

The Australian stockman – equivalent of the American cowboy – has a mythology all his own. These days, however, he may use a trail bike or a helicopter more often than a horse to round up the herds.

Moving a mob A group of stockmen pause with their cattle beside a river in a forest of huge gum trees. A cattle trail like this is known as a stock route.

Old and new Branding is still done the old way (left), but the helicopter can 'muster a mob' faster than men on horseback.

The cattle duffer

A cattle duffer is an Australian cattle rustler who alters the brand to conceal his ill-gotten gains. From the earliest days, thieves have rounded up cattle and driven them to hideouts, often in the mountains. There they altered their brands before driving the animals to market. In 1870, Harry Redford – 'Captain Starlight' – and two accomplices drove 1000 stolen cattle 1500 miles (2400 km) from Queensland to South Australia, pioneering a stock route through country where few Europeans had ventured before. Redford was caught in 1873, tried, acquitted by an admiring jury, and later immortalised in the novel *Robbery Under Arms*. Some station owners have also engaged in 'poddy-dodging' – rounding up their neighbours' unbranded calves ('cleanskins') and branding them with their own mark.

The Australian cattle business had an inauspicious start. The First Fleet arrived with two bulls and six cows, quickly reduced to one bull and one cow when the others strayed. More were procured from South Africa and India, but the herd became diseased. Prospects brightened with the discovery of good pasture on the far side of the Blue Mountains in 1813. Victoria's pasture lands were stocked and settled in the 1830s, allowing 'overlanders' to drive cattle into South Australia. Other intrepid men drove their animals north from New South Wales into Queensland, while in the 1870s the most adventurous penetrated ever deeper into the continent in journeys of epic proportions.

The goldrushes of the 1850s stimulated a huge demand for beef, which continued to grow for over a century. Canning and refrigeration opened up world markets, and cattle numbers peaked in the 1970s at more than 33 million, though they have subsequently fallen sharply as a result of persistent droughts. Most of the stock are Herefords or Shorthorns, sometimes crossbred with Brahmans to increase resistance to heat and pests.

Stockman jargon

Australian stockmen and American cowboys are much the same in outlook. Toughness is a matter of pride, though their terminology has many differences. In Australia, the cattle ranch is a 'station' and a herd is a 'mob'; animal pastures are 'paddocks'. Cattle barons, like the owners of big sheep stations, are 'graziers'. An apprentice stockman is a 'jackaroo'; these days, there are also female 'jillaroos'. A cattle roundup is a 'muster'.

Many stockmen use cattle dogs of a unique Australian breed combining collie, dingo and kelpie. But horses are increasingly being replaced by all-terrain motorbikes, jeeps and helicopters, especially on the bigger stations, one of which is the size of Belgium.

A nation of ports

For all its wide open spaces, Australia developed through its ports as a nation of maritime cities, a number of which double as state capitals. Most of the country's population lives on or near the coast.

The focal point of modern Australia is, appropriately, a port – Port Jackson, better known as Sydney Harbour. In 1788, Captain Arthur Phillip recorded 'the satisfaction of finding the finest Harbour in the world' near which to unload his cargo of convicts. Countless residents and visitors have since agreed with his opinion of Sydney Harbour – more than 20 000 sq miles (50 000 km²) of calm, deep waters, with numerous bays and inlets and a narrow entrance protected by cliffs. The harbour contains several islands, large and small, including a number which were used as prisons for recalcitrant convicts. During the 1850s and 60s, one of these islands was turned into a fort, and its name was changed from Pinchgut to Fort Denison.

Far-flung harbours

Only one important city – the politically sited federal capital, Canberra – is built away from the coast. Before federation, all six of Australia's colonial capitals were ports, each on a river, with its back to the bush or the desert. The far-flung nature of the continent as much as the 11 000 miles (18 000 km) separating it from 'home', dictated this; the great distances and barren terrain separating European settlements meant that going by sea was more practical and cheaper than 'overlanding'. To make exporting worth while, goods also had to be worth the cost of a long voyage. The first exports – whale oil and sealskins, then wool and gold – all had gratifyingly high value-to-weight ratios.

Maritime tradition   From the earliest days of European settlement, ships have been a vital supply line for Sydney.

Sheep liner   Sheep are sent live to markets in the Middle East. It takes two days to load 120 000 sheep onto this caged transport at Fremantle.

All-powerful dockers

The Maritime Union of Australia (MUA), the seamen's and dockers' trade union, exercises a near-monopoly over hiring in the nation's ports. This has enabled it to hold governments to ransom on more than one occasion. The union has achieved a great deal for its members, who are today among Australia's best-paid workers.

Since the end of the 1980s, the government has tried to make the ports more competitive by initiating a series of reforms to make working methods more efficient, and loosen the union's stranglehold. The union, in turn, is challenging it every step of the way.

Australia has about 70 ports, a remarkable number for a population of 18 million, but a reflection of the continent's size. Each has its own specialities, including bauxite mined in Queensland and exported from Weipa on the York Peninsula, and grain and livestock shipped from Fremantle – charming 'Freo' – the port of Perth. During the Second World War, 'Freo' also served as the Allies' principal submarine base in the Southern Hemisphere.

Southern fisheries: from lobster to orange roughy

Commercial fishing was always important to New Zealand, but for a long time Australians remained oblivious to the bounty of their oceans. Now success is threatening stocks. Fish farming may provide a solution.

Fishing in Australia had an even more inauspicious start than cattle farming. The convicts of the First Fleet included only one fisherman, who was put in charge of nets cast in Sydney Harbour. After he was caught running a black market with his catch, and given 100 lashes, he made off in the governor's cutter. This chastening experience is hardly enough to explain the century of inactivity that ensued, for everyone knew that they were on the edge of a wide ocean.

The first fishers

The Aborigines around Sydney ate large quantities of shellfish, but their fishing was limited by the fragile nature of their tree-bark canoes. In New Zealand, the Maori were a sea-going people for whom fishing was part of life; their fishing equipment was so painstakingly crafted that it became an art form. They used nets and lines with hooks made from the bones of large birds to catch ocean fish, and devised pots and traps to catch crayfish and crabs. Whalers, the earliest European fishermen, quickly picked up the local lore, but commercial fishing was tied to domestic needs until

Fishing port   Early colonial warehouses frame Victoria Dock, home to Hobart's fishing fleet (above). Tasmanian giant crabs (left) are much sought after.

Fish from over the seas

Trout and Atlantic salmon were introduced to Australia and New Zealand in the 19th century. Their eggs made the long voyage from England in beds of moss placed on blocks of ice. The trout thrived, especially in New Zealand, where they became giants. Salmon did well in New Zealand and Tasmania, where they are now farmed successfully.

Another introduced species adapted so well to Australian conditions that in some places it has become the aquatic equivalent of the rabbit. Carp, originally from Asia, were brought from Europe in 1872. They bred prolifically, and once established drove out local species through their method of feeding, which is to churn up the beds of rivers and lakes. This makes the water too cloudy for indigenous fish to survive.

A long tradition   Fishing has a long history in New Zealand's Cook Strait (below). Centuries before Europeans arrived, the Maori caught barracuda and red cod here.

depletion of stocks in other parts of the world opened up a wider market. Only then did the real potential of New Zealand waters, covering a huge continental shelf, become fully appreciated.

In 1992, the New Zealand government and the Maori negotiated a settlement to address grievances arising from the Treaty of Waitangi's provision of Maori fishing rights. The Treaty of Waitangi Fisheries Commission, or Te Ohu Kai Moana, was established to assist the Maori in the business activity of fishing. The major commercial fish is hoki, whose white flesh is suitable for processing into consumer products. The 1998 hoki catch was worth over NZ$186.4 million – up NZ$38.9 million from the previous year.

Compared with New Zealand's extensive fishing grounds, Australia's

Pearl lugger *This stoutly built wooden boat from the heroic era of pearling is now a pleasure craft.*

Broome and the pearlers

Once Australia's pearling capital, Broome is a dusty port trapped between the desert and the deep blue sea. Four hundred pearl luggers were based here in the early 20th century, their crews from all corners of the world engaged in desperate rivalry. Scores died in agony from 'the bends', a depth-induced malady, and cyclones took many more. Though the pearl fleet is reduced to one or two boats, the past endures in Broome's cosmopolitan population, Chinese merchants, mother-of-pearl workshops and pretty wooden buildings. Modern additions to Broome's multicultural atmosphere include an influx of tourists. The pearl-divers' cemetery is near the ocean, whose blue waters dance with surfboards; after sunset, the beach hosts twilight camel rides. Once a year, past and present unite at the Shinju Matsuri, the Festival of the Pearl, when cattlemen and miners from the outback augment the tourists and locals.

Sun-dried *Nets hung out to dry in the sun on the quiet South Australian coast, south-east of Adelaide.*

are limited. Despite its vast territorial waters, Australia's continental shelf is mostly narrow, and its waters are poor in nutrients. No attempt was made to develop an offshore fishing industry until early in the 20th century. Later, a consignment of frozen lobster tails shipped to the United States in 1947 pointed the way to a booming export trade in shellfish. By the mid 1970s, Australia was the world's largest supplier of rock lobster, and the second-largest supplier of abalone.

The national catch of 220 000 tons is modest by world standards, but its value is out of proportion to its size. Seventy per cent is exported. Tuna is important, but shellfish accounts for more than 85 per cent of exports, often flown to Asian markets, where it fetches high prices.

The orange roughy

The firm-fleshed orange roughy became a restaurant favourite around the world before it was appreciated that this success could doom the fish. Commercial fishing began in 1979 with a catch of 4200 tons, which increased to 45 000 tons in the 1990s. Scientists were late to discover that the orange roughy is an extremely slow-growing fish; it takes about 30 years to reach maturity and can live for more than 100 years. In an attempt to assure its survival, a catch quota has been fixed provisionally at 6500 tons in Australia and 21 000 tons in New Zealand.

The problem of overfishing

As in the rest of the world, overfishing is exhausting Antipodean stocks. About a quarter of commercial species are under threat, and poaching adds to the problem, despite heavy fines and prison sentences. Hopes rest on farming, already responsible for a quarter of the total value of Australia's catch. Rearing oysters, mussels, shrimps, salmon and barramundi (a large tropical perch) has proved successful. In New Zealand, quotas have been imposed on some species, such as rock lobster and paua.

Kiwi gold under the green

New Zealand's greatest natural resource is grass. But for a while in the 19th century, gold was the principal source of revenue. The boom lasted long enough to boost the European population from around 60 000 to almost 300 000, far surpassing the Maori numbers. When the hubbub died down, thousands of young adventurers stayed on to work the land, and the course of New Zealand history was fundamentally altered.

Greenstone, a hard green gemstone that polishes to an oily lustre, drew the Maori to the mountains of the South Island of New Zealand: with simple tools, they fashioned it into jewellery, known as *hei-tiki*, and blunt, lethal war clubs known as *mere*. Europeans followed the Maori trails to the same mountains, but in their case the lure was gold.

Population boom

Between 1861 and 1864, the European population tripled; during the single month of February 1864, 18 000 gold-seekers landed. Dunedin, with a population of 14 000 in 1870, was the largest town in New Zealand, and by 1871 the first university had been founded there. Gold accounted for 70 per cent of New Zealand's exports at the start of the 1870s. Not until the 1970s, when natural gas and oil were discovered, would minerals again figure significantly, but a few gold mines still function and the government is trying to encourage investment in prospects that have yet to be developed.

Gold fever *The 19th century search for gold (left) gave rise to the settlement of Arrowtown, which has been meticulously restored (above).*

Whaling, forestry and farming provided a foothold, but it was dreams of instant wealth that stimulated the population growth that would enable New Zealand to develop its agricultural base. The settlers knew from the Maori that there was gold about, and set out to find it, spurred by the sensational strikes in California (1849) and Australia (1851).

Excitement was directed first at the Coromandel Peninsula in the North Island, then around Golden Bay in the north-west of the South Island, followed by the creeks of the Southern Alps. On May 23, 1861, an Australian prospector named Gabriel Read filled his pan with gold from a creek now known as Gabriel's Gully. A newspaper printed the story in July, and by the end of the month 11 000 prospectors were working the creeks and rivers feeding Lake Wakatipu, which had been sighted by the first European explorer only eight years earlier. Among these streams, the Shotover River achieved fleeting fame as 'the richest river in the world'.

A century after the rush

Nowadays, gold mining accounts for no more than about 1 per cent of New Zealand's GNP. About 11 tons of the precious metal are recovered each year, much of it from unglamorous open-cut mining. The industry employs about 4000 people. Some of the 19th-century gold rush settlements, such as Arrowtown, have found a new lease of life by mining tourist dollars. Queenstown, once the prospectors' supply depot on Lake Wakatipu, attracts half-a-million tourists a year to its boutiques and wine bars, and by its claim to be the 'adventure capital of the world'. Where the prospectors once toiled, today's tourists go bungee-jumping and parasailing, and take jetboat rides up the Shotover River.

Australia's Eldorado

'Everything comes from the Earth – you dig or you die', said Lang Hancock, who discovered mountains of iron ore. An Australian is nicknamed 'digger' with good reason. The early gold strikes built the nation and mining now drives the economy, but mining has become a controversial political issue.

The dream of stumbling upon a fortune strongly exercises the minds of many Australians. If most nowadays pin their hopes on the lottery or the racing tipster, thousands of amateur prospectors spend their weekends 'fossicking' (searching for gold) around abandoned shafts and mines. The metal detector has replaced the pan of the old-time gold-digger, but fortunes can still be made. Out where the swagmen wandered, some of the world's richest mineral deposits are generating riches beyond an old-timer's wildest dreams.

Iron mountains

One day in 1952, a gathering storm forced a cattleman named Lang Hancock to fly low over the Hamersley Ranges of the Pilbara, in the north-west of Western Australia. He dipped his single-engined plane through a gorge and was intrigued by the ochre sheen of its rugged walls. 'Iron ore', he guessed – correctly, in the greatest concentration on Earth. Hancock's hunch made him hugely rich and transformed the fortunes of his state. His subsequent ideas ran to using nuclear bombs to blow up iron-rich mountains, damming the Indian Ocean to generate electricity, and hauling icebergs from the Antarctic to provide miners with water. None of these schemes were realised, and Hancock died in 1992. Others have made fortunes without budging from their desks. Joseph Gutnik, son of a Russian rabbi, spent dogged years investing in gold and diamond-mining companies that had yet to show results. Today, 'Diamond Joe' heads a mineral empire.

The pink diamonds of Argyle

Australia is a major source of uncut diamonds, thanks to the discovery in 1979 of a phenomenally rich diamond pipe in the far north of Western Australia. About 5 tons – around 40 million carats – are extracted annually at the Argyle Diamond Mine, in rugged hills overlooking what was once the home range of a pioneer cattleman of the Kimberley. About 95 per cent of the stones are industrial quality, but the other 5 per cent include exquisite white, champagne and unique pink gems. Auctions of the best specimens bring the world's major dealers to Perth each year.

The uranium of Jabiluka

Australia has a third of known world reserves of uranium, but what to do with them is cause for bitter debate. Major deposits lie in Kakadu National Park, whose unique wetlands are rated a 'heritage of mankind' by UNESCO. The Ranger Mine within the park has operated since 1977 and storage ponds contaminated with radioactive material are said to have leaked. In 1998, the government approved the mining of high-grade uranium at Jabiluka. Ecologists joined with local Aborigines in loud protest. The Mirrar people, traditional owners of the land, say that no offer of royalties can compensate for such a violation. Litigation continues. Australia's uranium exports have been limited to about 3000 tons of 'yellowcake' per year.

Keeping watch A group of Aborigines monitors operations at the Ranger Mine in Kakadu National Park.

From coal to gold

It all began in 1791 with humble coal, found north of Sydney by escaped convicts, who thereby condemned many of their fellows to labouring in the pits. The area is now an industrial landscape of smelters and big open-cast mines that once threatened to gobble up the vineyards of the Hunter Valley. Australia is still one of the world's biggest exporters of coal, with huge mining operations in Queensland, New South Wales and Victoria.

But it was gold that made Australia what it is. From the first find near Bathurst in 1851, a succession of gold rushes changed life through the rest of the century and caused roads, railways and towns to spring up across the continent. The population soared from 350 000 in 1851 to 2.5 million in 1881. Gold has since become of minor significance, but the quest for it led to other discoveries: tin in 1872, copper in the 1880s, and in 1883, in western New South Wales, one of the world's richest deposits of silver, lead and zinc, chanced upon by a boundary rider who described the spot as looking like a 'broken hill'. The name stuck and the town of Broken Hill sprang up as miners flocked to the area. The Broken Hill Propriety Company (BHP), with mining interests across the globe, is still Australia's largest industrial enterprise, though no longer based at Broken Hill.

In 1923, in the Queensland outback, a prospector topped the Broken Hill find when he discovered the first deposits of Mount Isa, which later proved to be immensely rich in copper, silver, lead and zinc. Mount Isa Mines are currently the world's largest single producer of silver, lead and zinc. The 1930s saw a revival of Western Australia's goldfields, including the discovery of the state's largest-ever nugget of gold, the 71 lb (32 kg) Golden Eagle.

New technologies, such as aerial surveying, led to a rash of further discoveries after the Second World War. The list reads like a metallurgical catalogue: copper, lead, zinc, nickel, manganese, bauxite, titanium, uranium, yet more coal and apparently limitless iron ore. This coincided with the development of massive earth-moving equipment and bulk carriers, and the emergence of Japan as an ore-hungry industrial superpower.

After 1969, minerals replaced wool as the country's main source of income from exports. And fresh finds were still being made. In the 1970s, one of the world's largest concentrations of copper, gold and uranium deposits was found in the desert of South Australia, at Olympic Dam, to the west of Lake Torrens. Mining began here on a commercial scale in 1988. Today, the only deficiency is in oil. Offshore fields in Bass Strait provide 60 per cent of Australia's needs, but are slowly running dry. Australians remain optimistic – new finds have been made in the Timor Sea and tests are encouraging. Also, Australia has enormous reserves of natural gas.

Opposition to mining

Since the beginning of the 1970s, the mining industry has operated within a changing social climate. The emergence of a powerful environmental

The iron terraces of the Pilbara

The ancient rocks of the Pilbara contain more than 300 billion tons of iron ore. The mines here are among the most remote in the world, and conditions are among the most inhospitable. At Mount Newman, a mountain is being removed with explosives. Giant trucks transport the rock to the crushing plant. Giant shovels scoop up 50 tons of ore with each lunge and load it onto freight trains more than a quarter-mile (400 m) long for the 270 mile (436 km) haul to Port Hedland, where bulk carriers dock.

Hidden dangers. Parts of the Australian outback are pitted with old mine workings, especially around Coober Pedy in South Australia, where opals (inset) are found.

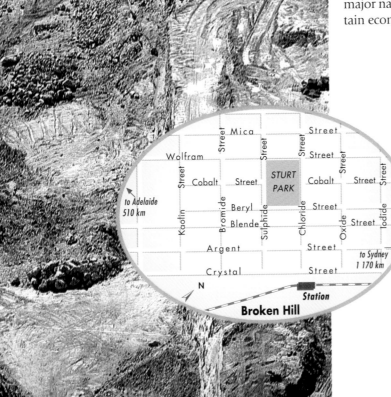

Mine tourism *Some mines welcome visitors, who perhaps dream of spotting a nugget like this one (right).*

Big hole *Mining at Broken Hill (left) is still going strong after well over a century. Many streets in the town centre (inset) are named after minerals.*

lobby has meant that it must now bear the costs of waste treatment and land restoration, and sometimes even abandon operations altogether, as happened with heavy mineral mines on Fraser Island, south of the Great Barrier Reef. Since vast stretches of the Northern Territory were declared Aboriginal land, companies have had to negotiate with Aboriginal owners to acquire mining rights. These talks usually conclude with a payment of substantial royalties, but sometimes the answer is a flat 'no'. This has become a major national issue, as has Australia's heavy reliance on the uncertain economies of South-east Asia.

The gold of Kalgoorlie

In 1893, Irish prospector Paddy Hannan was travelling from one gold strike to another in Western Australia when he made his own strike. At a spot that came to be called Kalgoorlie, he found gold lying in the surface dust, and another gold rush was born. Before long, two Adelaide prospectors discovered the Golden Mile, a lode so enormous that it is still being mined. The main difficulty in the early days was a shortage of water. Rainfall in the area is less than an inch (25 mm) per year, and many miners died of typhoid after drinking contaminated water from boreholes. In 1903, an ambitious pipeline was built bringing water to the town from

Perth, some 350 miles (560 km) away. Kalgoorlie has continued to grow, and in 1989 merged with its neighbouring settlement of Boulder, to form the city of Kalgoorlie-Boulder.

Counting sheep

Economically, Australia relied heavily on sheep throughout its formative years and deep into the 20th century, as did New Zealand. Although no longer the mainstay that it once was, sheep-rearing remains a major activity in both countries, which are the world's top two suppliers of wool and lamb.

More sheep graze the pastures of Australia and New Zealand than in any other part of the world: about ten for every human inhabitant. In the heyday of sheep, before man-made fibres challenged the dominance of wool, their numbers reached 250 million, the legacy of a few hardy creatures that survived the arduous ocean voyage penned up in a sailing ship.

Heroic image *The sheep-shearer is a tough, romantic figure, one of Australia's pioneering legends. Here, the champion shearer, or ringer, Jacky Howe has been immortalised in bronze.*

Sheep that gave birth to an industry

The first arrivals were a hairy, fat-tailed African breed, which had been loaded on board the First Fleet when it called at the Cape of Good Hope; 29 of the original 90 beasts survived the voyage to Australia. Twenty Bengal sheep, whose diminutive stature dismayed the governor, arrived from Calcutta three years later. Prospects brightened when two naval officers purchased 32 Spanish merino sheep at the Cape of Good Hope; only 13 survived to reach Sydney in June 1797. The purchasers included John MacArthur, a fiery-tempered, ambitious army officer who happened to be the son of a cloth merchant. The merino was prized in Europe for its fine wool, and on this MacArthur pinned his hopes. He also realised that the sheep would need to be infused with a touch of hardier Bengal and fat-tail blood to thrive in Australian conditions.

Gunning a sheep *Shearing is done manually in sweltering sheds. Wages depend on the shearer's tally of sheep.*

Top gun

Until 1888, all shearing was done with 'tongs' – a set of hand shears. In that year, electric 'gun' shears, like barbers' clippers, were introduced at the Dunlop station on the Darling River in New South Wales.

A champion shearer is called a 'ringer'. The most legendary was Jacky Howe, who in 1892 sheared 321 ewes in 7 hours and 40 minutes on a station in the Queensland outback. He did it with tongs, yet it was nearly 60 years before his record was broken in 1950. Shearing is hard, exacting work, and there is a growing shortage of people either prepared or able to do the job. As a result, other methods are being sought for getting the wool off a sheep, including injecting the animals with substances that will make them shed their fleeces at a given time.

The struggle against synthetics

To face the threat posed by man-made fibres, Australia created the International Wool Secretariat (IWS) in 1937. This was reconstituted in 1988 as the Woolmark Company, known around the world for its 'Woolmark', a quality label guaranteeing that the product it is applied to is made from 'pure virgin wool' – that is, not recycled wool, or some other fibre. Numerous research institutes press the fight by devising new ways to use wool, rather than cotton or a synthetic material. One is a jeans fabric with 11 per cent wool to 89 per cent cotton.

By a bizarre stroke of fortune, MacArthur was sent to London to face a court-martial after wounding his colonel in a duel. It was 1802, and Britain was at war with Napoleon. The Yorkshire woollen mills were starved of merino fleeces and MacArthur had with him samples from his own stock to raise the possibility of a new, British, source. Acquitted by the court-martial, he was permitted to buy some merinos from a small flock owned by King George III, then awarded a grant of the best land available in the colony. More impetuous behaviour forced him into exile again,

State fairs and agricultural shows

Agricultural shows are a feature of Australian rural life. Hundreds are held annually by district societies, while each state capital hosts a major show, usually with the prefix 'Royal'. Grandest is the Royal Easter Show in Sydney, with roots going back to 1822. In New Zealand, the high point of the rural year used to be the local A 'n' P (for Agricultural and Pastoral) Show, a great occasion to compete for best fleece and get together with neighbours. These are now fewer and smaller, but the tradition endures with an annual show circulating among major towns. New Zealand also has a big agricultural equipment fair. The Fieldway, held in Hamilton, exhibits the latest in everything from tractors to

On stage   Sheep-shearing is demonstrated in New Zealand.

clothing, which in 1998 included something for the avant-garde farmer's wife: a dress of growing grass.

River of wool
A flock pours down the lower slopes of Mount Cook in New Zealand (left).

unimagined in Europe and posed problems of control. Existing sheepdogs could not cope with the hot plains, so the kelpie, an alert, untiring, smooth-haired breed, was created in the 1870s. Its ancestry is disputed, but is mainly collie, with perhaps a dash of dingo. By the 1890s, Australia had more than 100 million sheep.

New Zealand lambs

The first flock arrived in New Zealand in 1834, and with fresh imports from Australia in the 1840s, sheep became increasingly important. When merinos did not fare so well in the damp climate, other breeds were introduced. Before long, a new variety, the corriedale, had been developed by crossing merino ewes with Lincoln rams. This sheep was first bred in the 1870s by Scottish-born James Little at Oamaru on the South Island. The corriedale is a dual-purpose animal, giving quality meat as well as wool, and it proved a boon with the development of refrigerated ships in the 1880s. Since the Second World War, New Zealand farmers have bred another cross – Southdown rams with Romney ewes – which has the advantage of giving more uniform lamb carcasses. At least twelve breeds of sheep are now raised on New Zealand farms.

Waiting their turn
In southern New South Wales (above), a small flock of sheep waits to be shorn.

In Australia, sheep-rearing boomed in the 1890s, but ended with a prolonged drought that halved the sheep population before conditions improved. There were further crises from droughts and pests like the blowfly, but nothing to compare with 20th-century competition from synthetic fibres. Breeders fought back as best they could. Average wool yields rose from under 3 lb (1.4 kg) a head to 10 lb (4.5 kg) in the course of a century.

Today, Australia is the world's top producer and exporter of wool, supplying 450 000 tons annually, or 70 per cent of world needs. New Zealand, in second place, sends abroad 95 per cent of the 200 000 tons or more it produces every year.

but in his absence his wife, Elizabeth, managed the estate so successfully that the MacArthurs became the founders of Australia's grazier aristocracy.

Imports of a hardier Saxony strain of merinos in 1825 completed the magic mix upon which Australia's fortunes were laid. The flocks multiplied and spread rapidly, even where the going was tough, in 'dingo scrub', so-named because it sheltered the sheep-slaying wild dog. For £10 a year, 'squatters' were able to claim all the land they wanted as sheep runs. Flock sizes were on a scale

Grain, sugar cane, fruits, nuts and poppies

Australia supplies the world with an amazing range of farm produce, thanks to ingenuity in making the most of its opportunities. Despite the continent's immensity, its arable land is no greater than that of France, and much of it is less fertile.

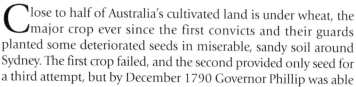

Close to half of Australia's cultivated land is under wheat, the major crop ever since the first convicts and their guards planted some deteriorated seeds in miserable, sandy soil around Sydney. The first crop failed, and the second provided only seed for a third attempt, but by December 1790 Governor Phillip was able to report a harvest of 8 tons.

Of the 940 convicts and Marines landed by the First Fleet, only one knew anything about farming – a diligent burglar named James Ruse, who was given 30 acres (12 ha) to clear. Ruse burned the felled timber, dug in the ashes, and planted wheat and some vegetables, which prospered to the extent that he was granted the land. Australian agriculture was on its way, with no ploughs and no draught animals for the first few years: only bare hands.

Once sheep were better established, farmers drove them into semi-arid regions with optimism as boundless as their ignorance of what they faced. Where there was no water, they fetched it by bullock cart from miles away. They believed the theory that rain would 'follow the plough'

Cane fire *Fire is used to 'clean' cane fields prior to harvesting.*

Raising cane in Queensland

The sugar cane of tropical Queensland is harvested by machine and shipped by rail to refineries at Mackay and Bundaberg. Nothing is wasted: the crushed fibre fuels the mill and residues left after extracting the syrup are turned into fertiliser, stock feed, and rum. Australia ranks third among sugar exporters, but a world surfeit makes the future uncertain.

The history of sugar in Australia is far from sweet. In the 19th century, tens of thousands of Pacific Islanders were 'recruited' by ruthless schooner captains, often at gunpoint, to work on the Queensland plantations. The activity, known as 'blackbirding', was gradually suppressed after evidence of a massacre of kidnapped workers came to light, and was outlawed from 1904. Descendants of the pressganged islanders, who were known as 'Kanakas', still live in Queensland.

once the soil was broken up and aired. Unpredictable as ever, rain did fall sometimes, and sometimes not. In large tracts of South Australia, the soil simply turned to dust and blew away. In parts of Victoria, there was such massive erosion that the dust clouds 'browned out' Melbourne. Elsewhere, removing the vegetation caused salts to rise to the surface and poison the ground. Everywhere, the thin soils were quickly exhausted, so that yields fell from promising beginnings. The lesson was eventually learned; more suitable crop strains were bred; phosphate fertilisers boosted the soil; and mechanisation facilitated harvesting. The wheatfields advanced and yields gradually increased.

The export trade

As agriculture became less labour-intensive and more productive, Australia was able to export ever greater amounts. From an experimental plot planted in Brisbane's botanic gardens in 1862, sugar became the country's second most important export crop. In 1905, Isaburo Takasuka, the son of a samurai, arrived in Melbourne and pioneered rice-growing on the banks of the Murray River. Takasuka used a Japanese strain, but American seed introduced in the 1920s proved more commercial. Australia now produces about 1 million tons of rice under irrigation and exports most of it. Coach-loads of Japanese come to marvel at the paddy fields of Murrumbidgee, 500 times the size of those in Japan, and seeded from aircraft.

Sugar, even more than wheat, has suffered from world over-production and the uncertainties of world markets. Britain's membership of the European Community initially caused

High-security crop *The opium poppy fields that bring a splash of pretty colour to Tasmania are closely watched.*

The formula *Irrigation (left) and mechanisation (above) are the keys to Australia's agricultural success.*

Saying it with flowers . . . from Australia

Growing international demand for Australia's exotic wildflowers has led to their commercial cultivation. One of the 'stars' of this industry is the kangaroo paw, whose natural habitat is the sandy woodlands of the south-western corner of Western Australia. The plant takes its name from its curiously shaped velvety flowers, which come in many brilliant colours and can be up to 4 in (10 cm) long. It is a favourite with honeyeaters and wattlebirds, which cling to its stem in order to drink the nectar. The most common, the red and green kangaroo paw (*Anigozanthos manglesii*), is Western Australia's floral emblem.

Another speciality is foliage for arrangements and bouquets – mainly eucalyptus, emu grass and koala fern. Japan is the major customer.

Nut-groves *The macadamia tree is grown in Queensland (left) for its delicious nuts. The white flesh, encased in a hard shell (below), has a taste reminiscent of the Brazil nut, but is not as dry in texture.*

New products: emus, camels and earthworms

Australia exports camels – to Arabia! It raises alpacas from South America for the wool, and ostriches from Africa for their meat and hides. The ostrich's local cousin, the emu, is also farmed for its meat. Crocodiles, protected in the wild, are bred in captivity for their skins and to satisfy a growing demand from restaurateurs with adventurous customers. The latest farming enterprise is perhaps the strangest: raising earthworms for sale to organic farmers and householders wanting to compost their vegetable waste.

Kangaroo meat is being promoted as a low-cholesterol alternative to beef or lamb, but is a sensitive issue. Animal rights advocates claim the shooting of kangaroos by night, using spotlights, is inhumane. They scored a victory in 1998, when a British supermarket chain pulled the meat off its shelves following protests.

severe disruption to Australian exporters, but ultimately led them to diversify imaginatively. Since the 1960s, the country has been self-sufficient in cotton, exporting any excess to South-east Asia. Grown mainly in irrigated zones in New South Wales and Queensland, cotton is a controversial crop in arid Australia.

In northern Queensland, Cairns is a centre for tropical fruits and vegetables, sold all over the world. Tasmania, at the other end of the climate scale, has supplemented its fruits and grain with crops for specialist markets: herbal essences, pyrethrum for insecticide – and poppies. Tasmania is the major world producer of opium for the manufacture of medicinal morphine. Figures are rarely published, but about 23 500 acres (9500 ha) are planted under licence. Monitoring is strict. The tourist who stops by a poppy field is quickly noticed and politely but firmly advised to drive on.

Changing times on the farm

New Zealand exports more dairy products than any other country and is second only to Australia in supplying the world with wool. However, it has been forced into an agricultural revolution by the loss of its protected British market. Famous for its butter and cheese, the country now also counts on fruit and vegetables, venison and timber.

Kiwi fruit, a local success story

Kiwi fruit, with its bright green flesh and furry brown skin, is the product of an Asian vine, originally imported from China as an ornamental garden plant. Around 1925, a grower named Hayward Wright developed the Hayward variety we know today. In the 1950s, vines were planted in the Bay of Plenty region of the North Island, where the climate and volcanic soil proved ideal. The fruit was then known as the Chinese gooseberry, or yangtao. In 1959, in a moment of inspiration, the name kiwi fruit was used for the first time. Sales were slow at first, but the exotic appearance, acid taste and high vitamin C content proved irresistible to the innovators of nouvelle cuisine. Fortunes were made before production spread to other countries and prices dropped. In 1997, the Zespri brand was launched to try to distinguish New Zealand fruit from those grown abroad.

Kiwi cultivation   The scale of the plantations are a measure of their success. Growers treat the fruit with tender care (inset).

After the Second World War, New Zealand continued to play an important role as Britain's 'overseas farm', but the horizon darkened when the United Kingdom joined the European Community in 1973 and bound by its trading rules. Remote from world markets, New Zealand struggled to compensate for the loss of such a major protected outlet. For a while, agriculture was sustained by high subsidies, but a permanent solution called for drastic reforms. Subsidies were cut dramatically, requiring farmers to rely on their own initiative. Many went bankrupt; others adapted and in the process earned a reputation for high-quality produce.

High production

Modern methods and mechanisation make New Zealand's farms among the most productive in the world. Conditions are ideal for raising livestock, since grass grows almost the whole year round and animals can remain

outdoors through the mild winters. New Zealand has more than 9 million cattle and more than 47 million sheep. It accounts for a quarter of world trade in dairy products, ranging from butter to 60 types of cheese.

Tobacco-growing, which was officially discouraged in the 1970s, has made a comeback. Horticulture has boomed: in 1998 exports of fruit and nuts alone earned NZ$888.7 million. Large areas have been reforested with fast-growing trees; one stand of American pines is the largest planted forest in the world. Even 'vermin' have been turned to profit. More than 1 million deer – which would previously have been shot as pests – are farmed for their venison and hides, in 1998 earning NZ$195 million.

Perfect conditions   Viniculture is one of New Zealand's most promising agricultural sectors. Both climate and soil are suitable for producing many fine wines, especially whites.

A wine revolution

Australians have discovered the pleasures of fine wine without abandoning their first love, beer. Across the continent, they now make, consume and export wines of great quality. New Zealand wines have also caught the attention of wine-lovers around the world, and an increasing number at home as well.

Grapevines were planted close to Sydney in 1790, without much success. A century later, wines from the Hunter Valley, north of Sydney, the Barossa Valley in South Australia and the Yarra Valley, near Melbourne, won praise in Europe, but the phylloxera blight and economic depression stunted the industry's growth. The 1970s saw a renaissance, thanks to the introduction of new grape varieties, an influx of immigrants from wine-drinking countries and the relaxation of drink laws.

Reliable quality

Australian viniculture is a flourishing, expanding industry at the forefront of technological advance, able to turn to advantage the challenge of hot

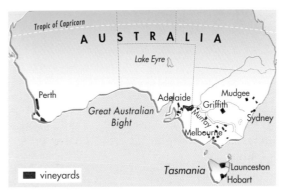

summers. It has achieved a consistency of quality which has endeared it to supermarket chains in Europe and America. The industry is extremely concentrated. Four main enterprises control 80 per cent of table wines, leaving 900 others to share the remaining 20 per cent. Production exceeds 132 million gallons (600 million litres) – about a tenth of the output of the world-leader, France.

South Australia accounts for about two-thirds of the national total. The Hunter Valley has about 70 wineries, including some of the oldest in the land. The Yarra Valley is noted for fine 'boutique' wines from small growers, while Western Australia has old-established vineyards along the Swan River.

Not forgetting the beer

Australians drink a lot of beer, though less than they once did. Leading brands have become popular in Europe and America, but with two giant companies now controlling the national market, 'boutique' breweries have sprung up to provide connoisseurs with local brews sporting colourful names like Dogbolter. Australian beer is sold in cans ('tinnies') or bottles ('stubbies' – 250 or 375 ml), or in bars by the glass (a 'butcher', 'pot', 'middie' or 'schooner', depending on size and location). New Zealand bars serve 'sevens', 'handles' or 'jugs'.

Wines from the Antipodes

The Australian wine industry is booming. Production has now passed 132 million gallons (600 million litres) a year, of which almost a quarter is exported. Such success is the result of technical skill, a willingness to blend different grape varieties – and a great enthusiasm for the drink itself.

New Zealand's wines also receive international acclaim. Long, warm autumn days and cool nights have proved ideal for many grape varieties, such as Sauvignon Blanc and Chardonnay. The most successful red wines so far have been Cabernet Sauvignons from Hawke's Bay. Prominent names include Montana and Cloudy Bay (at Marlborough), Millton (Gisborne) and Te Mata (Hawke's Bay). New Zealand has followed Australia in producing sparkling wines, some as joint ventures with French champagne houses.

Barossa classic *Australia's Grange Hermitage was created in 1951 by Max Schubert, a descendant of German immigrants.*

CHAPTER 5

TOWNS AND CITIES DOWN UNDER

Australians have room to breathe – a mere 18.5 million people occupy a land 25 times the size of Britain and Ireland – yet nothing could be more misleading than the image of Aussie fortitude in the lonely outback. This is an intensely urbanised society, and the majority of the population experiences the outback only through film or television. Nine out of ten cluster on the boomerang-shaped coastal plain between Adelaide and Brisbane. Each city cultivates characteristics that make it distinct. In the tourist guides, Sydney is 'cosmopolitan', Melbourne 'urbane', Adelaide 'serene', Brisbane 'tropical', Perth 'pleasure-loving'.
The pattern is much the same in New Zealand, with a steady drift to the cities. About 30 per cent of all New Zealanders now live in the Auckland area, and 85 per cent of the North Island population is urban.

Melbourne: with scullers, pleasure boats and church spires, this could be a scene of a European city.

Auckland and Wellington

Both Auckland and Wellington have magnificent harbour settings, but in mood the two cities are worlds apart. Their inhabitants take pleasure in a constant, cheerful exchange of insults.

Auckland is the largest and most cosmopolitan city in New Zealand. A million people live here – almost a third of the nation. It is the country's major port and commercial centre, and the hub for international air traffic. The city is also a melting pot: people flocking here from Pacific islands have made Auckland the largest 'Polynesian city' in the world, and it has acquired a substantial community from South-east Asia.

The setting could not be bettered. Auckland straddles an isthmus formed by volcanic eruptions, and so pinched that it is almost an island. With natural harbours on either side opening onto protected waters with sheltered anchorages and innumerable beaches, the city has a vast aquatic playground on its doorstep. The main thoroughfare, Queen Street, runs down to the city's spiritual heart, the lively waterfront area. From the rim of Mount Eden, an ancient crater, neat suburbs can be seen stretching for miles in either direction. The homes are mainly of wood; classic examples are made of kauri, with verandahs and doorways in a colonial Victorian style.

Evidence suggests that Auckland has been occupied by the Maori since the 14th century. They called this strategic isthmus Tamaki-makau-rau, or 'Tamaki of the hundred lovers', a reference to the many tribes who came to covet it. When Europeans first appeared, in the late 1700s, every volcanic hilltop was topped by a fortified village – a 'pa' – bearing witness to the tensions of the area. The spread of firearms and European diseases proved devastating, and the site was almost deserted by 1840 when, amid 'a few tents and huts and a sea of fern', the Union Jack flag was hoisted and Auckland founded as the colonial capital.

Twenty-five years later, the capital was moved to Wellington, on the southern tip of the North Island, a site more central to the country as a whole. Maori tradition credits the legendary voyager

Te Papa, a cultural celebration

Te Papa – the Museum of New Zealand – is not a national museum in the traditional sense, but part of a wider attempt to foster bicultural awareness between the country's two main peoples – Tangata Whenua ('people of the land') and Tangata Tiriti ('people who belong by right of treaty'). The museum covers an area the size of three football pitches and dominates the Wellington waterfront. A soaring lobby bridged by walkways leads into galleries that explore the heritages of the Maori and

Natural history *A whale skeleton in one of Te Papa's halls.*

Pakeha (Europeans) and the environment they share: warfare and music, earthquakes and volcanic eruptions, epic voyaging, national triumphs such as the conquest of Everest, and the history of the country's vibrant sporting life, including bungee-jumping. New Zealand art has its own gallery, and the museum has its own *marae* – a Maori meeting ground.

Kupe with discovering Wellington's splendid natural harbour, a volcanic crater flooded by the sea. In Maori myth, the harbour is the mouth of a fabulous fish that Kupe hooked and which pulled him to these islands.

Windy city

Wellington clambers up one side of the harbour and is cramped for space, despite 150 years of land reclamation, and an earthquake that raised the shoreline. The city proper has a population of 160 000, but many of its workers live in valleys to the north, boosting the population of greater Wellington to 345 000.

The setting is spectacular. A cable car climbs to the Botanic Gardens, from where, on a clear day, you can see the shore of the South Island, across Cook Strait. Wellington is more bracing than Auckland – sometimes too bracing, when the Roaring Forties tear through the strait to hit the city at gale force. Its sobriquet, Windy Wellington, is not to be taken lightly. In 1968, the wind caught the *Wahine*, an inter-island car ferry, and dashed it onto rocks at the entrance to the harbour; 51 lives were lost. Wellington's other main worry is earthquakes. In anticipation of 'the big one', new structures are built as quake-proof as possible, existing buildings are being braced, and some have been razed, to the despair of traditionalists.

Early Wellington was built of wood, the mightiest survivors being government buildings on what was formerly the quay; these are said to be the second-biggest set of structures in the world made entirely of wood (after a temple complex in Japan). Standing opposite is their modernistic counterpart, the cabinet offices designed by Sir Basil Spence and nicknamed 'the Beehive' for their distinctive shape. The Beehive has been a controversial landmark since its completion in 1980, but in terms of futuristic design it has been supplanted by the Te Papa, or Museum of New Zealand, opened in 1998. Te Papa is the new pride of a city that takes its culture seriously. Home of the national ballet and symphony orchestra, Wellington also sustains several theatre companies.

Ride to the top *A cable-car ride from Wellington's city centre to the Botanic Gardens provides memorable views.*

High point of the Southern Hemisphere

One of the main considerations in building Auckland's Sky Tower was that it should be taller than the Sydney Tower. Reaching a height of 1076 ft (328 m), it achieved this comfortably and became the highest structure in the Southern Hemisphere, as well as the sixth-tallest tower in the world, when completed in August 1997. It is designed to withstand an earthquake in the near neighbourhood, and to sway up to 3 ft (1 m) in cyclone-force winds without snapping. Like its rival in Sydney, the top deck of the tower incorporates a revolving restaurant.

It takes 40 ear-popping seconds for the tower's fast elevators to reach an observation deck, where visitors are rewarded with a vista of the two gulfs that pinch the isthmus of Auckland: Hauraki on the Pacific side, and Manukau Harbour,

opening onto the Tasman Sea. Powerful binoculars, weather monitors and audio guides are provided to enhance the experience, while solid glass plates set into the floor offer the thrill of stepping over a void, beneath which people in the street appear no bigger than ants.

The tower is in fact a giant minaret perched on top of Sky City. This is an entertainment complex featuring a 24 hour casino, whose gaming floor is done out in shades of green and blue, intended to evoke the undersea domain of the Polynesian demi-god Maui.

Going to the top of the Sky Tower costs NZ$15, plus an extra $3 for the upper viewing deck. Visiting the gaming halls down below costs nothing, initially.

The Sky Tower *A minaret atop a casino dominates Auckland's skyline.*

A British air

Devout Scots settled amid the penguins of the Otago Peninsula, and hand-picked English 'pilgrims' were shipped to the fertile Canterbury Plain. After 150 years, the bagpipes still skirl in Dunedin, and Christchurch is renowned for its English-style public gardens.

Scottish heritage
Gold built Dunedin and learning sustains it, amid a landscape reminiscent of the Scottish Highlands.

Christchurch character
The Wizard, a popular local eccentric, attracts an audience in the city's Cathedral Square.

The inhabitants of the South Island like to feel that they live on the 'mainland', reasoning that their island is the bigger one. Although today it has only a quarter of the nation's population, this was not always so. Dunedin (Gaelic for Edinburgh) was founded in 1848 by Scots Presbyterians, who took to the melancholy grandeur of the south-east. Canny exploitation of the gold rush made their city the biggest and richest of either island. When the gold ran out, Dunedin fostered frozen food exports which were New Zealand's salvation. Today, it rests on a patrimony of Victorian public buildings and institutes of higher education, not forgetting the Robbie Burns statue, and a whiskey distillery.

Punts on the River Avon

Christchurch, 200 miles (320 km) up the coast, now has a larger population than Dunedin (337 200 to 112 800) and is as English a creation as Dunedin is Scottish. Punts glide on the willow-shaded River Avon, winding around streets with names like Worcester, Gloucester and Oxford. The trams, withdrawn in 1954, are back again. It is sometimes called the garden city: close to a third of the central area is park, and its suburbs are renowned for their floral displays, typically of geraniums and chrysanthemums, set off by manicured lawns.

Yet Christchurch is more than an English idyll transplanted to the Pacific. It is a thriving commercial and industrial centre, and a major base for Antarctic operations. Dunedin has also spread its

roots. It has well-established Chinese and Lebanese communities, as well as more recent arrivals from Vietnam and Cambodia. Despite the city's Presbyterian origins, its many students ensure a lively pub and café life, as well as a vibrant music scene.

Lofty vision of the Canterbury pilgrims

Christchurch and Dunedin are monuments to experiments in planned colonisation inspired, like Adelaide in Australia, by the uplifting theories of Edward Gibbon Wakefield. One of Wakefield's disciples was a devout Anglican named John Godley, who envisioned a Church of England Utopia on a green swathe of the South Island appropriately named Canterbury. In 1850, the first 780 'Canterbury pilgrims', each with a vicar's certificate attesting to their 'sober, industrious and honest' character, arrived in four ships to take possession of a settlement that Godley named Christchurch, after his Oxford college. The streets are named after Anglican bishoprics and the neo-Gothic cathedral remains the central edifice of the city, but the 19th-century class system that Christchurch was intended to perpetuate failed to take root in New Zealand.

Neo-Gothic *The cathedral is at the heart of Christchurch.*

Perth, beyond the desert

The capital of Western Australia is the most isolated major city in the world. To the west, the next speck of land is Mauritius, 3700 miles (6000 km) away; to the north, the nearest big city is Jakarta, capital of Indonesia. Perth's closest major neighbour is Adelaide, a mere 1670 miles (2700 km) away, across the desert.

When America sent its first astronaut, Alan Shepard, into space in 1962, Perth switched on all its lights to greet him and, coincidentally, to remind the world of its existence. The city has not looked back since this inspired piece of publicity, which coincided with the discovery and rapid development of Western Australia's massive mineral deposits. Perth has stayed switched-on, perhaps a little too brightly at times. The mineral boom fostered the rise of multimillionaire entrepreneurs, such as the brewing, property and media mogul Alan Bond, whose downfall amid scandal was a chastening experience, but not one to dent the frontier spirit so cherished here. Slogans are encouraged in the 'City of Light' and the 'State of Excitement'. If Western Australia is the Texas of Australia, then Perth is its Dallas.

Perth's 1.4 million citizens occupy a balmy corner of the continent, entirely isolated by ocean and desert. The city was founded in 1829, when Captain James Stirling arrived with a party of gentry colonists motivated to emigrate by the desire to acquire land and thereby power. Their need for labour led to the introduction of convicts in 1850 just when transportation was being phased out in the rest of Australia. Roads, bridges and public buildings were built by convict labour until as late as 1868. The gold strikes of the 1890s boosted the population and created a sense of independence, which grew to such an extent that a massive majority in the 1930s favoured severing ties with the rest of Australia. It is still said that there are two kinds of Australians: Australians and West Australians (more than 70 per cent of whom live in the capital, Perth).

Contrasts *Modern skyscrapers loom behind shop façades that survive from an earlier age.*

City of beauty

Perth boasts of having 'the climate that California thinks it has'. It is a delicious Mediterranean variety, with a sea breeze called the Fremantle Doctor that wafts upriver to invigorate summer afternoons. The lazily flowing Swan has the dimensions of a lake, whose shimmering surface has been likened to a Monet painting. The city it reflects has been transformed by the mining boom, a fate not shared by the high ground of King's Park, which was saved from development in 1872 to enable people 'a thousand years hence to see what the bush was like'. In springtime, the park is a riot of native wild flowers. Viewed from here, the compact commercial centre seems puny in the face of the immensity all around.

Freo, for fishing and sailing

Waterfront *Perth sits on a broad stretch of the Swan River, which is in some ways reminiscent of Sydney's huge harbour. As in Sydney, there are many yacht owners, who make the most of the city's sailing opportunities.*

Perth's seaport is located 12 miles (19 km) to the south-west of the city centre, at the mouth of the Swan River. It was named Fremantle after a navy captain who landed here in 1829 and claimed Western Australia for Britain. The mood in Fremantle ('Freo' to the locals) is easy-going, as befits a population with a high proportion of free-thinkers. It owes its fine harbour to the 1890s gold rush, and a brilliant engineer, C.Y. O'Connor, who also constructed a pipeline to the gold diggings of Kalgoorlie, 350 miles (560 km) away in the desert.

Staging the America's Cup yacht race in 1987 shook Freo out of a slumber that had lasted since the gold rush faltered in the early 20th century. Now it is a busy yachting centre, with the past refurbished for tourists. Its attractions range from the lively, century-old Fremantle Market to the reassembled sections of the wreck of the *Batavia*, a Dutch East Indiaman that sank off Western Australia in 1629.

Melbourne, intellectual hub

*Melbourne is 'the other' great city of Australia: it is Boston to Sydney's New York.
It lacks the pace of Sydney, but makes up for this in spaciousness and a peaceful
opulence that offers an exceptionally comfortable way of life.*

The site of Melbourne was 'purchased' from local Aborigines for blankets, flour and various other items by an opportunist who famously declared: 'This will be the place for a village.' The Ballarat and Bendigo gold strikes of 1851 turned the village into a city, quadrupling its population in less than a year. The gold paid for churches, noble institutions and fine buildings, which were admired by many early visitors, including the novelists Anthony Trollope and Mark Twain.

Melbourne has long vied with Sydney for the right to be called Australia's premier city. Sydney may be older, but Melbourne can justly claim to be Australia's intellectual capital: its schools and universities the most prestigious; its clubs the most exclusive; its politicians and trade union leaders the most powerful. Most Australian prime ministers have had their base here. Laid out on flat ground by a military man, Melbourne is a parade ground of immaculate parks and broad avenues commanded by imperious Victorian buildings. It is Australia's most British city, helped to an extent by an unpredictable climate, though there is nothing British about the dreaded 'northerly', a scorching wind that rushes down from the interior.

A city with a conscience

The Arts Centre, an answer to Sydney's Opera House, is no architectural wonder, but is sumptuous inside. In Melbourne, content is all-important. A touch elitist, but with a keen sense of social responsibility, Melbourne has opened its heart to 'new Australians', to the extent that they represent a substantial proportion of its 3.5 million inhabitants. After Athens and Thessaloniki, Melbourne has the largest population of Greeks in the world. And the district of Carlton, home of a famous Australian beer, has a second identity as 'Little Italy'.

Melbourne may feel strongly British, but it is also vibrantly 'Continental'. It has thriving cafés, which spill out onto its wide pavements under colourful awnings. The variety and quality of food are staggering and are suitably appreciated by the inhabitants, who give every indication of knowing how to enjoy life to the full.

The city of the big event

American evangelist Billy Graham called Melbourne 'one of the most moral cities in the world'. Impressed by the huge turnout for his crusade, he might have reflected on Melburnians' addiction to public meetings of all kinds. As a sports venue, the city is unparalleled. It has hosted an Olympic Games; it stages the Australian Open, one of four Grand Slam events of world tennis; and the Formula 1 motor racing season begins here, with one of the few Grand Prix outside Europe. Melbourne is also the scene of the two most atmospheric events in Australian sport: the Australian Rules Football grand final, and the Melbourne Cup horse race. Cup Day at Flemington Racecourse (left) is when Melbourne kicks up its heels and becomes uncharacteristically light-headed.

Hobart and Adelaide, southern perspectives

The capitals of Tasmania and South Australia look towards the chill Southern Ocean. Diminutive Hobart is second only to Sydney in age, and second to none in its preservation of the past. Adelaide, shielded from the outback by rolling wheatfields and vineyards, is elegant, refined and orderly.

Victorian vision *Adelaide has elegant, wide streets, including some that have been turned into pedestrian malls.*

Hobart, capital of 'Tassie', confronts the Southern Ocean from its cosy position in a cove on the Derwent estuary. This does not prevent it from being battered in winter by bitter winds blowing in from the Antarctic. The city's origins in 1804 were largely strategic, as it provided a base from which to keep watch on prying French navigators, and on intrepid Yankee whalers who were already on the scene.

The waterfront remains the hub of a city whose isolation and modest population (195 000 people) have enabled it to preserve much of its 19th-century character, while at the same time allowing modern development, including even a casino. The state parliament, Town Hall and Theatre Royal ('best little theatre in the world,' reckoned Laurence Olivier) are all a short stroll from Constitution Dock. The mood is easy-going and friendly. The city is best observed on Saturdays, when colourful market stalls are set up before the Georgian warehouses of Salamanca Place. To round off the day, all that's needed is to down a glass of Cascade, the celebrated local beer, in a pub dating back to whaling days.

Freely settled

Serene and dignified, Adelaide is a mainland match for Hobart in terms of being relaxed, but it has cultural aspirations and a panache that can be traced to its pride in being wholly the creation of free settlers, with never a convict in sight. Once known as 'the City of Churches', it was the inspiration of Victorian reformer Edward Gibbon Wakefield, whose first shipload of 'persons of a superior class' arrived in 1836 to be handed an urban plan of geometric perfection, incorporating the world's first green belt. This was the brainchild of the colony's surveyor general, Colonel William Light, who based his plan, in part at least, on the Sicilian city of Catania, with its two main streets, one running north-south, the other east-west, meeting in a central square. City parks, beaches and suburbs stretching to the Adelaide hills all conform to this vision: no roof or fence is untidily out of line.

Now with 1 million inhabitants, Adelaide is still free of major traffic problems, and can claim to be Australia's most elegant, cared-for city. Since the Second World War, it has been enlivened by the arrival of a substantial Italian population, who have helped to make its cafés, bars and restaurants some of the best in the country. Adelaide also has a long tradition in cultural and artistic affairs, perhaps most evident in its biennial Arts Festival, which attracts writers, artists, musicians and performers from all over Australia, and the rest of the world.

The Sydney-to-Hobart, a gruelling race

The Sydney-to-Hobart is one of the world's great ocean races. The race begins in Sydney on Boxing Day, allowing the fastest boats to reach Hobart well before New Year's Day, when thousands of craft congregate in Storm Bay to escort them into Constitution Dock. Celebrations ensue for as long as it takes the last boat to arrive. For days, Hobart's tranquillity is shattered by hundreds of 'yachties' and their supporters. But these seas can be treacherous. In 1998, many boats capsized in mountainous waves, six competitors drowned and 55 had to be rescued.

Hobart *Mount Wellington broods over the Tasmanian capital.*

Protesters *Aborigines demonstrating in front of Parliament House.*

Canberra, a capital among the woods

The political, administrative and diplomatic capital of the Commonwealth of Australia was created out of the bush. An American architect's vision of geometric perfection set in bucolic seclusion, it has yet to acquire the lived-in look.

Parliament open to all

The Australian Parliament met in a 'temporary' building for 61 years, until the completion of a remarkable edifice, opened by the Queen in 1988. The new Parliament House cost well over a billion Australian dollars. It is in the form of a squat pyramid, with the roof grassed over so that it sinks into the landscape, except for a four-legged flagstaff 266 ft (81 m) high. The building houses the legislative chambers of the Senate and House of Representatives, together with the cabinet offices, and is filled with works of art. The atmosphere is engagingly informal, with guided tours and souvenir shops for the public, as befits an egalitarian society at ease with itself. Old Parliament House now houses the National Portrait Gallery.

Youthful city *Canberra is built around an artificial lake. Its imposing buildings include the National Gallery of Australia (inset).*

Australians love to mock their capital. It is a 'collection of suburbs in search of a city', or even 'a semi-dignified Disneyland' (complete with Captain Cook Memorial Water Jet). But when an outsider, the Duke of Edinburgh, dared to suggest that the city lacked soul, locals were outraged.

The meeting place

Canberra happened because Melbourne and Sydney both insisted on being the capital when the six colonies federated in 1901 to form modern Australia. After ten years of wrangling, a sparsely inhabited valley at an equally inconvenient distance between the arch rivals was proclaimed 'capital territory'. To the disgust of the Royal Institute of British Architects, an American urban planner, Walter Burley Griffin, won a contest to design a city in the virgin bush. He did so in Chicago, using maps. It took three years to agree upon a name. 'Shakespeare' and 'Eucalyptica' were considered, then someone mentioned 'kaamberra'

or 'nganbirra' as being an Aboriginal word for 'meeting place'. It was another dozen years before enough of Canberra existed for parliament to move here, in 1927.

Canberra is like no other Australian capital city. It is inland, so Burley Griffin provided a large artificial lake, around which he laid out his visionary road map of circles and octagons connecting public buildings and homes hidden under foliage. He planned for a population of 25 000, which was not achieved until after the Second World War. Government centralisation has since pushed the population to over 300 000.

The city remains true to Burley Griffin's dream: green, clean and unnaturally tranquil. The circular road system makes visitors dizzy, but traffic flows with ease. Homemakers are given trees to plant, and fences are banned as unaesthetic. Chilly and windy in winter, uncomfortably hot and humid in summer, Canberra is at its best in spring and autumn – in spring for its flowers and in autumn for the forest colours.

Sydney, from convict camp to Olympic city

In just over 200 years, Sydney has progressed from being a convict settlement to the self-styled 'best address in the world'. As brash as it is beautiful, it is certainly one of the great cities of the world, and its residents are justifiably proud of it.

Draped around its magnificent natural harbour, Sydney is the largest and the most stunning city in Australia. It is the country's leading business and financial centre, as well as its media hub. The city has two ports – Sydney Harbour and Botany Bay to the south – which together handle much of Australia's foreign trade. Almost a quarter of the continent's population live within the Sydney metropolitan area.

Yet Sydney has had to fight hard to retain its place as first city. In 1836, it had 25 000 inhabitants, against a mere 177 in a muddy river encampment named Melbourne. But 25 years later, Sydney's population had reached 95 000, while Melbourne's stood at 125 000, thanks to the discovery of gold nearby. In 1901, the two cities were neck-and-neck, at about 500 000 inhabitants apiece. At that point, Melbourne stole a march as the first federal capital, until Canberra was built.

Sydney Harbour Bridge
The city's beloved 'coat hanger' links the centre with the northern suburbs. It is 443 ft (135 m) high at the tip of its arch. On one side is a pedestrian walkway (below); on the other a cycleway. Between are two railway tracks and eight traffic lanes. Cars also use a tunnel which eases the bridge's load.

The bridge and the opera house

Sydney's progress through the 20th century can be summarised by reference to two remarkable pieces of architecture, an iron bridge and an opera house. The single-arch steel bridge across a narrow neck of the harbour was strongly influenced by New York's Hell Gate Bridge. Its designer, however, was a well-known English civil engineer, Ralph Freeman, working in close association with J.J.C. Bradfield of New South Wales's Public Works Department. It was finished during the Great Depression, when its construction provided much-needed work for many people. This, together with its grand size and distinctive silhouette, made it an icon as much as a major convenience as soon as it was opened in 1932.

Now the bridge has fitting company. The Opera House, conceived as a flight of fancy, was designed by Danish architect Jørn Utzon. It made pioneering use of computer technology, took 14 years to complete – it was opened in September 1973 – and ran a staggering 1500 per cent over budget. But it is one of the world's most spectacular structures. Like a ship with billowing sails, it seems to be launching itself upon the harbour with the sort of confidence that is appropriate for a city playing host to the first Olympic Games of the new millennium.

1. GOLDFISH BOWL

Kings Cross For many years, 'The Cross' was notorious as a den of iniquity. It is still a red-light area, replete with strip joints and gay bars, but has been made much safer for the benefit of tourists.

Chinatown This neighbourhood of Chinese restaurants and shops is expanding, thanks to money flowing in from Hong Kong.

Hyde Park
e Royal Botanic
) offer a green
eart of the city.

Mutiny ship An exact replica of HMS Bounty, *on which Captain William Bligh experienced the famous mutiny, takes tourists on voyages around Sydney Harbour. This ship was used in the 1984 film of the mutiny, featuring Anthony Hopkins as Bligh and Mel Gibson as the mutineer leader, Fletcher Christian.*

Status Symbol
Opened in 1973, the Opera House has five auditoriums, including the concert hall seen here. It is us for music, ballet and theatric productions, as well as opera.

In the heart of the city

The arch of Sydney Harbour Bridge, the Opera House, the sparkling blue waters create an image that remains fixed in the mind for ever. Where Captain Phillip envisioned a thousand ships of the Royal Navy at anchor, thousands of pleasure craft of all shapes and sizes bob quietly at their moorings, or race around the harbour at weekends. Sydney's inhabitants, the Sydneysiders, believe they have the best lifestyle in the world, and are quick to say so. The oldest part of Sydney is all ups and downs, winding streets, and sudden harbour views. Many of its streets and suburbs have names echoing those of London: Oxford Street, Paddington, Waterloo, Kings Cross. There is also a Hyde Park, laid out when the city was in its infancy. Other names – such as Woolloomooloo and Woollahra – reflect the Aboriginal heritage of the continent on which this city has grown up. Inland rise the Blue Mountains, offering an easy escape from city life into the wildness and grandeur of nature. Sydney's climate is close to ideal. Average temperatures range between 12°C (54°F) and 22°C (72°F).

Tranquil zone (above) and the Gardens (right) haven in the h

Old and new St Mary's Cathedral (in the foreground) was built between 1866 and 1913. Looming behind on the left is Sydney Tower, 1000 ft (305 m) high, which offers views over 60 miles (100 km) or more.

The big smoke Pitt Street (above) is one of the city's busiest. Looking north, you can see the Harbour Bridge between the buildings. Visitors include Japanese businessmen, American tourists and locals (left), who all contribute to the cosmopolitan air.

Sydney

Picnickers relax under an enormous fig tree at Watsons Bay, near the harbour mouth.

2. Paddington, with its rows of Victorian terraces, is a fashionable neighbourhood of art galleries and small, chic homes.

3. The harbour police patrol 190 miles (240 km) of inlets, coves and promontories, and numerous small islands.

4. The most affluent Sydneysiders tend to live on the harbour, sometimes with their own yacht and jetty.

5. A telephone box in the largely Aboriginal neighbourhood of Redfern bears an indigenous design.

6. Darling Harbour is an immense leisure zone built on abandoned dockland. It includes entertainment and exhibition centres, lively museums, restaurants and hotels.

7. Taronga Zoo on the steep northern foreshore affords its inmates a panoramic view of the city centre.

8. Seasoned morning commuters on a cross-harbour ferry seem oblivious to their spectacular surroundings.

4

5

6

8

7

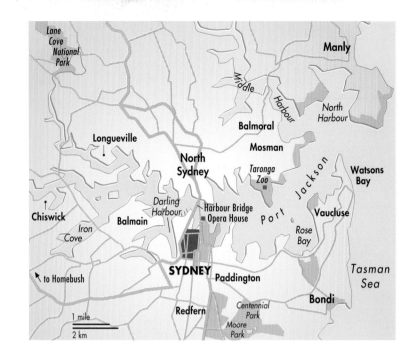

Business hub *Major national and international companies increasingly base their operations in Sydney, which has ousted Melbourne as business capital of the South Pacific region.*

Fish market *Fish and shellfish of every description are available fresh every day.*

Shopping in style *The Queen Victoria Building (the QVB to locals) was built in 1896. It was renovated in 1987, and is enjoying a new lease of life as a luxurious retail complex containing some 200 shops.*

Enjoying life *Country dancing in the square in front of the Opera House.*

Bins provided *Sydneysiders are very sensitive to the quality of their environment.*

The Rocks *In the 1980s, this oldest part of Sydney was a dilapidated area of warehouses and narrow cobbled streets. Restored, it now welcomes tourists (left). Pub-life is in the best Australian tradition (right).*

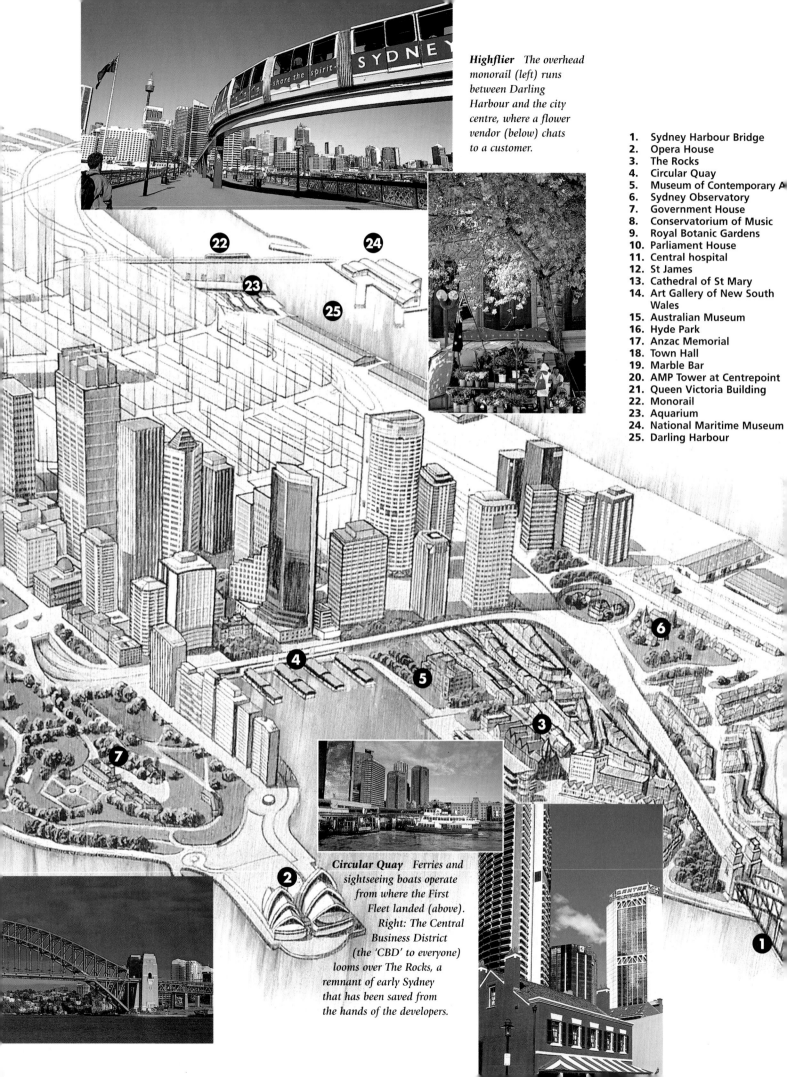

Highflier The overhead monorail (left) runs between Darling Harbour and the city centre, where a flower vendor (below) chats to a customer.

1. Sydney Harbour Bridge
2. Opera House
3. The Rocks
4. Circular Quay
5. Museum of Contemporary A
6. Sydney Observatory
7. Government House
8. Conservatorium of Music
9. Royal Botanic Gardens
10. Parliament House
11. Central hospital
12. St James
13. Cathedral of St Mary
14. Art Gallery of New South Wales
15. Australian Museum
16. Hyde Park
17. Anzac Memorial
18. Town Hall
19. Marble Bar
20. AMP Tower at Centrepoint
21. Queen Victoria Building
22. Monorail
23. Aquarium
24. National Maritime Museum
25. Darling Harbour

Circular Quay Ferries and sightseeing boats operate from where the First Fleet landed (above). Right: The Central Business District (the 'CBD' to everyone) looms over The Rocks, a remnant of early Sydney that has been saved from the hands of the developers.

Brisbane and the Gold Coast, the hot zone

The capital of Queensland is located in the state's south-east corner. First settled as a penal colony in 1824, then opened up to colonists in 1842, it has grown to be Australia's third-largest city, thriving on the popularity of the magnificent Gold Coast.

Sir Thomas Brisbane, a colonial governor, complained that the place they named after him was 'much too good' for the type of convicts it was created for – hardened second-offenders from Sydney. Situated some 12 miles (19 km) inland up a river – also named Brisbane – the city spread higgledy-piggledy over the surrounding hills of the Taylor Range. It entered the 1960s pleased to regard itself as 'the world's biggest country town', charmingly rickety, with fine colonial buildings and a lot of dirt roads.

The boom times of the 1960s had the impact of an earthquake in Brisbane. Conservative politicians, who opposed the 'permissiveness' of the other big Australian cities, nevertheless welcomed high-living entrepreneurs from the south, and the result was unbridled 'development'. The Brisbane of colonial colonnades and large, shaded verandahs was torn down to make way for a city of office towers. The state Parliament House was among the few edifices to escape the developers, but the city profited by equipping itself with superb cultural and recreational facilities. Mirroring the growth of American 'sunbelt' cities, migration from the south has seen Brisbane's population jump to 1.5 million, and some expect that it will soon exceed that of Melbourne.

Old ways survive

In spite of everything, 'Brizzy' has preserved some of its old ways, including wariness of 'meddling' from Canberra. The dress code for money-making is casual – big hat, open shirt and shorts – and old-world civilities are observed in a slow accent, with sentences often ending with an 'eh?'. There is a hint of New Orleans about its lazy river lined with houses on stilts, while the suburban hills sequester colonial homes with voluptuous gardens laden with the sweet perfume of frangipani.

Survivors   Some of Brisbane's fine old buildings remain, including the clock of its central station (above) and these wooden houses (right), with wooden slats that provide shade.

Surfers Paradise, a mini-Miami

Surfers Paradise ('Surfers' to every Australian) is the high-rise heart of the Gold Coast. The only natural element that remains here is the beach, which from late afternoon is cast in shadow by tower blocks of apartments. This hastens bathers to the shopping malls and nightlife that are its other attractions, along with easy access to a hinterland of theme parks, and casino gambling.

The name Surfers Paradise was coined by an estate agent, long before the rise of mass tourism. In 1936, the Surfers Paradise Hotel opened as a hideaway for the discerning. The hotel site is now engulfed by the Paradise Centre, a large shopping and restaurant complex lying between the beach and a strip of bars.

The lure of the Gold Coast

A short drive south from Brisbane and extending to the New South Wales border is a stretch of seashore with golden sands and rolling surf that was occupied in the 1950s by guesthouses. Now known as the Gold Coast, it is Australia's major holiday destination and the continent's most feverish zone of property speculation. The population is 400 000 and rising, as is the number of tourists – 3 million a year in the late 1990s.

A ribbon of apartment blocks, golf courses and motels is backed by 'canal estates' with a jetty for every home. Theme parks proliferate – Movie World, Sea World, Dreamworld, Frozen World, a Wet 'n' Wild Water World.

Gold Coast   Apartment blocks have replaced tropical vegetation.

Darwin, capital of the Top End

Darwin is a melting pot, in almost every sense. Multiracial, and steaming hot all year round, it is forging a distinctive lifestyle in its own relaxed way.

Darwin, near the top of the Top End, is as close to the Equator as urban Australia gets. Sydney is as distant as Singapore, Vietnam as near as Tasmania. Here is the Australia of tropical vegetation and swamp, of basking man-eating crocodiles, and two seasons, equally torrid: the Wet, when monsoon rains sweep in from the Ocean, and the Dry. The area can be torrid in another sense, as Cyclone Tracy demonstrated when it levelled the town on Christmas morning, 1974. That was more than the Japanese achieved in wartime raids that woke Australians to the realisation that their isolation was gone for ever. Most Australians still think of Darwin as a frontier outpost, while to Darwin 'the south' is somewhere to gripe about. Darwin has been the Northern Territory capital since 1911, but the territory has yet to gain full statehood, and sensitive matters such as Aboriginal affairs and uranium mining are handled from Canberra.

Battered by cyclones

Built around a huge natural harbour, twice the size of Sydney's, Darwin has battled extinction several times. Cyclones wrecked it in 1897 and 1937, the Japanese bombed it in 1942, and Cyclone Tracy forced its near-total evacuation. Darwin has been totally rebuilt since the cyclone, and so has the air of a brand-new town. Its new architecture is rather monotonous, but a lot safer than the old: all buildings have to conform to the Australian Cyclone Code, which determines their height, among other things.

Since 1974, the population has doubled to 85 000, and is now the most cosmopolitan in Australia, more transient than elsewhere, and the most racially tolerant. Aside from stalwart Aussie 'Territorians', there are all kinds of Asians and Pacific islanders, and every brand of 'New Australian' of European extraction: one count found 61 ethnic groups living in Darwin. Some Chinese families are fourth-generation Australian. The city has twice had a Chinese mayor.

The lifestyle is relaxed, even by Australian standards: this is Crocodile Dundee territory. Beer consumption is a matter of pride, made manifest in the Darwin stubby, claimed to be the largest and most potent bottle of beer in the world, containing as it does just under half a gallon (2 litres) of Northern Territory draught. Every August, the city of Darwin hosts its Beer Can Regatta for boats made entirely from beer cans. Most are sleek racing vessels, but one year a Viking longboat turned up. At sunset on Thursdays, much of Darwin's population decamps to Mindil Beach, to a food market under the coconut palms, exuding aromas from every corner of Asia.

Desert town *Alice Springs, nestled among the MacDonnell Ranges, stages such colourful events as the Camel Cup.*

Alice Springs, a bush oasis

The town called Alice Springs (usually just 'Alice'), 930 miles (1497 km) 'down the track' from Darwin, and 950 miles (1529 km) up the track from Adelaide, began as a telegraph relay station pitched beside a waterhole in the heart of Australia's Red Centre. Nowadays, there are hotels, restaurants a shopping mall, and the inevitable casino. Visitors who time things well can enjoy the town's Camel Cup races, held in July, or the Henley-on-Todd Regatta, a series of boat races held in October in the dry bed of the Todd River. All the boats are bottomless, allowing competitors to sprint along the course.

Looking north *Darwin was founded in 1869 as Palmerston, after the former British prime minister Lord Palmerston. It was renamed in 1911 after the naturalist Charles Darwin. Being so close to Asia, Darwin shows a strong Asian influence.*

CHAPTER 6

A NEW WAY OF LIVING

Unlike Europe, trapped in its history, and the United States, wrapped in its sense of destiny, Australia and New Zealand live in the present, pursuing a lifestyle shaped by a strong sense of equality. Little violence, a bearable unemployment rate, systems of social security for long the envy of the world and, above all, space . . . might as well take advantage of it all, and people do just that. In the cities, homes are spacious, with gardens large enough to welcome a tribe of friends around the barbecue and the pool. This is essentially a suburban civilisation, and an Australian's house and garden is his castle. Since the Second World War, millions of migrants from more than 120 countries have brought with them new ideas – and new cuisines. The tendency for most is to become absorbed rather than to form subcultures. After a couple of generations, a Sicilian-Australian will be playing cricket or rugby better than most Britons.

A Scottish rugby player vainly tries to halt the attack of Australian forwards.

Celebrating a sense of belonging

Party-loving Australians will seize upon any opportunity for a celebration, preferably on a Monday, so as to turn it into a long weekend. But in both Australia and New Zealand, the history behind the major national holiday stirs very mixed emotions.

The national holiday, Australia Day, marks the arrival in Sydney of the First Fleet on January 26, 1788. The convicts who disembarked to start clearing the bush had more reason to appreciate June 4 the following year, when the governor gave them the day off for King George III's birthday. Early colonial Australia was not something to boast about, and the first generations of locally born colonists continued to regard themselves as entirely British, though they called themselves 'currency lads and lasses' to acknowledge that they were not sterling – that is, from the 'motherland'.

By the 1820s, the anniversary of the landing was occasion for an official dinner party, and in 1838 – the 50th anniversary – it

Meaningful marks *Body paint is an essential element of Aboriginal ritual.*

was proclaimed a public holiday. Yet no one thought to name the holiday Australia Day until the 1930s, and only in the 1970s did it become an occasion of national self-awareness and pride. On the last Monday in January (to make a long weekend of it) Australians now celebrate their identity with zest. Sports events, exhibitions, parades and spectacles of all kinds foster a sense of belonging, of being special. In Sydney, the passenger ferries take part in a mad sprint across the harbour, and later in the day a flotilla of magnificent tall ships departs for an annual race around the harbour. Parties, fireworks, barbecues follow; it is summertime, and the country is on holiday. Conspicuous by their absence are the Aborigines, who hold a vigil of their own on a day that represents for them the loss of their land. A solution would be to change the date – to remove the explicit association with the arrival of the First Fleet – which may happen some day.

Days to remember

True to the tradition begun in 1789, the sovereign's birthday continues also to be a public holiday. A century of independence and growing republican sentiment are not reasons enough to forgo a holiday on the second Monday in June – except for Western Australia, which, having its own Foundation Day then, moves the Queen's birthday to September. Different states hold Labour Day – also sometimes known as Eight-Hour Day – at different times of the year. This commemorates 19th-century campaigns for decreased working hours, and pays tribute to Australia's strong trade union tradition. The most sacred day in the calendar is Anzac Day, on April 25. Courage, loyalty and sacrifice are the themes of this national holiday tied to the bloody Gallipoli landing in the First World War, which also honours the dead of subsequent wars. Other reasons are also found to pause and party.

Making a point *The Maori* haka *used to be a prelude to combat.*

Waitangi Day

Waitangi Day, February 6, is New Zealand's national day, although it was not declared a public holiday until 1973. That year, the government renamed it 'New Zealand Day', but under Maori pressure the old name was restored shortly afterwards.

A celebration is traditionally held on the lawn in front of the Treaty House at Waitangi, overlooking the Bay of Islands. This is where Maori chiefs and representatives of the British crown signed the Waitangi Treaty in 1840. For Maori nationalists, however, the treaty remains a deeply contentious event, and the holiday has become an occasion for noisy protests, particularly by Maori extremists.

Marches and demonstrations disrupt other events held throughout the country, as do displays of the traditional war dance, the *haka*. Waitangi Day is a useful barometer for gauging the state of relations between the government and the Maori people.

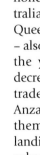

Bush picnic *In a strange mix of elegance and the basics, dinner-jacketed Australian picnickers carry their own chairs, plus a can of beer each.*

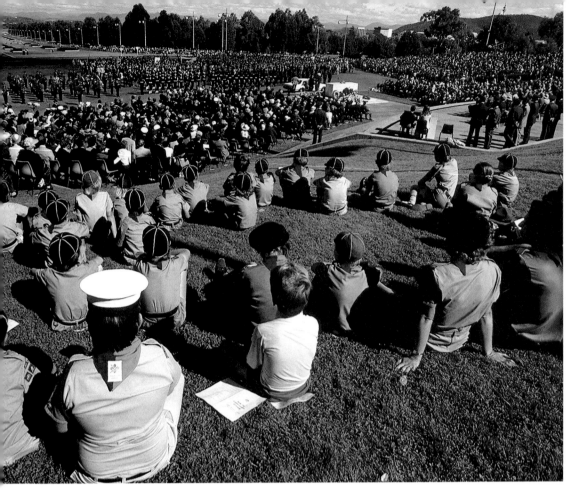

Patriotism and remembrance
An Anzac Day ceremony in Canberra honours the war dead.

Gay and Lesbian Mardi Gras takes place, also a month-long event which culminates in a colourful parade and an enormous party. Suppressed when first attempted in the early 1970s, the parade now draws over a million spectators and is claimed to be the largest event of its kind in the world. It is a stunning demonstration of the transformation of Australia's social climate.

Festivals for all – Irish, German, Chinese . . .

Anyone who feels Irish wraps up in green and drinks Guinness on St Patrick's Day, and those of German descent in the Barossa strike up their brass bands for local festivities. In January, or sometimes February, Australia's Chinese celebrate their New Year with parades of dragons and clashing gongs, as they have done since arriving in their thousands to seek 'mountains of gold' in the 1850s. In Bendigo are preserved a pair of colourful imperial dragons, Loong and Sun Loong, said to be the oldest (Loong) and longest (Sun Loong) in the world. In a highly Australian act of cultural fusion, they are brought out once a year to star in the local Easter Fair.

Substitute Waitangi Day for Australia Day, and New Zealand's national holiday schedule reads much the same as that of its neighbour across the Tasman Sea. The Queen's birthday (celebrated a week earlier in New Zealand), Anzac Day and Labour Day are also observed, while each province has its own anniversary day, usually adjusted to ensure a long weekend.

Some things new ... and some things old

The flood of 'New Australians' from continental Europe and Asia have added their traditions to the festive stew, while Aborigines are finding cause to celebrate after a long cultural exclusion. The Barunga Culture and Sports Festival, for instance, draws thousands to a remote site to the south-east of Katherine, in the Northern Territory. In New Zealand, Polynesian immigrant communities organise the most attractive celebrations, such as the Pasifika Festival in Auckland, an arts, entertainment, food and sports jamboree that combines all the island cultures.

New wave Australia's Asians celebrate their traditional festivals, adding to the multicultural mix.

In Victoria, a horse race is cause for a state holiday: Melbourne Cup Day. The race, on the first Tuesday in November, brings all of Australia, not just Victoria, to an expectant halt, gathered around television sets and barbecues; in stations and in trains, loudspeakers keep travellers informed.

Get together and have fun

It is customary in all parts of the country to hold local holidays on the occasion of agricultural shows, while wine regions have their vintage festivals, most lavish in the Barossa of South Australia. Summer festivals are organised in all cities. Moomba, in Melbourne, is one of the biggest, with concerts, theatrical performances, parades and dancing, as well as sporting events such as waterskiing championships. Moomba is said to come from an Aboriginal word meaning 'to get together and have fun'. The Festival of Sydney lasts for the month of January, and has hardly ended when the city's

Glad to be gay Groups from all over the world take part in the gay Mardi Gras parade in Sydney (above). Melbourne gays have their Midsumma Carnival; those in Auckland cavort at the Hero Parade.

117

A question of faith

Australia has no equivalent of the American motto 'In God We Trust', and its national symbols are devoid of all reference to the sacred. Likewise, New Zealand is a secular society, with increasing numbers professing to have no religion.

Guardian *The Buddha keeps watch.*

Statistically, Australians and New Zealanders are not very religious. The mood might be said to have been set from the start. Captain Cook had no time for chaplains. Later, the First Fleet did have an Anglican chaplain, whose baggage included 4200 religious books, but it was five years before he was able to build a church. This cost him £67 out of his own pocket, and after only a month it was burned down – the convicts had strongly resented being ordered to attend his services, Irish Catholics especially. Catholic numbers grew rapidly, especially after an uprising in Ireland in 1798, yet priests were banned from the colony, and permission to celebrate Mass was not granted until 1803.

Poor examples

The harsh realities of life in the early colony were probably not conducive to spiritual contemplation; nor could the convicts have been encouraged by such representatives of the Church as the Reverend Samuel Marsden, nicknamed 'The Flogging Parson'. He had a particular hatred of Irish Catholics, whom he regarded as 'always alive to rebellion and mischief', and would readily sentence suspected troublemakers to 300 lashes.

The result was that Australia never acquired an established Church, as in England. If anything, there are today more Catholic than Anglican Australians.

Scottish and Dutch Presbyterians, Methodists and German Lutherans leavened the mix, but religious enthusiasm waned in the sunshine. The prudish churchgoer was a figure of ridicule, and 'dull as a month of Sundays' became a popular expression.

Out of 18 million Australians, 12.5 million consider themselves Christians, with Greek and Serb immigrants accounting for half a million adherents of the Eastern Orthodox Church. There are also around 200 000 Muslims, 80 000 Jews, 67 000 Hindus, and some 200 000 Buddhists. Yet more than a quarter of all Australians profess to have no religion at all.

New Zealand, despite a history of Church-sponsored settlement, is also very secular. A study in 1989 found less than 20 per cent of the population involved in any religious activity, with the trend pointing downward. Between the 1976 and 1991 censuses, those professing no religion rose from 3.3 per cent to 20.1 per cent.

A political and moral force

The churches may not have attracted large crowds of worshippers, but they have exerted great influence in Australia all the same. One in three children attends a private school, usually affiliated with a religion. The churches are also quick to throw their weight behind crusades against alcoholism, racism and the recent challenge of legalised euthanasia. The Australian Labor Party has deep roots in communities of Irish origin, and it suffered its greatest crisis in the 1950s, when the Catholic Church turned against the party over communism.

Living faith *Young Catholics in Darwin pose after taking their First Communion (above). The entrance to St Patrick's Cathedral in Melbourne (right).*

Missionary impact *Christian missions to Aborigines, here in the Northern Territory, go back a long way.*

Very British *In both Australia and New Zealand (here, in Christchurch), many schools still insist on uniforms.*

Education – the traditional and the new

The churches played an important role in setting up education in both Australia and New Zealand, but it has had a different legacy in the two countries. The role of the two national governments is also very different.

In Australia, early colonial governors put the Anglican clergy in charge of schooling, which infuriated Catholics, dissenting Protestants, and everybody who was anti-establishment. By the time that the Australian colonies federated, in 1901, Church-sponsored schools of any denomination were excluded from government grants, becoming the core of a private school system that continues to this day. In addition there are a handful of prestigious and expensive private schools (in Melbourne they are called public schools) which provide high-quality education and can be almost as tradition-encrusted as the British model on which they are based. One of the most famous, Geelong Grammar, near Melbourne, counts the Prince of Wales among its former pupils. Sydney and Melbourne have the two oldest universities, founded in the 1850s.

State schools also provide quality education – a fusion of British standards and broader, American-style curriculums – but they are run by the individual states under systems differing to the extent that Australia has no common national examinations. Schooling was not compulsory until the 1940s, and it was not until the 1970s that the Federal Government began to contribute, meagrely, to its cost. The issue is a cause for heated debate. Canberra does provide much of the budget for higher education, and Australia

Cultural coaching *Maori children are often taught in their own language, as here in Rotorua.*

has prestigious institutes and research centres that regularly scoop Nobel prizes. Rich Asians have long come to study in Australia, but the economic crisis in the region has recently jeopardised this form of indirect subsidy.

The example of New Zealand

The path to learning in New Zealand was considerably smoother. Missionaries laid the groundwork, and from 1847 a portion of government revenues was earmarked for education. An act of 1877 established a centralised system of 'free, secular and compulsory' education for all children between the ages of 7 and 13 (raised to 15 in 1944). Secondary education was effectively opened to all in 1903, when the government funded a 'free places' bursary scheme. Today, elected education boards control New Zealand's state primary and secondary schools.

Maori schools were integrated into the state system in the 1960s, but under a strategy to ensure the preservation of their culture, Maori preschool centres and language schools were established later.

Schools of the air: teaching by radio

Extending education to sparsely populated reaches of the outback is a big challenge. Richer families can afford to board their children at private schools, and some states operate hostels. Correspondence courses were the only alternative until, in 1951, the Schools of the Air began using two-way radio to reach children directly.

Transceivers connect pupils with teachers at consoles in a dozen centres, such as Alice Springs. Radio, television and video recorder equipment is supplied on loan, sometimes with an 'Esky', a portable beer cooler for dad: parental enthusiasm is crucial.

Teachers make a flying circuit of their 'classrooms' several times a year, and annual holiday trips are usually arranged for pupils. Inculcating social skills is an important and difficult part of the task. Children who think nothing of fighting a bush fire can be terrified of crowds and traffic.

Clean, green and nuclear-free

Neither Australia nor New Zealand makes use of nuclear energy, but 'clean and green' New Zealand has gone very much further, with an anti-nuclear policy that incurred the wrath of the United States and became a defining aspect of its international image.

Anti-nuclear protest *Demonstrations such as this led to New Zealand banning nuclear-powered warships from its ports.*

in French Polynesia, the ancestral home of the Maori, had enraged public opinion. In 1973, it sent a frigate with a cabinet minister on board to the test site, and took France to the International Court of Justice.

Nuclear-free zone?

When American warships resumed their visits, they were met by flotillas of protest boats, and pressure grew to declare New Zealand a nuclear-free zone. In 1984, the government denied access to both nuclear-powered and nuclear-armed ships. Official US policy was to refuse to confirm or deny that a vessel had nuclear weapons on board, so the ban was extended to ships considered 'nuclear-capable'. Infuriated, the United States declared New Zealand to be in breach of the ANZUS Treaty, a security pact guaranteeing American protection for Australia and New Zealand.

France was meanwhile deeply embarrassed by the *Rainbow Warrior* incident, in which its agents confessed to sinking a Greenpeace ship in Auckland harbour. For New Zealand, what had begun as an environmental issue had become a challenge to its pride and sovereignty by two of the world's nuclear powers. In an emotionally charged atmosphere, the country refused to sacrifice its principles in spite of enormous pressure to do so.

For 50 years following the bombing of Hiroshima and Nagasaki, the Pacific area was used for hundreds of atomic tests conducted by the United States, Britain and France. Remote South Seas atolls were the preferred sites, but the Montebellos – small, flat islands off the north-west coast of Western Australia – were used for British testing in 1952 and 1956. The extent of radioactive contamination was never formally established, but the fallout in terms of public opinion continues to be felt. Australians remain wary of anything nuclear. After years of planning, a decision was taken in 1968 to build a nuclear power plant at Jervis Bay in New South Wales. Three years later, the project was deferred indefinitely. No reason was given. With abundant coal, Australia had no pressing need for a controversial new power source.

In New Zealand, feelings ran stronger, and when Australia was putting its energy plans on indefinite hold, the government in Wellington was placing a temporary ban on visits by American nuclear-powered vessels. New Zealand's real concern, however, was over France, whose testing of atomic weapons

France sinks the *Rainbow Warrior*

In July 1985, at the height of French nuclear testing in the Pacific, the flagship of the environmental organisation Greenpeace suffered a mysterious explosion and sank while docked in Auckland harbour. A photographer,

Fernando Pereira, was killed. Police quickly determined that the *Rainbow Warrior* had been mined. Two French secret-service agents, Alain Maffart and Dominique Prieu, were eventually arrested, tried and imprisoned. France was obliged to pay heavy compensation to Greenpeace and to New Zealand.

Internationl sabotage *The explosion blew a huge hole in the* Rainbow Warrior's *hull.*

Television, radio, newspapers – a passion for information

It need come as no surprise that Rupert Murdoch, the most powerful media mogul in the world, honed his skills in Australia's lively domestic arena. Australians are dedicated media consumers, and competition is intense.

Local mogul *Kerry Packer, a power in commercial TV, is the richest man in Australia.*

Years of isolation made Australians avid for information, a disposition that continues to this day. The race to cross the continent was spurred mainly by the need to establish a telegraph link with the rest of the world; the line was completed in 1872. Each state has several daily newspapers, often long-established. Melbourne's *The Age* and *The Sydney Morning Herald* are the major city dailies, while Rupert Murdoch owns the only national daily paper, *The Australian*. Lurid tabloids, 120 ethnic newspapers and 1200 magazines cram newsstands. Australia has the highest per capita readership of magazines in the world.

The excellent government-funded Australian Broadcasting Corporation (ABC) is the only national TV and radio network. Like the BBC, its model, it is sometimes fondly referred to as 'Aunty'. It is also an important patron of the arts, especially music, sponsoring a symphony orchestra in each state. SBS (Special Broadcasting Service) serves the country's ethnic minorities with programmes in a range of languages, including Arabic and Russian, on both radio and TV. And Imparja TV beams Aboriginal programmes from Alice Springs over much of outback Australia.

Commercial TV channels, however, attract up to 80 per cent of total viewers. There are three of them in each big city, and they are fiercely competitive, loading their schedules with imported programmes and sport. Among the most successful is Kerry Packer's Channel Nine network. Like his rival Rupert Murdoch, Packer is the son of an Australian press baron, Sir Frank Packer, who founded the popular magazine *The Australian Women's Weekly* in 1933 and ended up owning a stable of papers and magazines, including Sydney's *Daily Telegraph*. His son now heads a vast broadcasting empire as well as owning 60 per cent of all magazines sold in Australia.

Media in New Zealand

Radio stations proliferate everywhere in both New Zealand and Australia. New Zealand has no national newspaper. *The New Zealand Herald*, published in Auckland, has the largest circulation; and *The Press*, in Christchurch, is well respected. Two of the four national television channels are state-owned, but all of them carry commercials. New Zealanders can also subscribe to Rupert Murdoch's Sky TV, while in Australia, Murdoch's Foxtel is involved in a fight for the emerging pay-TV market.

Global mogul *Rupert Murdoch (above, right) is Australia's richest son, although now a US citizen. He tapped into the Australian passion for newspapers and magazines (right).*

Rupert Murdoch: media phenomenon

Rupert Murdoch's News Inc. extends over 75 per cent of the world, yet still has a battle on its hands at home, where Kerry Packer's Press and Broadcasting (PBL) empire keeps up relentless competition. The son of Sir Keith Murdoch, a leading local journalist and newspaper proprietor, Rupert Murdoch began, at age 22, with his father's newspapers in Adelaide. Soft-spoken and shy, he revealed a driven personality and a talent for spotting a bargain. He used major newspaper acquisitions in London as a lever to gain control in 1984 of an American TV network and the Twentieth Century-Fox studios in Hollywood. In 1999, he followed up his triumph with the movie *Titanic* by purchasing the LA Dodgers baseball team. His ambition is to encircle the world with a satellite network beaming transmissions from his own stations.

Sun, sea and surf – where water sports reign supreme

Including Tasmania, Australia has some 23 000 miles (37 000 km) of coastline. Most people live within reach of a beach, and water sports are the supreme national pastime. New Zealand's shores are wilder and more rugged, but they nourish among New Zealanders an equally fervent love of the sea.

When a surf is running, the sea bobs with 'surfies' all looking to 'catch a big one'. This most Australian of arts was first introduced in the 1880s by Tommy Tanna, a Melanesian gardener, who amazed onlookers by hurtling to shore on a breaking wave. At the time, Tanna was taking more than the obvious risks, for sea-bathing in daylight was then illegal. In 1902, a newspaper editor forced the issue by repeatedly bathing at noon. He was not prosecuted, despite complaints of indecency from homeowners who feared a drop in property prices, and a Sydney alderman who objected to violation of 'the rapture of the lonely shore'. Rapture took a new form as Australians flocked to some of the loveliest beaches on Earth.

Better boards

The surfboard came from Hawaii and was originally a cumbersome affair made of wood. Boards became lighter, until the demonstration of the glass-fibre-coated Malibu board revolutionised Australian surfing in 1956 and Australians entered international competitions. In 1964, Australians Bernard 'Midget' Farrelly and Phyllis O'Donnell became the first official amateur world champions. Within ten years, half a million Australians had surfboards.

There is a downside to this world of fun, however: Australia has the world's highest incidence of skin cancer, with New Zealand not far behind. Since the dangers of sunburn were appreciated, prevention campaigns have had an effect. Zinc-based creams, an Australian invention, are used, and children often wear swimsuits that cover their upper bodies – anything to avoid abandoning the beach, or the waters beyond. Marinas continue to multiply and the Sunday yacht race is a staple of life. The Royal Hobart Regatta is the largest aquatic event in the Southern Hemisphere, while Auckland in New Zealand has more private pleasure craft than any other urban area on earth.

Credo of the surf lifesaver

The beach guard in Australia is a heroic figure: a tanned, muscular embodiment of self-sacrifice for the common good. Unlike their US counterparts, the 82 000 Australian surf lifesavers are not paid. Instead, they give time voluntarily to risk their lives for others. This risk is real. Swift currents and undertows make many beaches as dangerous as they are alluring, while sharks are another problem. Most urban and resort beaches are protected by anti-shark nets, while spotter aircraft look out for the creatures from the air.

The world's first lifesaving clubs were formed in Sydney and the first surf rescue boat was developed at Manly and Bondi beaches early in the 20th century. Efficiency contests to keep lifesavers at the peak of fitness led to 'iron man' competitions, which test competitors to the limits of endurance. During the Second World War, Australians passed their knowledge to Americans, and international competition evolved. For 43 years, Australia retained the world title. It lost, in 1998, to New Zealand.

Surfies *The surf on this occasion is not great, but offers a chance to practise basic skills.*

Modesty boxes *No one bats an eye if bathers don their costumes on the beach, but some prefer to disrobe in private.*

Social sizzle *The ever-popular 'barbie' – the perfect social gathering for Australia's easy-going outdoor lifestyle.*

Barbie and hangi

The word barbecue, from the Spanish *barbacoa*, was first used in the Caribbean. In New Zealand, the Maori, from their Polynesian background, enjoy the barbecue's big brother, the hangi (pronounced 'hungi'). For this, a whole pig is roasted in a coal-filled pit covered by leaves or wet sacking.

Living the good life

'No worries' is not just a popular expression in Australia; it is a life formula. Clustered around the backyard barbecue, and in the pub, Australians revel in fellowship without social barriers, while New Zealanders sometimes prefer to get away from it all by enjoying, or challenging, nature.

You come casually dressed, and bring the children with you. The aroma of grilling meat guides you towards the garden, where a sizzling barbecue awaits. You dump your contribution of beers into a tub full of ice, and join the crowd on the lawn. Bursts of laughter punctuate the birdsong. The hosts make sure that you know everyone by their first names, and with your plate and your glass both well filled, you mingle among the other guests. 'G'day, mate', someone says. You relax. You belong.

You are careful not to put on any airs and graces. Australians have an expression for people who get too high and mighty: 'tall poppies', they call them, and with obvious displeasure. This, after all, is the land of the 'fair go', a fellowship of equals. The place where this rule is most scrupulously observed is the pub. You drink, you talk sport, you play a game of pool, you join in the joking banter. 'No worries' perfectly captures the mood that must be maintained, in all circumstances.

Overseas experience, a rite of passage

The many young Australians and New Zealanders serving behind the bar in London pubs bear witness to an Antipodean tradition: that of experiencing life in the former mother country, as part of growing up. In polite New Zealand society, one is not properly adult without completing OE, or Overseas Experience. This a journey of initiation, essentially, including a visit to London, which is used as a base from which to inspect continental Europe. With the advent of cheaper air fares, the OE is going global, the best itineraries including Asia, and a return from Europe via the USA. An OE needs to last from six months to a year to be credible. Then it is time to go back home and loudly declare that nowhere compares with 'Godzone', short for 'God's own country'.

Death-defying New Zealanders

Social cohesion is less of a priority in New Zealand. Men meet easily around beer and rugby, but communal enterprise is less important to them than it is for their Australian counterparts. For many, real happiness lies in facing a raging winter sea or contemplating a beautiful summer night, or in sitting snugly in a cabin, waiting for the kettle to boil for a 'cuppa'.

The cabin in the wild is where New Zealanders get away from it all. In the north, it is called a crib; in the south, it is a bach, pronounced 'batch', as in bachelor – originally, it was a fairly basic dwelling occupied by a man on his own, especially in more remote areas. But wherever you are in New Zealand, nature is never very far away, and often it has a dramatic, wild quality. New Zealanders have responded to this by developing a range of 'extreme' outdoor pursuits, such as bungee-jumping, achieving pleasure in a death-defying 'adrenaline rush'.

Kiwi idyll *Close to nature and remote from the rest of the world, many New Zealanders have a sense of being the privileged possessors of a corner of Eden. Opportunities for picnics abound, especially on long summer evenings.*

Sport, a national passion

By any standard, Australia occupies a place in the first rank of sporting nations; in terms of the size of its population, it is supreme in the world. New Zealand, with fewer people, concedes nothing, and has its own fields of dominance.

Sport in Australia is more than a matter of fun and exercise. It is a fixation. When not watching or betting on sport, the Australian male is talking sport. It is the lubricant that oils the conversation on most social occasions. An outdoor lifestyle, a coastal climate made for play, and a general belief in the prime importance of leisure have combined to create a nation of sports fanatics.

A love of cricket

By the 1880s, most city workers had sufficient time off to be able to indulge in their favourite pastime, long before this was possible in the Northern Hemisphere. Cricket, played since at least 1803, was the first national sport, and a potent force in binding the country together. Through the first half of the 20th century, cricket Test matches were the main means of national expression, and in Sir Donald Bradman Australia produced a player second to none. In 1998, at the age of 90, 'The Don' endured as a national treasure and living legend.

In the sun-and-beer-charged passions of its cricket crowds, Australian camaraderie – 'mateship' – finds its full expression. In winter, the Melbourne Cricket Ground is turned over to another local obsession, Australian Rules Football. 'Footy' probably originated as a form of Gaelic football amongst gold diggers. Played by teams of 18 on an oval field with an oval ball, it is a fast, skilful and furious brawl, though it is not the only kind to please Australians. In Sydney and Queensland, 13-a-side Rugby League is favoured, while universities and private schools foster 15-a-side Rugby Union. Australia regularly beats other countries in both rugby codes.

Sporting heroes

The country's sporting prowess remained a secret of the English-speaking world until the 1950s, when Australians found they could run, swim and play tennis better than anyone else. John Landy, Herb Elliott (athletics), Dawn Fraser, Murray Rose (swimming), Lew Hoad and Ken Rosewall (tennis) were a few of the heroes in an era that climaxed in 1956, with a 5-0 sweep of the United States in the Davis Cup and 35 medals in the Melbourne Olympic Games. The next generation proved this was no lucky streak. In Rod Laver, Australia produced arguably the best tennis player ever, and individuals shone in almost every sport, from motor-racing (Jack Brabham) to golf (Greg Norman). In the run-up to the Sydney Olympics, Australia's domination of the Commonwealth Games in 1998 verged almost upon the embarrassing.

Aussie Rules In 'Footy' (left), the ball can be kicked, caught, punched or bounced. The game has a fanatical following. The championship Grand Final, usually in September, has the charged atmosphere of an American Superbowl. Above: Evonne Goolagong Cawley wins Wimbledon for the second time in 1980.

A need to compete Fresh air and sunshine encourage all sections of society to take part in sport. Bowls extends the challenge into retirement (left). Cathy Freeman, twice a world 400 m champion (below), is an Aboriginal star.

Black, the colour of sport in New Zealand

The name that has become a legend in sport was coined out of a printer's error in the 1890s. 'They are all backs', a New Zealand reporter wrote, in an attempt to convey the fleet-footed play of the national rugby team. Next day, the newspaper printed this statement as: 'They are all blacks'. The name stuck, and was enshrined in the team colours. Ever since, New Zealand teams have spread terror around the rugby world as the All Blacks.

Rugby in New Zealand verges on a religion, with Eden Park stadium in Auckland its temple, and its own distinctive rituals. The All Blacks precede their matches with a *haka*. With eyes bulging and tongues hanging out, the team beat on their chests, stamp on the pitch, and chant the Maori challenge. The spine-tingling performance gives New Zealand sides a psychological advantage even before the kickoff. Public support is intense. When an American sportswear sponsor hinted, in 1999, at a desire to have the all-black kit altered, there was universal public consternation.

Other sports have adopted black as their colour. New Zealand athletes wear all-black clothes; even the white-flannelled national cricket team have black caps; hence their unofficial name 'the black caps'. When, in 1995, New Zealand captured the most coveted prize in world sailing, its yacht was painted black, and named *Black Magic*.

While Australia vaunts the 'battler' spirit, Timaru in the South Island of New Zealand has produced more sporting battlers than any place of its modest size in the world. They include Bob Fitzsimmons, a middleweight boxer who captured the world heavyweight crown from the American Jim Corbett in a historic fight in 1895, and Jack Lovelock, New Zealand's most outstanding athlete until modern times. But the town's most celebrated athlete was a horse, called Phar Lap, which won the Melbourne Cup in 1930. The phrase 'A heart as big as Phar Lap' is still used as an expression of admiration in Australia, which would like to think of this legendary thoroughbred as one of its own.

The tug of war over Phar Lap continues still. New Zealand has the skeleton; Australia has the skin, stuffed in the Museum of Victoria, and the heart, preserved in the National Museum in Canberra. With less than a fifth of Australia's population, New Zealand gives as good as it gets. 'Underarm delivery' is an expression sometimes used to describe something that is unfair. It hearkens back to 1981, when Australia won a game of cricket by 'bowling' the final ball of a match in a controversial manner, thereby denying New Zealand a chance to tie. The memory lingers on.

No longer America's cup

Australia and New Zealand are the only two nations ever to have wrested sailing's prestigious America's Cup from the United States. Nicknamed the 'auld mug', the trophy had been won continuously by the United States since the inaugural race

in 1851. It was virtually considered to be American property when the yacht *Australia II* scored a narrow victory in 1983. A crowd of 400 000 greeted the victors on their return to Perth, and the national celebrations were the greatest since the end of the Second World War. In 1987, racing off Fremantle, the United States regained the cup amid accusations of cheating, but in 1995, off San Diego, the New Zealand yacht *Black Magic* swept aside challengers from all other nations including the United States. The defence of the cup is scheduled for 2000, on a course to be set in the Hauraki Gulf, off Auckland.

Ocean-racing fervour
Sailing has become increasingly popular since Australia won the America's Cup in 1983. Here, yachts set out on the Sydney-Hobart race.

Strength and speed
All Black player Jonah Lomu barrels through the Wallaby pack. Lomu is of Tongan origin.

Road trains, monsters of the outback

From Adelaide to Darwin, via Alice Springs, 'The Track' arrows through the desert. To haul heavy goods and livestock across central Australia called for a different kind of vehicle, and a special kind of driver. Enter the road train, and the 'truckie', the kind of man who can barrel across a continent twice in ten days wrestling a juggernaut named High and Mighty.

Nothing in Australia is more daunting than being overtaken by a road train. Rumble. Roar. Flying grit and blanketing dust. The wise motorist slows to a crawl, and cowers, until the enormous dark bulk has vanished, and the dust settles. And as for overtaking a road train, this is hazardous at any

Juggernaut *A road train is built like a bulldozer, with heavily reinforced bumper and massive 'roo bars' to deflect kangaroos and similar obstacles. The driver can never simply slam on his brakes for fear of losing control.*

time. Tourists pulling a caravan are warned never to attempt this foolhardy manoeuvre.

Behind the wheels of these huge monsters are men like Eddie Holland. Eddie, 46, has been a truckie for 30 years, and he rides The Track, the Stuart Highway, which bisects Australia from north to south. In Britain, Eddie would be called a long-distance lorry driver, a hopelessly inadequate term to describe this uniquely Australian means of moving masses of freight and mobs of livestock over thousands of miles of outback. A road train is to a lorry what a supermarket is to a corner shop. A new, fully equipped rig with 'dogs' (trailers) costs about A$500 000. Its four tanks hold 640 gallons (2910 litres) of fuel. A fill-up costs about A$2000. The monster averages about 3 miles to the gallon (1 km per litre).

High and Mighty

Eddie lives in Adelaide. The son of a truckie, he acquired his heavy-vehicle licence at the age of 16. Now he has his own transport business, with three road trains that he fixed up to his liking in his workshop. His great pride is his Mack Titan: 610 horsepower,

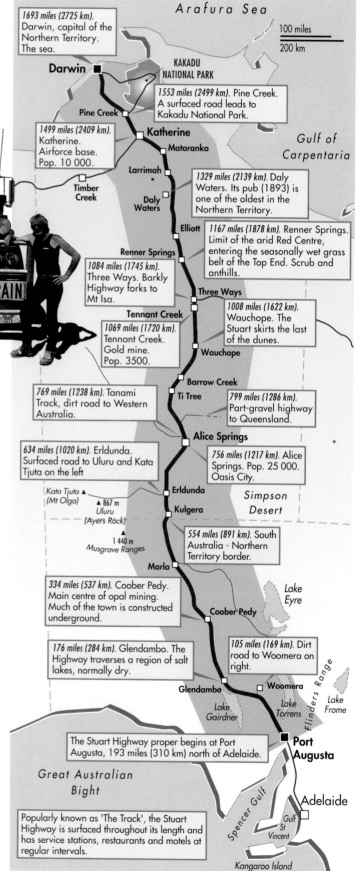

1693 miles (2725 km). Darwin, capital of the Northern Territory. The sea.

1553 miles (2499 km). Pine Creek. A surfaced road leads to Kakadu National Park.

1499 miles (2409 km). Katherine. Airforce base. Pop. 10 000.

1329 miles (2139 km). Daly Waters. Its pub (1893) is one of the oldest in the Northern Territory.

1167 miles (1878 km). Renner Springs. Limit of the arid Red Centre, entering the seasonally wet grass belt of the Top End. Scrub and anthills.

1084 miles (1745 km). Three Ways. Barkly Highway forks to Mt Isa.

1008 miles (1622 km). Wauchope. The Stuart skirts the last of the dunes.

1069 miles (1720 km). Tennant Creek. Gold mine. Pop. 3500.

769 miles (1238 km). Tanami Track, dirt road to Western Australia.

799 miles (1286 km). Part-gravel highway to Queensland.

634 miles (1020 km). Erldunda. Surfaced road to Uluru and Kata Tjuta on the left

756 miles (1217 km). Alice Springs. Pop. 25 000. Oasis City.

554 miles (891 km). South Australia - Northern Territory border.

334 miles (537 km). Coober Pedy. Main centre of opal mining. Much of the town is constructed underground.

105 miles (169 km). Dirt road to Woomera on right.

176 miles (284 km). Glendambo. The Highway traverses a region of salt lakes, normally dry.

The Stuart Highway proper begins at Port Augusta, 193 miles (310 km) north of Adelaide.

Popularly known as 'The Track', the Stuart Highway is surfaced throughout its length and has service stations, restaurants and motels at regular intervals.

18 gears, 115 tons, three trailers, 62 wheels; total length: 180 ft (55 m). The cab is painted grey, with red trimmings incorporating the name 'High and Mighty'. To Eddie's obvious delight, High and Mighty made the centrefold of *Truckin' Life* magazine in May 1998.

Eddie and High and Mighty are in direct line of descent from Afghans and their camels, brought to Australia in the 19th century to provide the outback with its first transport service. By the 1930s, a cumbersome arrangement of diesel truck and trailer, dubbed the Government Road Train, was

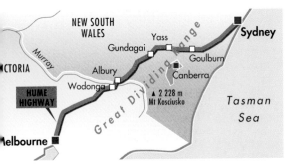

Australia's Main Street The Hume Highway is the fast track between Melbourne and Sydney, cutting through the historical and agricultural heartland of the nation.

hauling supplies to isolated communities. Following the Second World War, a trucker named Kurt Johannsen used an army-surplus tank transporter to pull a string of eight cattle trailers, but regulations now limit road trains to three 20 ton trailers. These monsters provision Darwin and much of the outback, and haul farm produce to the populated south. Until the 1950s, cattle were moved in herds by mounted stockmen, making a few miles a day, then thousands of miles of dirt roads were pushed through the bush, enabling road trains to do this job too.

Nights on the road

Eddie operates to a tight schedule, and sleeps wherever he halts. The cab is equipped with sleeping quarters, refrigerator, television, video, CD-player and cooking facilities. He prefers driving at night, when the roads are clear, and he is spared the sight of the desert, which he considers 'boring'. He listens to music and chats with his mates, other truckies, over the radio-telephone. On each trip, he clocks up around 5000 miles (8000 km). Outward bound, he hauls construction materials to Darwin, then he makes a detour to Kununura, in the north of Western Australia, to load melons for the markets of Adelaide and Melbourne.

He sets out on Friday evening, planning to reach Darwin on Monday morning, after 55 hours on the road. 'Easy', he calls this, now that the Stuart Highway has been surfaced. Until 1987, a 760 mile (1200 km) stretch from Port Augusta to Alice Springs was still dirt, and almost impassable when it rained; once he broke down 36 times. By Wednesday, he is at Kununura. By Saturday, he needs to have recrossed the continent, to spend Sunday at home with his wife, Julie, and children. Julie Holland was the first woman to qualify to drive road trains; sometimes, still, she accompanies her husband. Their 16-year-old son has already begun to drive.

Great Ocean Road The world's most scenic war memorial, this 125 mile (200 km) spur of the Princes Highway is dedicated to the dead of the First World War.

Highway 1, the Hume and Princes Highways

You can drive almost all the way around Australia on Highway 1. Australia is not a land of multi-lane motorways: the amount of traffic does not justify them, and distances are far too great. The exceptions are the approaches to state capitals and large stretches of the Hume Highway, which links Sydney and Melbourne, with a spur to the federal capital, Canberra.

A longer, more scenic alternative to the Hume Highway is the Princes Highway, which is the section of Highway 1 that curves around the coast from Sydney to Melbourne then on to Adelaide. It crosses magnificent forests and national parks.

Ready to roll A fully laden road train prepares to depart. At Coober Pedy (inset) truckers can rest in an air-conditioned underground motel.

Little colonial gems in the bush

Early graziers, farmers, prospectors and mariners endowed Australia with a scattering of magnificent small towns laden with flamboyant colonial architecture. Today, some are living museums; others are ghost towns.

Time warp   Nineteenth-century Ballarat is brought back to life at Sovereign Hill theme park.

In Australia, between the cities of the coast and the deserts, there is a zone of what elsewhere might be described as 'countryside'. From early in the 19th century, stockmen and farmers began to clear the trees and scrub. In the 1850s, the gold diggers followed in their tracks. These pioneers have left Australia dotted with marvels of colonial town planning. Some of these places have been abandoned; some have thrived; some have been carefully restored to bear witness to the iron will of a people determined to plant a distinctively British civilisation in the bush. A solid courthouse, historic jail, ornate pub-hotels, a racecourse, and a botanic garden are characteristic features.

Market towns, gold towns

Wool gave the continent its market towns. Goulburn (with a population of 22 000) is one of the oldest, glad now to be bypassed by the Hume Highway. There is a single main street, wide and very long. The principal commercial buildings are banks, built in purest Victorian style; corner pubs; a cathedral for the Anglicans and one for the Catholics; stockyards; a brewery built in 1836. The inner cluster of homes are 19th century, with corrugated iron roofs, cast-iron balconies and immaculately tended gardens.

Invariably, a town began as a clump of tents, duly replaced by wooden shacks, then more substantial structures, and finally noble public buildings, according to the degree of prosperity achieved. At each stage, some towns would falter, sometimes to die back into the bush. The gold rush quickened the process. Ballarat, now an easy

Ghost towns, raised and restored

When the lode ran out, the gold diggers moved on, leaving broken mining gear and abandoned pubs to be reclaimed by the bush. Some substantial towns died in this way, though some limped on. Ravenswood, in Queensland, has tumbledown buildings and cows grazing deserted streets, but it also has two restored pubs and mining has recommenced in the area. Not satisfied with dusty relics, Australia has re-created the past at Sovereign Hill, a theme park in Ballarat with an underground mine and a reconstructed 19th-century village, including hotel, post office, blacksmith, apothecary, newspaper office, theatre, and a cast of 'residents' in period costume. Tourists can pan for gold in the creek, take a stagecoach ride, and watch re-enactments of the historic stand at Eureka Stockade.

The tropical towns of coastal Queensland

The steamy coastal belt of Queensland has produced a distinctive tropical architecture, which includes delightful buildings known as 'Queenslanders'. Built of wood, with corrugated iron roofs and expansive verandahs, they stand on stilts to allow air to circulate, and to provide protection from tropical floods. The towns up the coast date from the mid to late 19th century. Rockhampton ('Rocky') lives off cattle now, but once it was gold, to which splendid structures like the Criterion Hotel bear witness. Townsville manages to be relaxed, even though a busy commercial centre and a military base. Cairns used to be the most beautiful of all. Locked in by rain forest and nudged by the Great Barrier Reef, it had everything to please, but it has had to pay a price for its popularity. It attracts hundreds of thousands of visitors, and its colonial architecture is giving way to highrise tourist hotels.

Off to the Reef Tourism thrives in Cairns (left).

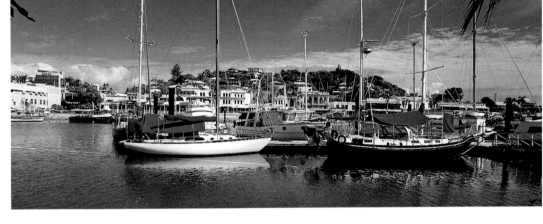

hour's drive from Melbourne, was an isolated farm settlement in 1851, when gold was discovered. Within months, it somehow managed to accommodate 20 000 fortune-hunters. More than 600 tons of gold were extracted before its reefs gave out in 1918, at which point Ballarat was content to rest on its laurels. The consequence is a charming, intact period-piece: wide streets with verandahs and iron-lace balconies, and a central bandstand – the Titanic Memorial Rotunda. About 50 pubs survive, including elaborate palaces such as Craigs Royal Hotel. Next to the mining exchange, the art gallery has the tattered remnants of the flag flown in 1854 at nearby Eureka Stockade, during Australia's only armed uprising; the gallery is older than the flag. The botanic gardens are dotted with pavilions and white marble sculptures (donated by a digger who once was a Glasgow post office clerk), and a little paddle steamer plies the ornamental lake.

Tranquil air   Townsville has a busy port but manages to keep relaxed.

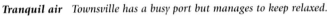

Bendigo's Pall Mall

The gold reefs at Bendigo were even richer and lasted longer, with a consequent raising of aspirations. It has a Pall Mall and Charing Cross, whose central Alexandra Fountain was named after the then Princess of Wales. Much of the wealth dug up from beneath Bendigo's streets was ploughed back into increasingly extravagant architecture, including a Gothic cathedral which took almost a century to build. Other gold towns faltered much earlier. Castlemaine is stuck charmingly in the 1860s, with a former market

*Historic transport
Bendigo's tram runs
along Pall Mall.*

designed like a Greek temple, and particularly impressive botanic gardens. Nearby Maldon has preservation orders to conserve its historic architecture; even Clunes, with a population of 800, retains fine buildings from its 1850s heyday. It is the same story wherever gold was found. Charters Towers, in north Queensland, has its complement of fancy old homes and classic architecture, and even a stock exchange (now a shopping arcade) dating from the 1890s, which was open 24 hours a day, seven days a week, during the height of the town's boom years.

Tasmania, thanks to its out-of-the-way location, has the best-preserved colonial villages. Battery Point, in Hobart, retains the quaint atmosphere of a colonial port, with a maze of mariners' cottages and merchants' homes, a little village green and a church – St George's – with box pews. Inland, tiny Richmond is a rural gem of the 1820s, complete with waddling ducks. Even its convict jail is perfectly preserved; famous inmates included Ikey Solomon, reputed to have been the model for Charles Dickens' Fagin.

*Iron lace   Behind its verandah decorated
with iron lace, the Richmond Arms Hotel
in Richmond, Tasmania, is a simple structure
made from local yellow sandstone.*

*Goldfields pride   Bendigo's first
Shamrock Hotel was a gold diggers'
café, whose floors were washed down
to collect gold dust from the miners'
boots. As money from the mines
flooded the town, the hotel was
rebuilt (for a third time) in 1897 in
French Renaissance style, so as not to
be outdone by the grandiose post
office and law courts across the
street. When it reopened, the
hotel boasted an electric light
and electric bell in every room.*

Colonial architecture

The simple elegance of the Georgian style sat well in the dusty grey-green and brown of the Australian landscape. By the 1830s, distinctive features had emerged – an overhanging roof, to protect the walls from damaging downpours, and shady verandahs. In the 1840s, cast-iron became available, and with it the galvanised iron roof and delicate iron columns to prop up the verandah. From the mid 19th century, iron was cheap and local taste ran to the fanciest designs of decorative iron lace. The gold rush coincided with a flood of materials from the factories of Britain and Europe, and sudden wealth was channelled into ever more extravagant architecture until a ruinous drought and depression in 1892 brought all to a grinding halt. Surviving ironwork in urban neighbourhoods, such as Paddington in Sydney and Carlton in Melbourne, adds greatly to a property's value.

Eating out   Restaurants and bistros serving all manner of exotic fare spill onto city streets.

A taste of everything, including the bush

Meat – grilled, roasted, barbecued or made into pies – was the mainstay of Australian cuisine until a culinary revolution swept the country. South-east Asia has had a particularly strong influence, contributing to the local style known as 'new Australian' cuisine. In many pubs, too, much has changed.

The meat pie topped with tomato sauce is a hallowed Australian tradition. Until recently, so was steak, beef being readily available and cheap. In fact, in 1894 Australians were the world's biggest meat-eaters, their annual consumption dwarfing that of their nearest rivals, the Americans. As in other affluent countries, times – and eating habits – are now changing. But true to the traditions of an earlier time, when shearers and stockmen would often eat steak at every meal, a truckie at a roadhouse will mumble 'Make me up a plate, thanks, mate', then tuck into a 'cooked brekkie' of steak, sausages, bacon and eggs, and just a few hours later, wolf down another steak.

Yet something miraculous has occurred in the past 25 years. All those migrants from Mediterranean countries, coupled with the eye-opening experience of air travel, have weaned many Aussies from reliance on the staples of their Anglo-Saxon ancestors. Until the 1960s, a night out at a Chinese café was high adventure, whereas Australia is today a shop window of world cuisines – among them Italian, Greek, Lebanese and Asian. Many a traditional Australian 'milk bar' now pro-

claims itself a 'milk bar delicatessen', and many chefs are acquiring celebrity status as they develop a 'new Australian cuisine' – a style that fuses European and Asian ingredients and cooking styles and increasingly features the now fashionable 'bush food'. For all the innovation, at the basis of this new cuisine is an abundance of fresh, high-quality local produce. Meanwhile, the country pubs remain strongholds of the steak-and-chips tradition, and the meat pie, generously smeared with tomato sauce, still reigns supreme in sports stadiums across the country.

Lamb and Pinot Noir

New Zealand, long a land of roasts and boiled vegetables, but blessed with superb produce, is experiencing a similar culinary transformation. Sophisticated diners fuss over their cervana (venison), or rack of lamb served with a soft Martinborough Pinot Noir, and demand the finest Bluff oysters and green-lipped mussels. The Sugar Club, one of London's top gourmet restaurants, had its beginnings in a Wellington backstreet.

Bush tucker

All manner of indigenous foods known as 'bush tucker', have come into vogue as 'native cuisine'. Trendy Australian restaurant-goers can now tuck into emu paté, crocodile steaks, kangaroo-tail soup and even pan-fried witchetty grubs, while chefs continue to discover new ingredients among the 5000 species of edible native plants, with results ranging from 'bush salad' to ice cream flavoured with wattle seed. Leading chefs vie to create ever more exotic dishes. Specialist shops sell berries, fruits, nuts and roots once known only to the Aborigines.

Fresh taste   The Red Ochre grill in Cairns (below) features native fruits, such as the quandong (left).

Aussie elixirs

Vegemite – 'concentrated extract of yeast' – is a thick, dark, salted paste spread on toast at breakfast. Since its creation in 1923, it has become a national institution, along with pavlova (meringue fruit-and-cream pie) and lamingtons (sponge cake covered with chocolate and coconut). New Zealanders insist the pavlova is theirs.

Mixed emotions Australians love to make jibes about the British, whom they refer to as 'pommies', yet many retain a sentimental attachment to Britain and the Crown. When the Queen visited Australia in 1992, crowds of wellwishers turned out to greet her (left). Others would prefer to have an elected president as head of state in Canberra (below).

Towards a republic?

Australia entered the 21st century with the Queen as its head of state. Many Australians are in favour of cutting this last colonial tie to Britain, but others question the merits of a republic over the present constitutional monarchy. Despite a referendum on the issue in 1999, the debate is far from over.

In 1975, Australian politics was shaken to its foundations when the prime minister, Gough Whitlam, was dismissed from office by the governor-general, acting under his powers as the representative of Queen Elizabeth II. In fact, the Queen, whose role was symbolic, had nothing to do with these events; rather, they were engineered by the prime minister's domestic foes. Such a coup could not happen again, yet this crisis cast into sharp relief Australia's anomalous position as an independent democracy with a distant, hereditary monarch as its head of state.

Polls in the 1990s showed that a small majority of Australians were in favour of their country becoming a republic, but a referendum in 1999 resulted in defeat for the republicans. In fact, the defeat had as much to do with disagreement over how a president should be elected as with support for the monarchy – many want a nationally elected president and opted to retain the status quo rather than accept a president chosen by a majority of the two major political parties, as proposed in the referendum. Meanwhile, the governor-general would take the royal role of opening the Olympic Games in September 2000.

Changing the flag?

It is the Union Jack in the corner of the Australian flag that many people find most irksome, seeing this as the badge of a 'colony'. Many New Zealanders feel the same about their very similar flag. Some want to see it replaced by a black standard bearing the silver fern worn by its sportsmen; others say that would be too much like a 'pirate flag'. There is less of an urge here to get rid of the monarchy, although economic woes have revived an old idea. A radical Maori minority dream of having their own state.

New Zealand women at the helm

In 1893, the women of New Zealand were the first in the world to gain the vote. In 1997, they scored another first, with women heading both the Government and the major opposition party. In power was Prime Minister Jenny Shipley (National Party), a mother of two children; in opposition, Helen Clark (Labour Party), a former political scientist. The circumstances could not have been more testing. Economic difficulties had strained the comprehensive social welfare system that had been New Zealand's pride. Shipley, in her previous position as health and social welfare minister, had the task of making the country accept reforms, and as prime minister her intention was to complete this process. In contrast, Clark's aim was to restore the old social priorities. Making the situation more difficult was a change in the system of parliamentary election. In a 1993 referendum, New Zealanders opted for a degree of proportional representation. As a result, the 1996 election saw the emergence of a small ultra-liberal party, ACT, and the strengthening of New Zealand First, a breakaway group led by a Maori maverick, Winston Peters.

First lady Jenny Shipley became premier of New Zealand in 1997.

CHAPTER 7

A CULTURAL AWAKENING

Australia and New Zealand long shared a sense of cultural isolation, from which escape was the only option for a talented individual. The critical year of change was 1973, when Patrick White won the Nobel prize for literature and the Sydney Opera House was completed. Creative artists of every sort shared in an awakening, and before long Australians and New Zealanders were winning Oscars and Booker prizes, while the 'Australian sound' and 'Dunedin sound' were rocking the airwaves everywhere. Coincidentally, an Australian-born mogul emerged to exert enormous influence in the world's media: Rupert Murdoch. The new confidence has infused all sectors of society. Among the Maori, it brought about a cultural renaissance that has restored dreams of bicultural partnership on which the country was supposed to have been founded. In Australia, the Aborigines, too, have rediscovered their artistic talents and sense of pride.

A display of Aboriginal art at the National Gallery, Canberra.

Australia's new-wave cinema

The supremely enterprising Australian cinema was once throttled by a monopoly of Hollywood imports, but now it is Hollywood that is at the receiving end. Films, more than anything else, have made the world sit up and take notice of Australian culture.

Movie-making took off in Australia with a film of the 1896 Melbourne Cup, made within a year of cinematography's debut in Paris. *Soldiers of the Cross*, a story of early Christian martyrs with intervals for slide-lectures and prayers, was made in Melbourne in 1900 and shown across the United States. Melbourne led the world again with *The Story of the Kelly Gang* (1906). Its screening time of more than 60 minutes made it by far the longest feature film of its day.

Australian film-makers turned out hundreds of bushranger adventures, comedies and documentaries, only to be slowly squeezed out as local distribution companies

TERENCE **STAMP**   HUGO **WEAVING**   GUY **PEARCE**   BILL **HUNTER**

The Adventures of

PRISCILLA

Queen of the Desert

Outback lark   *Stephan Elliot's comedy* The Adventures of Priscilla, Queen of the Desert *(1994) tells the story of a group of drag artists touring the outback in a bus called Priscilla.*

Oscar winner   *The Piano was an Australian-New Zealand co-production, set in New Zealand and directed by a New Zealander, Jane Campion.*

fell under American control. Independent producer Charles Chauvel persevered with outdoor adventure movies. His *Forty Thousand Horsemen* (1940) contained the most spectacular cavalry charge ever filmed. But the Australian feature film died with him, until resurrected with government help in the late 1960s, just when the country was in creative ferment. A national film and television school opened, and thanks to a theatrical resurgence and a spate of new novelists, there was no lack of script material, or of actors and directors ready for the challenge.

International recognition

The directors Peter Weir (*Picnic at Hanging Rock*, 1975), Gillian Armstrong (*My Brilliant Career*, 1979) and Bruce Beresford (*Breaker Morant*, 1980) helped to secure the critical recognition the industry needed in order to become an international force, while George Miller (*Mad Max*, 1979) proved that Australia could deliver films that would appeal to mainstream mass audiences. Among the many writers supplying plots, dramatist David Williamson had numerous plays made into movies and also wrote several scripts specifically for films, including *Gallipoli* (1980). Success was so great that the industry lost talent to Hollywood, and had to

regroup. Further international hits, such as *Crocodile Dundee* (Peter Faiman, 1985) and *Strictly Ballroom* (Baz Luhrmann, 1991) secured its position, while 1990s films like *Babe*, *Muriel's Wedding* and *Shine* demonstrated a range in the Australian cinema to match its vitality.

A circuit of festivals provides a useful outlet for new talent, and keeps competition on the boil. The festivals also help film-makers to obtain new funding, which can at times be a problem. Television, too, has put Australian entertainment on tap for the world through a flurry of 'soap operas' exported worldwide. In Britain, *Neighbours* and *Home and Away* became big hits.

The lure of Hollywood

For many years, the fact that Hollywood star Errol Flynn was Australian was often forgotten. The same, on a grand scale, could be happening again as Australian personalities are absorbed abroad. The director Peter Weir last made an Australian movie (*The Year of Living Dangerously*) in 1982; 16 years later, he was nominated for an Oscar for *The Truman Show*, a quintessentially American movie. Mel Gibson is known for his *Lethal Weapon* portrayals rather than the string of Australian successes that brought him to Hollywood. The list continues with stars like Olivia Newton-John, Nicole Kidman, 1997 Oscar-winner Geoffrey Rush and Cate Blanchett, nominated for an Oscar for her portrayal of Elizabeth I.

Hit series   *The Mad Max films starring Mel Gibson drew world audiences.*

Australian literature abandons the bush

Australian authors, until recently, were fixated upon the hostile wonders of the outback – usually from a comfortable distance. Now they are active, in unprecedented numbers, in holding up a mirror to life in their bright cities and leafy suburbs.

Australia's first, and for a long time only, attempt at self-identity was through ballads and yarns extolling heroism in the face of forbidding nature. The prime early exponents were 'Banjo' Paterson and Henry Lawson. Paterson grew up in the outback (Banjo was the name of his favourite horse), and besides penning the words of 'Waltzing Matilda', he wrote 'The Man from Snowy River' and a string of other jaunty ballads. Lawson wrote poems and stories telling of the lonely 'mateship' of bushmen, exalting the 'battler' and the underdog. These themes were echoed in the novels of Joseph Furphy, writing under the pen name Tom Collins, who used the alleged last words of bushranger-folk hero Ned Kelly as the title of his best-known work, *Such Is Life*.

This literary tradition continued well into the 20th century. Possibly the best 'outback' novelist was the prolific Katharine Susannah Prichard, active over four decades, while Xavier Herbert's *Capricornia* (1938) is an epic treatment of life in the far north. The best-sellers of Colleen McCulloch (notably *The Thorn Birds*) still keep the spirit alive at airport bookstalls all around the world.

Outback as backdrop

In Patrick White, Australia found an author who used the outback as backdrop for monumental works that explore the human soul. *The Tree of Man* (1955) deals with the struggles of a farmer amidst drought, fire and flood; *Voss* (1957) explores the mind of an explorer. Later works explore spiritual and sexual confusion. In real life, White disliked bush life, and the generation that succeeded him turned their backs on it entirely, to find inspiration in modern urban life and in re-examining cherished myths. With government encouragement, there has been a constant flow of new titles, and around 50 per cent of books sold in Australia are by local authors. Peter Carey, David Malouf and Thomas Keneally have a world readership. Keneally, one of whose main themes is oppression, became a focus of attention when his novel *Schindler's Ark* was made into a major movie. Peter Corris, who favours Sydney settings, the wry Elizabeth Jolley, Helen Garner and Tim Winton are among other leading authors.

The tormented world of Patrick White

Australian literature is dominated by the figure of Patrick White (1912-90), who wrote the first of his eight novels in 1939 and was awarded the Nobel prize for literature in 1973, being cited for 'epic and psychological narrative art which has introduced a new continent into literature'. Several of his works explore the individual's search for meaning in a harsh land at odds with itself. White was born into a prosperous grazier family and educated in England; he served in the RAF through the Second World War. He was as complex as his novels. Feared for his trenchant sense of humour and abrupt mood-swings, he confided in his biography that he could not come to terms with his fellow Australians and found consolation in the landscape.

Contemporary voices Peter Carey (below) and David Malouf (right) have both won major international awards.

Revolutionary Like Miles Franklin before her, Germaine Greer chose to live abroad.

Feminist tradition

Australia's top literary prize is named after Miles Franklin, a feminist who gained fame by writing *My Brilliant Career* aged 20. Franklin lived abroad for 20 years before returning to her native land in 1927. A tradition of strong-minded literary women continued with Germaine Greer, whose *The Female Eunuch* (1970) advocated revolutionary empowerment for women.

A culture on the edge

The achievements of the land that is under Down Under are often lost, or confused with those of its big neighbour, but New Zealanders thrive under the challenge. With a population of scarcely 3.8 million, it is a country of creative as much as natural surprises.

Katherine Mansfield She was one of the greatest-ever short-story writers.

Jane Campion New Zealand's most distinguished film director achieved success at Cannes and an Academy Award for **The Piano,** *about a mute woman's struggles in pioneering days.*

Ask any New Zealander who invented the aeroplane and you will be told how Richard Pearse, a South Island farmer, flew his home-made aircraft in 1902, thus beating the Wright Brothers off the ground by 21 months. Eyewitnesses swore to it, but it was too far away for the outside world to take notice. In 1999, the prime minister, Jenny Shipley, sought to turn this geographical dislocation to advantage and, with an eye to the millennium celebrations and New Zealand's proximity to the international dateline, declared: 'We live on the edge of the Earth . . . the leading edge.'

Being part of the world's most isolated community of any size has encouraged creative enterprise, and it has been said that given a length of fencing wire, a New Zealander can make anything. It is in keeping with this can-do spirit that a bee-keeper and a young Maori girl should have become the best-known living New Zealanders . . . one as the world's most famous mountaineer, and the other as an opera star. Edmund Hillary leapt from obscurity to immortality in 1953, when he conquered the world's highest peak. Kiri Te Kanawa was a teenager in Gisborne, singing at weddings and funerals, when she won a radio contest in 1965; within a year, she was studying music in London. A sublime soprano with a breezy personality and captivating lack of pretension, she became internationally celebrated for her roles in the operas of Verdi, Mozart and Strauss, yet remains happy also to sing pop songs and jazz.

New Zealand's Chekhov

Katherine Mansfield, born in Wellington in 1888, was about the same age as Te Kanawa when she ventured to London. She was only 35 when she died, yet her writing is compared with that of Chekhov. Other internationally recognised authors include Frank Sargeson, thriller-writer Ngaio Marsh and historical novelist Maurice Shadbolt. In the late 20th century, a distinctively New Zealand literature emerged, greatly stimulated by the contributions of Maori authors such as Witi Ihimaera, Patricia Grace and Keri Hulme, who won the 1985 Booker Prize

for her novel *The Bone People*. Poet and novelist Janet Frame came to notice when her autobiographical *An Angel at My Table* was made into a movie directed by Jane Campion, while Maori author Alan Duff's *Once Were Warriors* inspired the film of the same name. The New Zealand film industry dates only from the 1970s, but has grown steadily. *Sleeping Dogs*, released in 1977, set actor Sam Neill on the path to a major Hollywood career. Director Campion sealed her reputation with the Oscar-winning *The Piano* in 1993.

A New Zealander, Ernest Rutherford, pioneered nuclear physics and revealed the structure of atoms. Other New Zealanders have achieved breakthroughs in electronics, medicine, agriculture, boat-design, even space rocketry, but have often had to work abroad to do so, and had their achievements credited to another country. New Zealand authors and scientists are mistaken for Britons, their film-makers for Australians, and their rock bands too, Split Enz and Crowded House, composed mainly of Kiwis, are among the biggest names in a rash of internationally known rock groups.

Diva Dame Kiri Te Kanawa took the role of Donna Elvira in the 1980 film of **Don Giovanni,** *directed by Joseph Losey.*

All smiles Tenzing and Hillary after their epic climb.

On top of the world

Sir Edmund Hillary, born in Auckland in 1919, honed his mountaineering skills on New Zealand's Southern Alps. With Sherpa Tenzing Norgay, he was the first to reach the summit of Everest (29 028 ft/ 8848 m) on May 29, 1953. He later played a leading role in the first land crossing of Antarctica, reaching the South Pole on January 4, 1958. This was the first time anyone had got to the Pole since Scott's tragic expedition in 1912.

The band plays on *A pub tradition of live music enabled thousands of Australian groups to take a first step towards festival appearances and hoped-for international success.*

From songs of the outback to pub rock

From bush pub to Wembley Stadium, Australian popular music has broken free of its tangled origins to sweep the world. The sound is vibrant and exultant.

A bush band belting out folk tunes like 'Click Go the Shears' with fiddle, tin whistle and 'lagerphone' (made from beer-bottle caps) accompaniment, is a living link with the beginnings of Australian popular music, created by early settlers out of their rich store of folk airs, London street songs and sea shanties. The melodies lingered on, but the lyrics of early popular songs like 'Moreton Bay', 'Jack Donahue' and 'Bound for South Australia' celebrated the exploits of convicts and bushrangers, pioneers and stockmen. The most famous of all, 'Waltzing Matilda', has been traced to an old Scottish tune, 'Craigielea', adapted and reborn in a Queensland outback pub in the 1890s.

Aussie hillbilly

In the 20th century, the bush songs faded in the face of an American counterpart, Country and Western, whose popularity was stimulated by the impact of American movies and American culture in general. The American model was quickly adapted to create 'Aussie hillbilly', with its own songs of bushrangers and pubs and tall tales of the outback, its own stars (with Americanised names) and its own radio stations. The prime exponent was Slim Dusty, born David Gordon Fitzpatrick, who learned to yodel

by listening to records in his outback home. In 1957, Slim Dusty's 'The Pub with No Beer' was an international hit, and an encouragement for others like Frank Ifield and 1960s pop groups such as the Easy Beats, the Seekers and the Bee Gees to venture abroad, where they received plaudits that reverberated at home. Singers like Olivia Newton-John and Helen Reddy later followed in their footsteps.

Throughout Australia, young people crammed live-venue pubs to hear local bands, and the excited, intense atmosphere was an ideal stimulant for the creation of a vibrant Australian sound, typified by the throbbing patriotism of the hit 'Down Under', from Men at Work, a group born in a Melbourne pub. Successes multiplied. Skyhooks, the Little River Band, AC/DC, Midnight Oil and Silverchair are among dozens of groups to make it big overseas. But 40 years on, Slim Dusty still continues to produce more records than any other recording artist in Australia.

Rock crusader *Peter Garrett, lead singer of the group Midnight Oil, campaigns for nuclear disarmament, Aboriginal rights and the environment.*

Aboriginal rock, the 'blackfella' sound

The impact of Aboriginal groups and singers is the big story of Australian popular music in recent years. Traditional Aboriginal music, consisting of sacred chants and songs, sometimes accompanied by the deep rhythms of the hollow-tube didgeridoo, confounded early Europeans. The Aborigines had no such problem: the country music of the outback, the rock of the cities and reggae have all been embraced, and a string of singers enjoyed success. On the rock scene, the success of groups like Warumpi has been crowned with the international impact of Yothu Yindi, whose sound combines chant, didgeridoo and electronic effects. The song 'Treaty' addressed political wrongs with telling effect. The group's lead singer, Mandwuay Yunupingu, was named Australian of the Year in 1992.

The Maori art of life

Traditional Maori culture was rescued from the brink of oblivion to become an influential factor in New Zealand life. It has to struggle with a disaffected younger generation infused with modern pop culture, but benefits from government encouragement.

Classical Maori culture – *maoritanga* – was steeped in oratory, song and chant, with an artistic tradition expressed principally through elaborate designs carved on buildings, tools, weapons and ornaments, and even tattooed on the bodies of the people themselves. Our word 'tattoo' comes from the Tahitian *tatua*; it was in Tahiti in 1769 that Captain Cook first encountered this indelible form of body art.

Warrior designs

In New Zealand, Cook found a highly sophisticated warrior society with a complex set of values and a rich store of poetic fable and history. Fundamental to everyone was their *iwi*, or tribe, with genealogies tracing back a thousand years to a particular migration voyage and even a specific canoe and its captain. Tattoos – *mokos* in Maori – were status symbols. All men except slaves were decorated on face, body, buttocks and thighs with patterns of circles and curves; women of rank usually only on the chin and lips. The prolonged operation was performed with a bone tool dipped in dark pigment and a mallet. With the pain came honour.

The Maori had welcomed Europeans for their technology and goods, but were demoralised by the impact. A century ago, Maori culture seemed about to expire, along with the Maori as a distinct people. It did not. By skilled parliamentary lobbying for resources, and achievements in sport and military service in the world wars, the Maori clawed back their self-esteem and their numbers began to recover. In recent years, Maori literature and art have flowered. While only about 153 000 New Zealanders speak Maori as their home language, more than 520 000 identify themselves as Maori. Today's Maoris are largely urbanised, but are experiencing a renaissance of cultural awareness. Many take holidays at a rural *marae* (traditional communal centre) and new *marae* pop up in cities, sometimes in a backyard or garage. Traditional crafts, such as carving in wood or jade, are encouraged through apprenticeships. Even tattooing has made a comeback, encouraged by the movie *Once Were Warriors*.

Meeting place Maori culture was transmitted through a tradition of song, here kept alive at a marae.

Kia ora! Welcoming back the Maori language

Fundamental to cultural revival is the restoration of the Maori language to everyday use. Maori is being taught in schools; old place names are being restored and government departments given Maori names alongside the English. (The Inland Revenue Department translates evocatively as *Te Tari Taake*.) Representing something of a challenge, however, is the world's longest place name, Taumatawhakatangihangakaoauauotamateauturipukakapikimaungahoronukupokaiwhenuakitanutuha. This translates roughly as: 'The place where Tamatea the land eater, the man who scrambled, climbed and swallowed up mountains, played his flute to his loved one.'

Aboriginal art – ancient and modern

Art has been integral to Aboriginal culture for millennia, but the creations of modern artists were largely ignored until quite recently. In the late 1970s, a schoolroom mural in a dusty Northern Territory settlement catapulted Aboriginal works onto the world stage.

Subtle allure *A painting to delight collectors carries a secret message.*

The first Aborigine to be granted Australian citizenship was an artist. Within a year, he was jailed, and the year after that he died, in despair. Albert Namatjira's Westernised watercolours of desert scenes had won him an international reputation and made him the darling of the authorities, who accorded him many rights then denied to his people. True to tribal obligation, he shared his wealth with his kin; likewise his alcohol – forbidden to Aborigines – for which he was imprisoned. The widespread shame caused by his death in 1959 helped to bring about a re-examination of official policies towards Aborigines.

'Honey Ant Dreaming'

Missionaries in the remote fastness of Arnhem Land began to encourage people to make paintings derived from the secret and sacred Dreamtime art all around, on rocks, tree bark and everyday objects, and as body decoration.

In the early 1970s, at Papunya ('Honey ant place'), a desert community to the west of Alice Springs, a white teacher named Geoffrey Bardon gave his Aboriginal pupils some polymer paints with which to decorate a wall of their classroom with traditional motifs. He had already established close ties with the local Aborigines, to the extent that he was allowed to take part in some of their rituals. In this way, he had become aware of their rich artistic heritage. The children in his school told their parents, who consulted the tribal elders, for children were uninitiated in such matters. After

Paintings out of time

An explosion of Aboriginal art since the 1970s has given contemporary voice to the oldest creative tradition on Earth. The paintings are largely abstract, but dip into a storehouse of tribal wisdom and secret information, hidden in complex symbolism. While the significance of the symbols is generally understood – concentric circles, for instance, usually signify a Dreamtime site – their precise interpretation remains a secret shared only by the artist and an intimate group. In this way, sacred stories can be publicly displayed without

Continuity *Modern artists display work in an ancient rock gallery.*

revealing their meaning. In cities, a hybrid art with strong European influences has evolved. Rock-painting in its traditional form is still practised in remote areas.

lengthy discussions on what could and what could not be displayed, the elders themselves undertook the task and transformed the wall into a captivating mural, entitled 'Honey Ant Dreaming'. Bardon followed up by distributing canvas and acrylics to the community, which became fired with enthusiasm.

This success spurred other communities across Australia to put traditional artistry to new purpose. The government started to give support, helping with materials and by setting up contact points for remote communities. The results were stunning enough to gain global recognition. The first wave of artists remained true to ancestral themes; a second wave has been creatively adaptive, producing effects as contemporary as they are timeless. Demand for Aboriginal art has increased dramatically, with some works selling for large sums, especially when they are sold in the major cities, or in galleries overseas.

Captured dream *Artists like Clifford Possum (left) work in traditional communities, and their works are sold in city galleries.*

MAPS, FACTS AND FIGURES

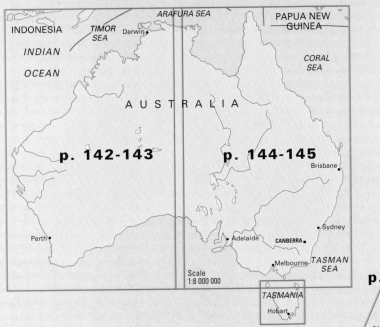

INDONESIA

INDIAN OCEAN

TIMOR SEA

Darwin

ARAFURA SEA

PAPUA NEW GUINEA

CORAL SEA

A U S T R A L I A

p. 142-143

p. 144-145

Brisbane

Perth

Adelaide

CANBERRA

Sydney

Melbourne

TASMAN SEA

Scale
1:8 000 000

TASMANIA

Hobart

p. 146-147

NORTH ISLAND

Auckland

NEW ZEALAND

WELLINGTON

Christchurch

SOUTH ISLAND

CHATHAM ISLANDS

Scale
1:4 200 000

Scale
1:2 500 000

Map key

Tourist sites

★ *ULURU*   Park or reserve

Topography

▲ Kata Tjuta
1 069 m   Peak

BLUE MTS   Mountain range

Borders

———   States and Territories

– – –   Maritime national borders

Depth tints for Australia

Metres

	0
	- 200
	- 2000
	- 4000

Depth tints for New Zealand

Metres

	0
	- 200
	- 1000
	- 2000

Elevation tints

Metres

	3000
	2000
	1500
	1000
	500
	200
	0
	- 200

Place names

■ **CAPITAL**

● Major city

• City

· Town

INDONESIA
TIMOR SEA
INDIAN OCEAN
SAWU SEA
BALI
Denpasar
Mataram
Praya
LOMBOK
SUMBAWA
LESSER SUNDA ISLANDS
SUMBA
Waikabubak
Waingapu
SAWU
ROTI
SEMAU
Kupang
TIMOR
Soe
ASHMORE ISLANDS
CARTIER ISLANDS
BROWSE ISLAND
ADÈLE ISLAND
BUCCANEER ARCHIPELAGO
BONAPARTE ARCHIPELAGO
Cape Leveque
Collier Bay
Admiralty Gulf
Cape Londonderry
Drysdale
DRYSDALE RIVER
Joseph Bonaparte Gulf
Queens Channel
BATHURST ISLAND
MELVILLE ISLAND
Beagle Gulf
Clarence Strait
Cape Croker
CROKER ISLAND
Cobourg Peninsula
Van Dieman Gulf
Darwin
Humpty Doo
Point Blaze
Rum Jungle
Daly
Pine Creek
Katherine
Jabiru
KAKADU
Birdum
Daly Waters
Newcastle Waters
L. Woods
Victoria
GREGORY
Victoria River Downs
Wave Hill
TANAMI DESERT
NORTHERN TERRITORY
Tanami
L. White
L. Wills
L. Mackay
L. Macdonald
Mt Leister 897 m
Mt Liebig 1 524 m
Mt Zeil 1 511 m
MACDONNELL RANGE
Papunya
L. Neale
Kings
Kununurra
Ord
L. Argyle
BUNGLE BUNGLE
Halls Creek
Wyndham
DURACK RANGES
KIMBERLEY PLATEAU
GEIKIE GORGE
Mt Ord 937 m
KING LEOPOLD RANGES
Fitzroy Crossing
Fitzroy
Derby
Broome
Lagrange
Canning Basin
GREAT SANDY DESERT
L. Gregory
Percival Lakes
L. Auld
L. Dora
Lake Disappointment
RUDALL RIVER
Cape Latouche Treville
Eighty Mile Beach
Shay Gap
Marble Bar
Nullagine
De Grey
Goldsworthy
Port Hedland
Pilbara
Wittenoom
HAMERSLEY RANGE
Mt Meharry 1 251 m
Newman
Mt Bruce 1 235 m
Paraburdoo
Tom Price
Mt Brockman 1 132 m
MILLSTREAM CHICHESTER
Roebourne
Karratha
Dampier
DAMPIER ARCHIPELAGO
Fortescue
Pannawonica
Ashburton
MONTEBELLO ISLANDS
BARROW ISLAND
Onslow
MUIRON ISLANDS
Exmouth
Exmouth Gulf
North West Cape
Point Cloates
116°
120°
124°
128°
132°
12°
16°
20°

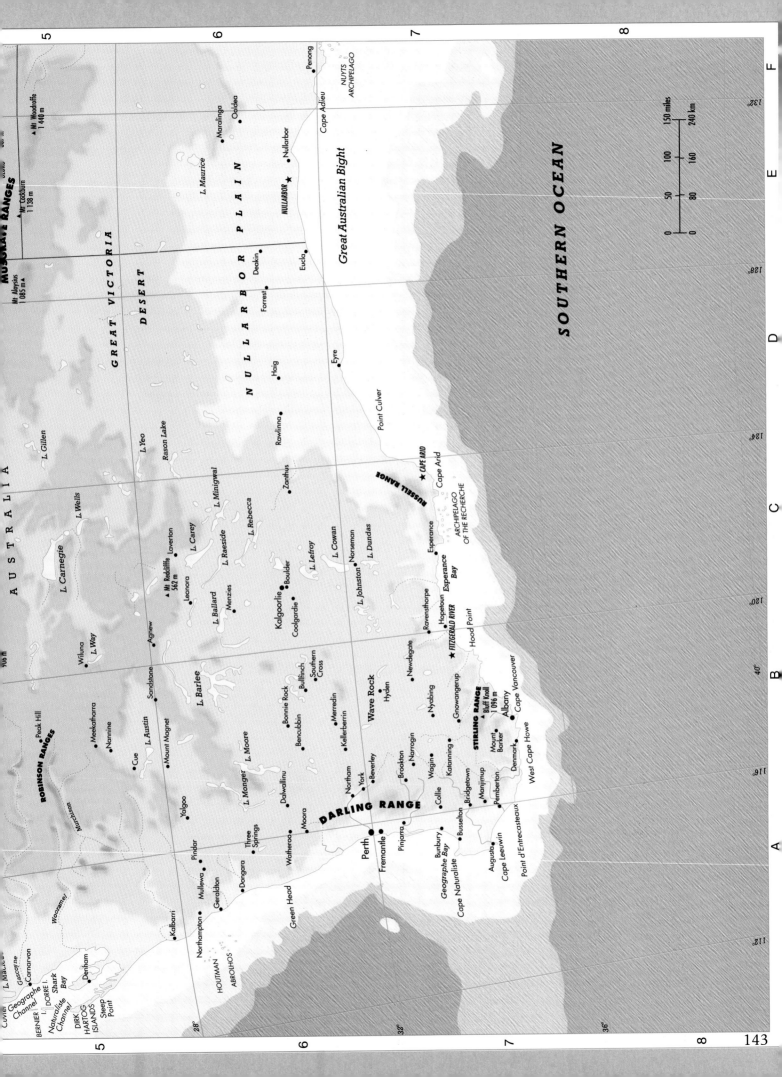

MUSGRAVE RANGES

▲ Mt Woodroffe
1 440 m

▲ Mt Cockburn
1 138 m

Mt Aloysius
1 085 m▲

GREAT   VICTORIA

DESERT

AUSTRALIA

L. Gillen

L. Carnegie

L. Wells

L. Way

Wiluna

L. Yeo

Rason Lake

L. Maurice

Maralinga
Oldea

Penong

NUYTS
ARCHIPELAGO

Cape Adieu

N U L L A R B O R   P L A I N

NULLARBOR ★

Nullarbor

Deakin

Eucla

Forrest

Haig

Eyre

Point Culver

Great Australian Bight

SOUTHERN OCEAN

Rawlinna

Zanthus

L. Minigwal

L. Carey

Laverton

▲ Mt Redcliffe
562 m

Leonora

Menzies

L. Raeside

L. Rebecca

L. Cowan

L. Dundas

L. Johnston

Norseman

RUSSELL RANGE

★ CAPE ARID

Cape Arid

Esperance

ARCHIPELAGO
OF THE RECHERCHE

Esperance
Bay

Hopetoun

Ravensthorpe

Hood Point

★ FITZGERALD RIVER

L. Ballard

L. Lefroy

Kalgoorlie
Boulder

Coolgardie

Southern
Cross

Bullfinch

Bonnie Rock

Merredin

Kellerberrin

Wave Rock

Hyden

Newdegate

Nyabing

Gnowangerup

STIRLING RANGE
▲ Bluff Knoll
1 096 m

Mount
Barker

Albany

Cape Vancouver

West Cape Howe

Denmark

Narrogin

Wagin

Katanning

Collie

Bridgetown

Manjimup

Pemberton

Augusta

Cape Leeuwin

Point d'Entrecasteaux

Geographe Bay

Bunbury

Busselton

Cape Naturaliste

Pinjarra

Brookton

Beverley

York

Norham

DARLING RANGE

Perth

Fremantle

Moora

Dalwallinu

Wubin

L. Moore

L. Monger

Three
Springs

Watheroo

Green Head

Dongara

Geraldton

Northampton

Mullewa

Pindar

Kalbarri

HOUTMAN
ABROLHOS

Yalgoo

Cue

L. Austin

Mount Magnet

Sandstone

Agnew

Nannine

Meekatharra

Peak Hill

ROBINSON RANGES

Murchison

Wooramel

Carnarvon

Gascoyne

Geographe
Channel

BERNIER I.
DORRE I.

Naturaliste
Channel

DIRK
HARTOG
ISLANDS

Denham

Shark
Bay

Steep
Point

Cuvier
L. MacLeod

L. Barlee

Bencubbin

28°

32°

36°

112°

116°

120°

124°

128°

132°

0   50   100   150 miles
0   80   160   240 km

143

Australia • East

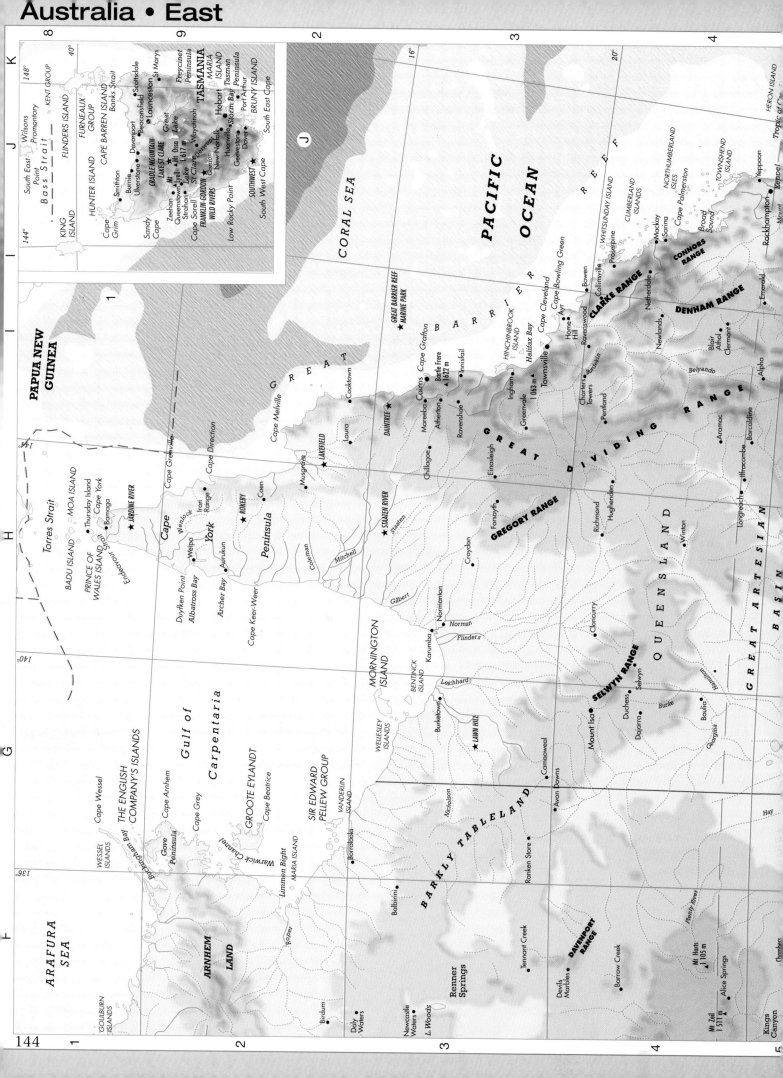

Inset: Tasmania

KING ISLAND
Cape Grim
Smithton
Stanley
Burnie
Ulverstone
Devonport
Sandy Cape
Cape Sorell
Zeehan
Queenstown
Strahan
FRANKLIN-GORDON WILD RIVERS
Low Rocky Point
SOUTHWEST
South West Cape

Wilsons Promontory
South East Point
KENT GROUP
FLINDERS ISLAND
FURNEAUX GROUP
HUNTER ISLAND
CAPE BARREN ISLAND
Banks Strait
Bass Strait

St Marys
Scottsdale
Beaconsfield
Launceston
Great Lake
Lake St Clair
CRADLE MOUNTAIN-LAKE ST CLARE
Mt Lyell
Mt Ossa 1617 m
Gordon
Lake
Derwent
New Norfolk
Huonville
Geeveston
Dover

Freycinet Peninsula
MARIA ISLAND
TASMANIA
Tasman Peninsula
BRUNY ISLAND
Hobart
Storm Bay
Port Arthur
Wayatinah
South East Cape

Main map

ARAFURA SEA

PAPUA NEW GUINEA

Torres Strait

GULF OF CARPENTARIA
Gulf of Carpentaria

ARNHEM LAND

GOULBURN ISLANDS
WESSEL ISLANDS
Cape Wessel
Buckingham Bay
Gove Peninsula
Cape Arnhem
Cape Grey
Cape Beatrice
GROOTE EYLANDT
Warrick Channel
THE ENGLISH COMPANY'S ISLANDS
MARIA ISLAND
SIR EDWARD PELLEW GROUP
VANDERLIN ISLAND
Limmen Bight
Roper

BADU ISLAND
MOA ISLAND
Thursday Island
PRINCE OF WALES ISLAND
Cape York
Bamaga
JARDINE RIVER
Endeavour Strait
Duyfken Point
Albatross Bay
Weipa
Aurukun
Archer Bay
Cape Keer-Weer
Coleman
Mitchell

Cape
York
Peninsula

Cape Grenville
Cape Direction
Wenlock
Iron Range
Coen
ROKEBY
Musgrave
Staaten
STAATEN RIVER
Gilbert
Norman
Normanton
Flinders
Karumba

Cape Melville
LAKEFIELD
Laura
DAINTREE
Cooktown

CORAL SEA

GREAT BARRIER REEF MARINE PARK
Cape Grafton
Cairns
Mareeba
Atherton
Chillagoe
Ravenshoe
Einasleigh
Forsyth
Croydon

GREAT BARRIER REEF

PACIFIC OCEAN

HINCHINBROOK ISLAND
Innisfail
Battle Frere 1622 m
Ingham
Halifax Bay
Cape Cleveland
Townsville
1 063 m
Greenvale
Charters Towers
Pentland
Hughenden
Richmond

Cape Bowling Green
Ayr
Home Hill
Ravenswood
Burdekin
Belyando

WHITSUNDAY ISLAND
CUMBERLAND ISLANDS
Bowen
Collinsville
Proserpine
Netherdale
CLARKE RANGE
Newlands
Blair Athol
Clermont
Alpha

NORTHUMBERLAND ISLES
Mackay
Sarina
Cape Palmerston
Broad Sound
CONNORS RANGE
DENHAM RANGE
Emerald
Aramac
Barcaldine

TOWNSHEND ISLAND
Cape
HERON ISLAND
Yeppoon
Keppel
Rockhampton
Mount
Tropic of C

GREAT DIVIDING RANGE

GREGORY RANGE

QUEENSLAND

GREAT ARTESIAN BASIN

Winton
Longreach
Ilfracombe
Hamilton
Boulia
Georgina
Hay

Cloncurry
SELWYN RANGE
Mount Isa
Duchess
Selwyn
Dajarra
Burke

BARKLY TABLELAND

MORNINGTON ISLAND
BENTINCK ISLAND
Leichhardt
Burketown
LAWN HILL
WELLESLEY ISLANDS
Camooweal
Avon Downs
Ranken Store
Nicholson
Balbirini
Borroloola

Camooweal

Renner Springs
Tennent Creek
Devils Marbles
DAVENPORT RANGE
Barrow Creek
Mt Harts 1105 m
Plenty River
Mt Zeil 1511 m
Alice Springs
Kings
Chamber

Birdum
Daly Waters
L. Woods
Newcastle Waters

144

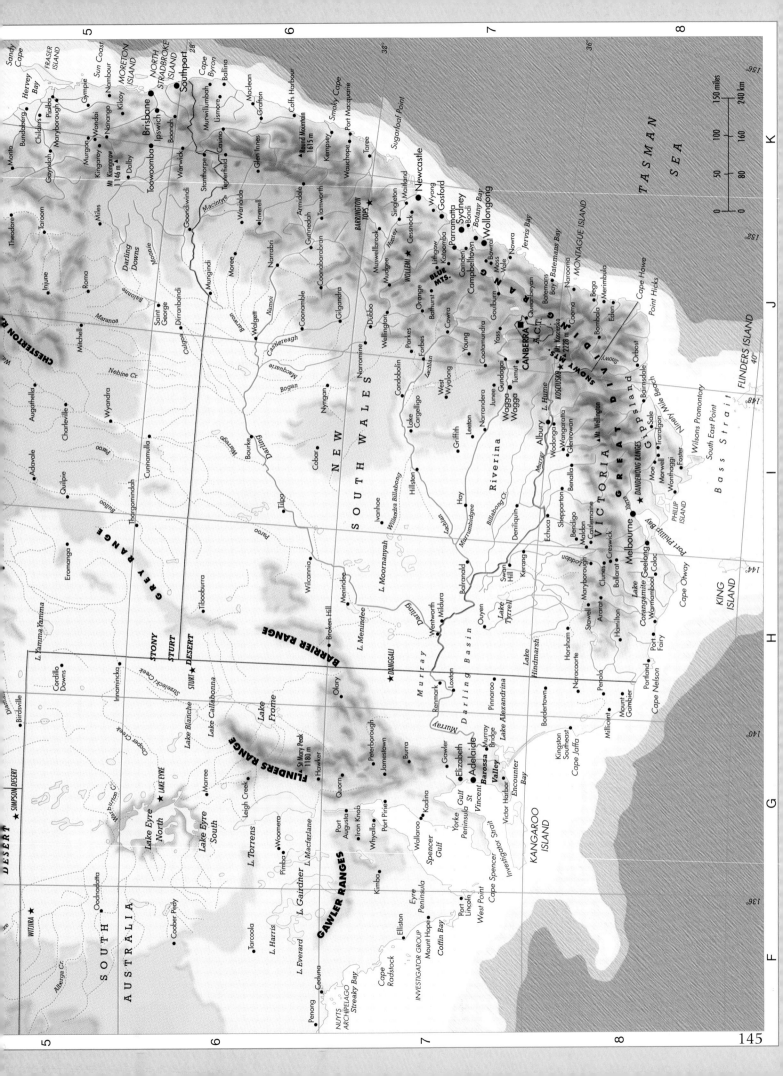

New Zealand

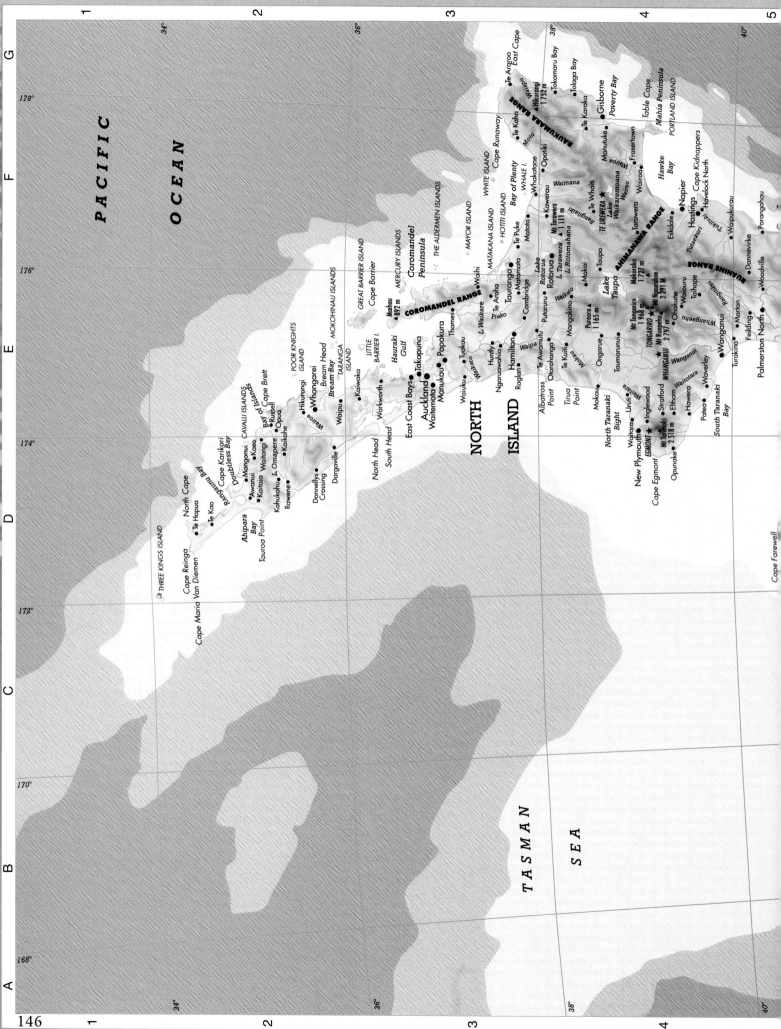

PACIFIC

OCEAN

TASMAN

SEA

THREE KINGS ISLAND

Cape Reinga
Cape Maria Van Diemen
North Cape
Te Hapua
Te Kao
Ahipara Bay
Tauroa Point
Rangaunu Bay
Cape Karikari
Doubtless Bay
Mangonui
CAVALLI ISLANDS
Kaeo
Awanui
Waitangi
Kaitaia
L. Omapere
Kohukohu
Kaikohe
Rawene
Bay of Islands
Cape Brett
Russell
Opua
Donnellys Crossing
Dargaville
POOR KNIGHTS ISLAND
Hikurangi
Whangarei
Bream Head
Bream Bay
Waipu
Kaiwaka
Maunu
Warkworth
North Head
South Head
East Coast Bays
MOKOHINAU ISLANDS
LITTLE BARRIER I.
TARANGA ISLAND
GREAT BARRIER ISLAND
Cape Barrier
Hauraki Gulf
Takapuna
Papakura
Auckland
Waitemata
Manukau
Waiuku
Tuakau
Waikato
MERCURY ISLANDS
Coromandel Peninsula
THE ALDERMEN ISLANDS
MAYOR ISLAND
WHITE ISLAND
Mehau ▲892 m
COROMANDEL RANGE
Maratoto
Waihi
Waihi
L. Waikare
Te Aroha
Thames
Piako
Tauranga
Te Puke
Matata
Opotiki
Cape Runaway
Te Araroa
East Cape
Waiapu
Hikurangi ▲1752 m
RAUKUMARA RANGE
Te Kaha
Tikitiki
Tokomaru Bay
Tolaga Bay
Karaka
Gisborne
Poverty Bay
Table Cape
Mahia Peninsula
PORTLAND ISLAND
Hamilton
Ngaruawahia
Huntly
Cambridge
Putaruru
Matamata
Morrinsville
Lake Rotorua
Rotorua
L. Tarawera
L. Rotomahana
Mt Tarawera ▲1111 m
Kawerau
Whakatane
Waimana
Koweru
Te Ureweera
Lake Waikaremoana
Te Whaiti
Wairoa
Frasertown
Wairoa
Manutuke
Waikaremoana
Hawke Bay
Cape Kidnappers
Havelock North
Napier
Hastings
Eskdale
Tutaekuri
Te Puke
Roglan
Te Awamutu
Otorohanga
Te Kuiti
Mangakino
Waipa
Ongarue
Taumarunui
Mokau
North Taranaki Bight
Tirua Point
Albatross Point
Waipa
Pureora ▲1165 m
Lake Taupo
Taupo
Mokai
Mangakino
Ohakune
Taihape
Makaraka ▲1727 m
Mt Tongariro ▲1968 m
Mt Ngauruhoe ▲2291 M
TONGARIRO ★
Mt Ruapehu ▲2797 m
WHANGANUI ★
Wanganui
Raetihi
Waiouru
Whangaehu
Rangitikei
Marton
Feilding
Woodville
Palmerston North
Dannevirke
Woodville
Waipukurau
Porangahau
RUAHINE RANGE
KAIMANAWA RANGE
Turakina
Waverley
Patea
Waitotara
Hawera
Eltham
Stratford
Inglewood
EGMONT ★
Mt Taranaki ▲2518 m
New Plymouth
Cape Egmont
Opunake
Waitara
Uruti
Mokau
South Taranaki Bight
Waverley

NORTH

ISLAND

Cape Farewell

178°
176°
174°
172°
170°
168°

34°
36°
38°
40°

34°
36°
38°
40°

G F E D C B A

1 2 3 4 5

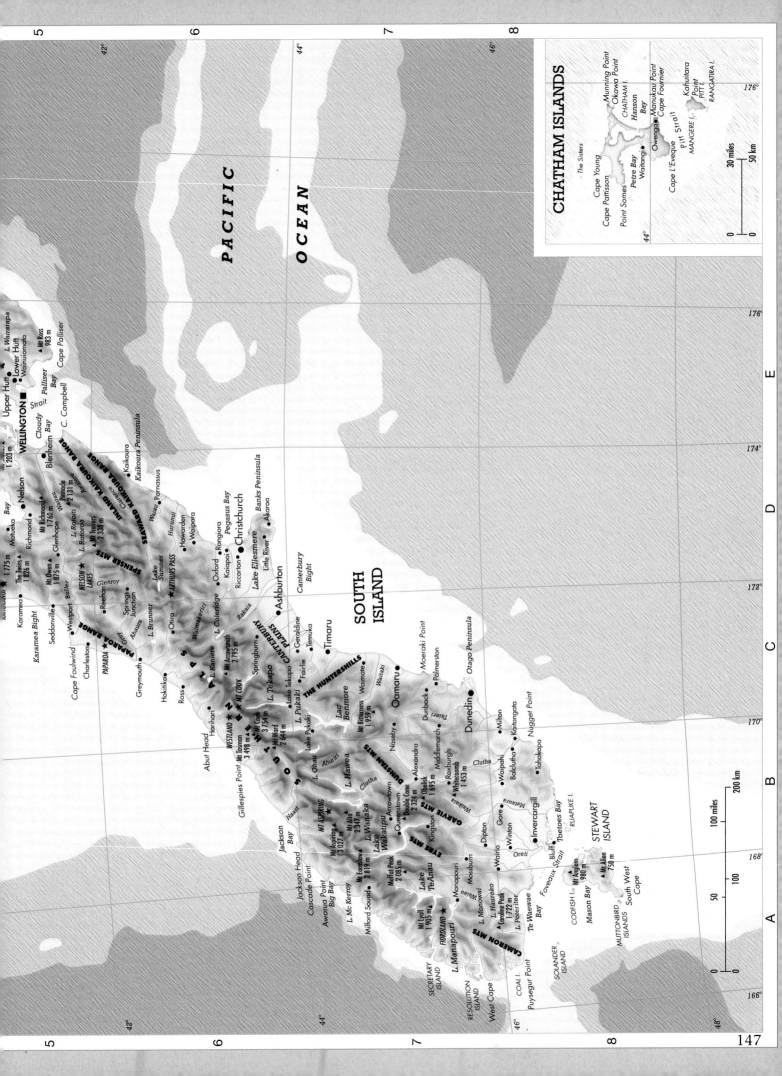

42°

44°

176°

176°

174°

172°

170°

168°

166°

E

D

C

B

A

CHATHAM ISLANDS

The Sisters

Cape Young
Cape Pattisson
Point Somes

Munning Point
Okawa Point

CHATHAM I.

Hanson
Petre Bay   Bay
Waitangi

Owenga   Manukau Point
                  Cape Fournier

Cape L'Eveque   Pitt Strait
MANGERE I.   PITT I.

Kahuiara
Point
RANGATIRA I.

44°

0   30 miles

0   50 km

PACIFIC

OCEAN

L. Wairarapa
Lower Hutt
Upper Hutt
WELLINGTON
Mt Ross
983 m
Wainuiomata

Cloudy
Bay
Blenheim

Palliser
Bay
C. Campbell
Cape Palliser

Strait

1 203 m

Kaikoura Peninsula

Motueka
Bay
Nelson
Richmond
Mt Richmond
Glenhope   1 760 m
Mt Owen
1 875 m

The Twins
1 826 m

INLAND KAIKOURA RANGE

SEAWARD KAIKOURA RANGE

Clarence

Te Pinnacle
2 131 m

Kaikoura

Wairau
Waiau
Parnassus

1 775 m

Karamea
Bay

Karamea Bight

Seddonville
Westport
Charleston

Cape Foulwind

L. Rotoiti
L. Rotoroa
Mt Travers
2 338 m

NELSON ★
LAKES

SPENSER MTS

Glenroy

Springs
Junction

Waiau
Ahaura

Hanmer

Howarden
Waipara

Reefton
L. Brunner

ARTHUR'S PASS

Rangiora
Oxford
Kaiapoi
Riccarton

Christchurch

Pegasus Bay

Banks Peninsula

Akaroa

Greymouth
Hokitika
Ross

PAPAROA RANGE

Otira

Waimakariri

L. Coleridge
L. Kaniere

Lake
Sumner

Springburn

Lake Ellesmere
Little River

Ashburton

Canterbury
Bight

Abut Head

Harihari

WESTLAND ★

Mt Tasman
3 498 m

MT COOK

Mt Cook
3 754 m

Mt Ward
2 644 m

L. Pukaki

Lake Tekapo

L. Tekapo

Geraldine
Fairlie

Temuka

Timaru

SOUTH
ISLAND

Gillespies Point

Mt Arrowsmith
2 795 m

CANTERBURY
PLAINS

Rakaia

Jackson Bay

Gillespies Point

Haast

L. Ohau

Ahuriri

Lac
Benmore

Mt Brunner
1 959 m

Waimate

Waitaki

Oamaru

Moeraki Point

THE HUNTERSHILLS

Cascade Point

Awarua Point
Big Bay

MT ASPIRING ★

Mt Aspiring
3 027 m

Mt Alta
2 347 m

L. Hawea

L. Wanaka

Clutha

Arrowtown

DUNSTAN MTS

Naseby

Alexandra

Middlemarch

Palmerston

Dunback

Dunedin

Otago Peninsula

Jackson Head

L. Mc Kerroy

Milford Sound

Mt Earnslaw
2 819 m

Double Cone
2 324 m

Lake
Wakatipu

Queenstown

Obelisk
1 695 m

Roxburgh

Whitecomb
1 453 m

Clutha

Waipahi

Balclutha

Kaitangata

Nugget Point

Tahakopa

GARVIE MTS

Kingston

Moffat Peak
2 085 m

EYRE MTS

Lumsden

Gore
Dipton

Winton

Clinton

Mataura

STEWART
ISLAND

Mt Lyall
1 905 m

FIORDLAND ★

Caroline Peak
1 722 m

Lake
Te Anau

L. Monowai

L. Hauroko

L. Poteriteri

CAMERON MTS

Manapouri
Mossburn

Wairio

Oreti

Invercargill

Bluff

Foveaux Strait

Toetoes Bay

RUAPUKE I.

CODFISH I.

MUTTONBIRD
ISLANDS

Mason Bay

Mt Anglem
980 m

Mt Allen
750 m

South West
Cape

SECRETARY
ISLAND

RESOLUTION
ISLAND

West Cape

L. Manapouri

Te Waewae
Bay

Puysegur Point

COAL I.

SOLANDER
ISLAND

42°

44°

44°

46°

46°

48°

0   50   100   200 km

0   50   100 miles

AUSTRALIA

Political system: Federal
parliamentary monarchy

Capital: Canberra
Area: 2 966 153 sq miles
(7 682 307 km²)
Official language: English
Total population: 18.5 million
Population density: 6.2 people
per sq mile (2.4 per km²)
Monetary unit: Australian
dollar
GNP per inhabitant: US$17 822

NEW ZEALAND

Political system: Parliamentary
monarchy

Capital: Wellington
Area: 104 454 sq miles
(270 534 km²)
Official languages: English
and Maori
Total population: 3.76 million
Population density: 36 people
per sq mile (14 per km²)
Monetary unit: New Zealand
dollar
GNP per inhabitant: US$16 851

Under the Southern Cross

*On the eastern flank of the South Pacific, two nations share the same
colonial heritage, language and cultural values. One has a continent
to itself; the other occupies an archipelago of two large and several
small islands. They face similar challenges in a rapidly changing world.*

THE FLAGS

The Australian flag

The basic design of the Australian flag emerged
from a competition run in a Melbourne magazine,
The Review of Reviews, in 1901. It was approved by
King Edward VII in 1903 and slightly modified in

Aboriginal flag
*It is intended to
encourage a sense of
pride and identity.*

1909. It is a British Blue
Ensign, a blue flag incorporating the Union Jack
in the upper quarter
next to the staff, with
the addition of a large
seven-pointed white star
in the centre of the
lower quarter next to
the staff, and five white
stars in the fly, or outer
half of the flag. The
large star represents the
Australian state and
dependent territories.
The five stars represent
the constellation of the
Southern Cross.

The flag competition attracted 32 823 entries.
The rules laid down that the design 'should be
based on the British Ensigns, . . . signalling to the
beholder that it is an Imperial Union Ensign of
the British Empire'. In other words, entries without the Union Jack would be rejected out of hand.
The winning design was submitted independently
by five competitors, who shared £200 in prize
money put up by the Australian government, the
magazine and a tobacco company. The winners
included a Melbourne schoolboy, Ivor Evans.

Each of the six Australian states also has its own
flag, as do the Aborigines, whose flag was created
in 1972. It consists of a black and a red band, representing the people and the Earth, with a large
yellow circle in the centre to symbolise the Sun.

National holidays and anthems

AUSTRALIA: Australia Day (January 26)
commemorates the arrival in Sydney of the
First Fleet under Governor Arthur Phillip.
National anthem: 'Advance Australia Fair'.
It replaced 'God Save the Queen' in 1984.

NEW ZEALAND: Waitangi Day (February 6)
commemorates the 1840 treaty under
which Britain assumed sovereignty.
National anthems: 'God Defend New
Zealand'; 'God Save the Queen'.

Anzac Day (April 25) commemorates soldiers
from both nations who gave their lives in war.

New Zealand's birthplace   *The Treaty
House at Waitangi stands on a lawn
facing the sea. It is now a museum.*

The New Zealand flag

The first official flag of New Zealand was a Maori
one, incorporating a St George's Cross with a star
in each quadrant; it was recognised by Britain in
1836. With the signing of the Treaty of Waitangi in
1840, this flag was replaced by a Union Jack bearing the initials 'NZ'. British flags were used until
1865, when an ensign incorporating the stars of
the Southern Cross was adopted for merchant
shipping. A version of this was adopted for use on
shore in 1902 and became the national flag. It is a
blue ensign with a Union Jack in the top left-hand
corner and four five-pointed red stars edged in
white to represent the Southern Cross.

The future of both the Australian and the New
Zealand flags is in doubt. Their 'colonial' connota-
tion has led to calls in both countries for them to
be replaced, and specifically for the Union Jack to
be removed.

AUSTRALIA
2 966 153 sq miles
(7 682 307 km²)

**UNITED STATES
(main body)**
3 081 717 sq miles
(7 981 647 km²)

NEW ZEALAND
104 454 sq miles
(270 534 km²)

UNITED KINGDOM
94 217 sq miles
(244 022 km²)

By comparison *Australia is approximately the
same size as the main body of the United States
(without Alaska and Hawaii). New Zealand
is slightly larger than the United Kingdom.*

Contrasting neighbours

Australia is flat and geologically stable. New Zealand is mountainous and geologically unstable. Australia has a generally arid climate. New Zealand has a moist climate. A story of contrasts with a common consequence: the populations of both countries are concentrated along the coasts.

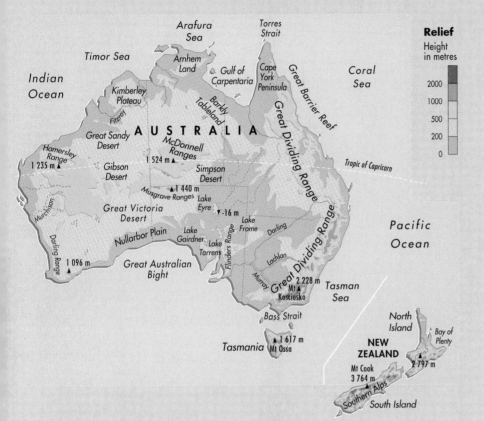

TIME ZONE CONFUSION

New Zealand is 12 hours ahead of Greenwich Mean Time. Clocks go forward an hour in summer for Daylight Saving Time. **Australia** has three time zones. Eastern Standard Time (GMT +10 hours) covers New South Wales, Queensland, Victoria and Tasmania. Central Standard Time (South Australia and Northern Territory) is a half-hour behind the east, and 1½ hours ahead of Western Australia's Western Standard Time (GMT + 8 hours). Time goes haywire in summer. States apply Daylight Saving Time over differing periods. Queensland and Western Australia do not observe it at all.

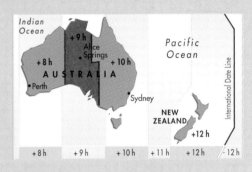

Literally 'down under' Europe

Australia and New Zealand are on precisely the opposite half of the globe from Western Europe; hence their frequent designation as the Antipodes and the popular expression 'Down Under'. Although twinned as neighbours, they are more than 1000 miles (about 1600 km) apart. Sydney is about as far from Auckland as London is from Moscow.

SOME GEOGRAPHICAL DATA

Australia
Dimensions: 2300 miles (3700 km) from north to south and 2500 miles (4000 km) from east to west
Highest point: Mount Kosciusko, 7310 ft (2228 m)
Lowest point: Lake Eyre, 50 ft (15 m) below sea level
Longest river: Murray/Darling, 2310 miles (3718 km)
Length of coast: 22 827 miles (36 735 km)

New Zealand
Dimensions: 1029 miles (1660 km) from north to south
Highest point: Mount Cook, 12 316 ft (3754 m)
Lowest point: Sea level along the coast
Longest river: Waikato, 264 miles (425 km)
Length of coast: 9404 miles (15 134 km)

Explosive forces, inert immensities
New Zealand is perched on the 'Ring of Fire', the result of two plates on the Earth's surface colliding under the Pacific Ocean. It literally heaves and buckles under the stresses. The North Island is ribbed with volcanoes. Some of these are extinct, like Mount Egmont (Taranaki); others are active, like Mount Ruapehu. The South Island has a backbone of high and steep mountains that are still growing: the multi-peaked Southern Alps, whose deep, glacier-gouged valleys contain lakes, or are invaded by the sea to form spectacular fiords. Both islands have numerous rivers, though not all are navigable.

Australia is the flattest landmass in the world after Greenland. After aeons of geological tor-

pidity, most of its mountains have weathered down to stumps. Two-thirds of the continent's mountainous terrain consists of a low plateau, covering about 3 million sq miles (5 million km²). The highest ground is part of the Great Dividing Range, which runs parallel to the east coast for 2300 miles (3700 km), from Cape York Peninsula to western Victoria.

New Zealand has a mild, moist, oceanic climate. As in Australia, the seasons are in reverse calendar order to those of the Northern Hemisphere. The hottest months are January and February, with an average temperature of 17°C (63°F). July is the coldest month, with an average of 8°C (46°F). Both islands are subjected to strong winds all the year round, but temperatures in the interior can reach 30°C (86°F) in summer. Chill southerly winds bring snow in winter. Rainfall ranges from

less than 16 in (400 mm) in parts of Otago, in the south-east of the South Island, to more than 50 in (1270 mm) in the Southern Alps.

Sprawled over more than 30 degrees of latitude, Australia has a more varied climate. The centre is the largest and hottest zone (over 50°C/122°F); it receives the least rain and experiences extreme temperature fluctuations between day and night. From north to south, conditions pass from tropical to temperate, with the gradations most evident down the east coast. There is a pocket of Mediterranean-type weather in the south-west corner of Western Australia.

Australia has the world's driest climate. Large areas of the interior receive on average less than 10 in (250 mm) of rain per year, the point at which a zone is characterised as desert. Averaged overall, the continent receives just 18 in (450 mm) of precipitation; the world average is 28 in (711 mm).

CLIMATES ▼

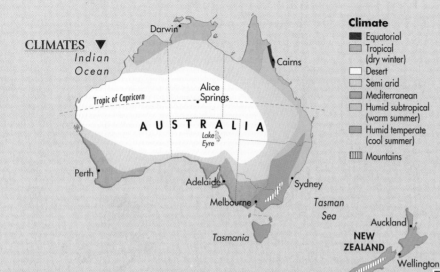

Indian Ocean

Climate
- ■ Equatorial
- Tropical (dry winter)
- □ Desert
- Semi arid
- Mediterranean
- Humid subtropical (warm summer)
- Humid temperate (cool summer)
- ▥ Mountains

CLIMATIC VARIATIONS IN NEW ZEALAND		
	Auckland	Dunedin
Average temperature in January (°C)	23.8	15.1
Average temperature in July (°C)	18.9	9.9
Bright sunshine per annum (hours)	2071	1595
Annual rainfall (in)	43.6	31.5
(mm)	1106	799

Drought and deluge

Discounting ice-locked Antarctica, Australia is the driest continent on the planet. Around 70 per cent of it is arid, and its 11 principal deserts cover 20 per cent of the landmass. Humid conditions prevail only in the tropical north-east and in the south-east.

New Zealand receives moderate to abundant average rainfall, ranging between 25 and 60 in (635 and 1525 mm) each year. Milford Sound in the south-east had almost 200 in (about 5000 mm) in 1998.

Why New Zealand smokes and shudders

New Zealand spans a split in the Earth's crust, where the Indo-Australian plate and the Pacific plate grind together. This results in constant volcanic activity and frequent earthquakes – at least one per year measures 6 on the Richter scale. On the plus side, volcanic activity is a source of renewable geothermal energy.

CLIMATIC VARIATIONS IN AUSTRALIA				
	Sydney	Darwin	Hobart	Canberra
Average temperature in hottest month (°C)	24	32.5	19.6	26.9
Average temperature in coldest month (°C)	15.3	29.4	10.5	10.6
Average daily sunshine (hours)	6.8	8.5	5.9	7.4
Annual rainfall (in)	48.1	60.5	24.1	24.9
(mm)	1220	1535	624	633

DEMOGRAPHICS OF THE TWO POPULATIONS

Where people live

New Zealand has been experiencing a steady movement of people from the south to the north. In 1997, 75 per cent of New Zealanders, including more than 90 per cent of the Maori population, were living on the North Island. The North Island also has a higher natural population growth, and a higher urban concentration.

Australia is the most sparsely populated of the inhabited continents. Four out of five Australians live in temperate coastal zones that make up no more than 3 per cent of the land area.

THE AGE PYRAMID ▼

Australia and New Zealand both have ageing populations, a circumstance that is common among developed countries. Encouraging increased immigration from abroad offers one answer to this problem. It is an issue that generates much debate, particularly in Australia.

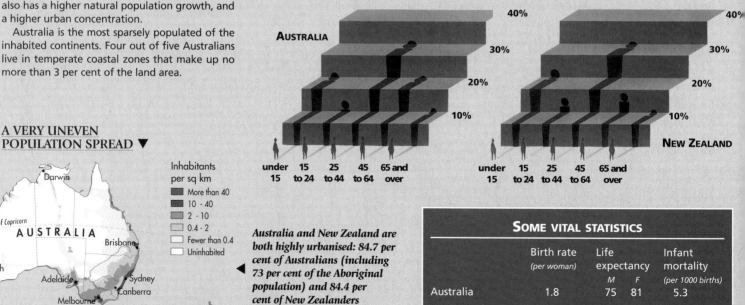

AUSTRALIA

NEW ZEALAND

40% / 30% / 20% / 10%

under 15 / 15 to 24 / 25 to 44 / 45 to 64 / 65 and over

A VERY UNEVEN POPULATION SPREAD ▼

Inhabitants per sq km
- More than 40
- 10 - 40
- 2 - 10
- 0.4 - 2
- Fewer than 0.4
- Uninhabited

Australia and New Zealand are both highly urbanised: 84.7 per cent of Australians (including 73 per cent of the Aboriginal population) and 84.4 per cent of New Zealanders (including 75 per cent of the Maori population) live in towns and cities.

SOME VITAL STATISTICS				
	Birth rate (per woman)	Life expectancy M	F	Infant mortality (per 1000 births)
Australia	1.8	75	81	5.3
New Zealand	2	74	80	6.7
Britain	1.7	74	80	6

THE FOREIGN-BORN POPULATION: COUNTRIES OF ORIGIN ▼

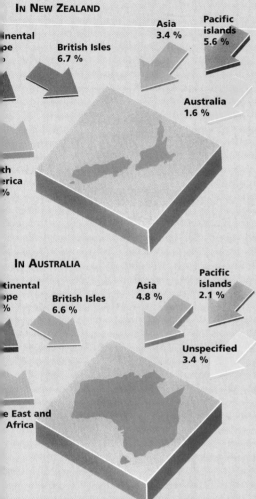

IN NEW ZEALAND

Asia 3.4 %
Pacific islands 5.6 %
...inental ...pe ...
British Isles 6.7 %
Australia 1.6 %
...th ...rica ...%

IN AUSTRALIA

Pacific islands 2.1 %
Asia 4.8 %
...inental ...pe ...
British Isles 6.6 %
Unspecified 3.4 %
...e East and Africa

▲

Immigrants make up around 16 per cent of the New Zealand population. In Australia, the proportion rises to more than 26 per cent.

The ethnic make-up of Australia and New Zealand

Australians and New Zealanders are overwhelmingly of European origin: 94 per cent, in the case of Australia. Aborigines account for 2.1 per cent of the Australian population, whereas 14.5 per cent of New Zealanders are Maori. At census time in both countries, there is a significant leap in the number of people claiming to be Aborigines or Maoris. The reasons for this phenomenon are not fully understood.

Chinese gold-seekers founded the first non-European settler communities in both countries. A 'White Australia' policy then closed the door on that country until the 1970s, when immigrants began arriving from South-east Asia. By the late 1990s, South-east Asians made up almost 4 per cent of the Australian population. This is expected to reach 7 per cent by 2010. In New Zealand, 5.6 per cent hail from the Pacific islands.

Population movements between New Zealand and Australia

New Zealand has a tendency to suffer a loss of skilled people, mostly to Australia. The situation was most extreme in the 1980s, when more people left New Zealand than arrived to settle. New Zealanders account for 1.6 per cent of Australia's population and about the same proportion of Australians live in New Zealand (1.6 per cent in 1998) – an almost 6:1 drift in favour of Australia, when population size is taken into account.

Closing a gender gap

A preponderance of males migrating to New Zealand resulted for many years in a shortage of women. A balance of the sexes was not achieved until 1971. Today, women slightly outnumber men. A 1998 UN survey found that women in NZ enjoyed a greater degree of executive power than women in any other society except Scandinavia.

DISTRIBUTION OF POPULATION

by state in Australia in 1997

	number of inhabitants	% of population	density (per sq mile/ km²)
New South Wales	6 274 400	33.9	20.3 7.8
Victoria	4 605 100	24.8	52.4 20.2
Queensland	3 401 200	18.4	5 2
Western Australia	1 798 100	9.7	1.8 0.7
South Australia	1 479 800	8	3.9 1.5
Tasmania	473 500	2.5	17.9 6.9
Australian Capital Territory	309 800	1.7	340 131
Northern Territory	187 100	1	0.4 0.1
Total	18 532 200	100	6.2 2.4

in New Zealand in 1997

North Island	2 837 400	75.4	64 25
South Island	923 700	24.6	16 6
Total	3 761 100	100	36 14

The politics of immigration

Immigration controls are being tightened in both countries. Current policy is to attract people with professional qualifications or financial means, and to discourage those relying solely upon a family connection, or asylum-seekers. Dissuasive measures include increased filing charges and limiting the appeal process. The Australian figures fell from 85 751 in 1995-6 to 77 300 in 1996-7. In New Zealand, immigration peaked in 1995-6 at 55 000 (principally from Asian countries). Migration has since become a major political issue, and the migrant population declined by over 9000 in the year to February 1999.

RELIGIOUS PRACTICE ▼

Patterns of 19th-century immigration explain to a great extent the slightly differing religious make-up of the two nations. In both, 'Other beliefs' – including those with no religious faith – is a fast-growing segment.

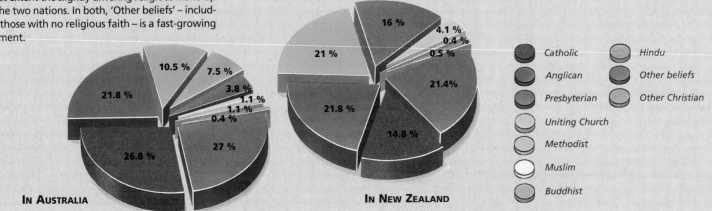

IN AUSTRALIA
21.8 %
10.5 %
7.5 %
3.8 %
1.1 %
1.1 %
0.4 %
26.8 %
27 %

IN NEW ZEALAND
16 %
21 %
4.1 %
0.4 %
0.5 %
21.4 %
21.8 %
14.8 %

Catholic
Anglican
Presbyterian
Uniting Church
Methodist
Muslim
Buddhist
Hindu
Other beliefs
Other Christian

Trade swings from west to east

Australia and New Zealand grew up supplying the factories and larders of Britain, but nowadays they focus their energies on the markets of the Pacific rim.

AGRICULTURAL RESOURCES ▼

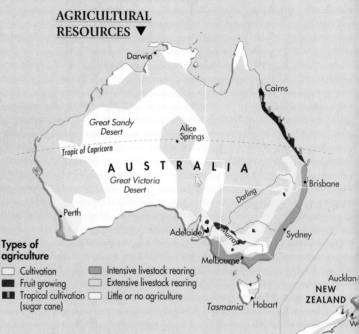

WEALTH UNDER THE GROUND ▼

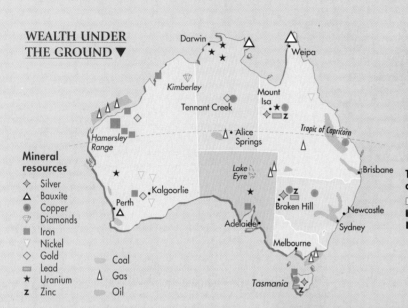

Mineral resources

◇ Silver
△ Bauxite
● Copper
▽ Diamonds
■ Iron
▽ Nickel
◇ Gold
▭ Lead
★ Uranium
z Zinc

▬ Coal
△ Gas
▬ Oil

Types of agriculture

▢ Cultivation
■ Fruit growing
▣ Tropical cultivation (sugar cane)
▨ Intensive livestock rearing
▢ Extensive livestock rearing
▢ Little or no agriculture

The two economies in essence

Despite exploiting its great mineral wealth and making strides in manufacturing, Australia still relies heavily on livestock and agriculture for its prosperity. Nowadays, however, wool accounts for less than 5 per cent of the country's total export income.

The New Zealand economy is based upon stock-rearing and dairy farming, using the latest equipment and technology to maximise productivity. Forestry and fishing are also significant.

TRANSPORT SYSTEM ▼

AIR TRANSPORT
(international airports)
Australia: 12
(202 domestic)
New Zealand: 5

ROAD NETWORK
Australia: 498 850 miles
(802 800 km), of which about one-third is surfaced
New Zealand: 57 350 miles
(92 300 km)

MOTOR TRANSPORT
(number of vehicles)
Australia: 11.7 million
New Zealand: 2.5 million

RAILWAYS
Australia: 21 455 miles
(34 530 km)
New Zealand: 2608 miles
(4197 km)

FOREIGN TRADE

Australia in 1996-7

Imports : A$78 998 million
consumer goods, machinery, fuels, chemicals

Exports : A$78 932 million
ores and minerals, coal, gold, machinery, cereals, wool, meat

Asian countries have become both the major supplier and customer, taking more than 70 per cent of Australian exports, as against 45 per cent in the 1980s.

• world's largest producer of bauxite (aluminium ore), diamonds, lead, zircon
• largest exporter of black coal
• second-ranked exporter of alumina and uranium
• third-ranked exporter of aluminium, gold

New Zealand in 1996-7

Imports: NZ$21 324 million
machinery, textiles, motor vehicles, plastics, iron and steel articles

Exports : NZ$21 033 million
dairy produce, meat, forestry products, fruit and vegetables, fish, wool

Principal trading partner: Australia, with over 20 per cent of overall trade. New Zealand is a leading exporter of foodstuffs.

DISTRIBUTION OF THE WORKFORCE ▼

SERVICE SECTOR
Australia: 74 per cent
New Zealand: 66 per cen[t]

INDUSTRY AND MINING
Australia: 21 per cent
New Zealand: 24 per ce[nt]

AGRICULTURE AND FISHING
Australia: 5 per cent
New Zealand: 10 per ce[nt]

TOURISM

New Zealand (1996): 1 441 838 visitors, of whom 32 per cent were Asians (10.7 per cent Japanese), 28.4 per cent Australians, 12.2 per cent Americans and 9.3 per cent British.
Australia (1996): 4 164 800 visitors, of whom 50 per cent were Asian (20 per cent Japanese), 16 per cent New Zealanders, 11 per cent Americans and 9 per cent British.

Social and political life

Democratic rights and working conditions that are often taken for granted were first introduced in New Zealand and Australia. The two countries also led the world in social services, but tougher economic conditions have brought a reappraisal.

Political systems

Both New Zealand and Australia are parliamentary democracies, each with a governor-general representing the Queen as head of state but with power vested in a prime minister. Australia is a federation of six states and two dependent territories. Its system of government combines British and American elements. The Federal Parliament consists of a Senate and House of Representatives; each state also has its own parliament. The New Zealand system is like that of Britain, but with no upper house, only a House of Representatives.

Health systems

Australia has compulsory national health cover, Medicare, partly funded by a levy on the pre-tax income of all but the lowest paid. It provides free hospital treatment and a partial refund on the cost of visiting private doctors. Private health insurance is available to cover private hospitals. In New Zealand, hospital and medical care are included in a non-contributory package of social security benefits financed from general taxation. State hospitals are free; out-patient treatment is free for the poor.

HEALTH SERVICES ▼
(in 1996)

■ NEW ZEALAND
■ AUSTRALIA

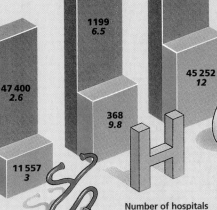

47 400
2.6

11 557
3

Number of doctors
In italics: number per 1000 inhabitants

1199
6.5

368
9.8

Number of hospitals
In italics: number per 100 000 inhabitants

148 300
8

45 252
12

Number of nurses
In italics: number per 1000 inhabitants

80 965
4.4

22 488
6

Number of beds
In italics: number per 1000 inhabitants

EDUCATION IN NEW ZEALAND ▼

Literacy rate: 99 per cent

Primary and secondary schools
712 276 pupils

Technical and further-education colleges
94 201 students

Universities
106 486 students

Unemployment problems

Unemployment rates in Australia and New Zealand rose above 10 per cent in 1993. Thanks to stepped-up economic activity, the numbers declined to stabilise at around 8.5 per cent in Australia (1995) and 6.9 per cent (1996) in New Zealand. The crisis afflicting Asian economies that began in 1997 threatened to have very serious consequences for both countries. In the event, however, they seem to have weathered the storm remarkably well.

Primary and secondary schools
3 171 624 pupils

Technical and further-education colleges
1 844 200 students

Education systems

Schooling is compulsory to the age of 15 in New Zealand and most of Australia (in Tasmania it is compulsory up to 16), and is available free. In New Zealand, 75 per cent stay on longer than the law requires, and a third of school leavers go to university. In Australia, about 30 per cent of pupils attend private schools, most run by the Catholic Church. About 40 per cent of school leavers attend some form of further education or training institution, full-time or part-time.

EDUCATION IN AUSTRALIA ▶

Literacy rate: 99 per cent

Universities
658 827 students

	IN AUSTRALIA		IN NEW ZEALAND
	4.5 %	health	2.9 %
	5.6 %	clothing	4.4 %
	1.4 %	education	4.6 %
	6.6 %	household goods	13.9 %
	13.2 %	leisure	2.2 %
	18.4 %	food	16.6 %
	15.5 %	transport	17.5 %
	22.2 %	housing	19 %
	12.5 %	other	18.9 %

THE HOUSEHOLD BUDGET ▲

IN NEW ZEALAND

IN AUSTRALIA

New Zealand and Australia: two social pioneers

New Zealand, a century ago, was hailed as a 'social laboratory' and the 'birthplace of the 20th century'. After pioneering the eight-hour working day in the mid 19th century, it became in 1893 the first country in the world to give the vote to women. In 1898, it led again with an old-age pension. The high point came in 1938, with a 'cradle-to-grave' Social Security Act, encompassing medical, maternity, unemployment, widow and family benefits as a universal right. Australia was not far behind in regulating working conditions, giving women the vote (1902) and instituting old-age pensions (1909) and family allowances well ahead of Europe and America.

Since 1984, previously sacrosanct ideals of social equality and the welfare state have given way to new economic realities. Many social services have been scaled down, or privatised, and means-testing introduced for students. Income gaps have widened. Australia's social welfare programmes have also been cut back, with unemployment benefits subject to more stringent criteria. A great stain on Australia's record was its denial of citizenship rights to Aborigines until 1967. In making amends, it now makes voting compulsory for everyone over the age of 18.

HOME APPLIANCES ▼

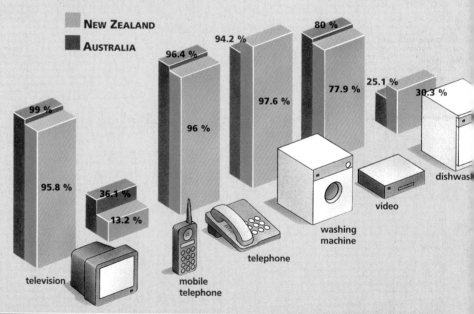

NEW ZEALAND
AUSTRALIA

- television: 99 % / 95.8 %
- mobile telephone: 36.1 % / 13.2 %
- telephone: 96.4 % / 96 %
- washing machine: 94.2 % / 97.6 %
- video: 80 % / 77.9 %
- dishwasher: 25.1 % / 30.3 %

How the indigenous populations fare

Maori and Europeans are integrated in New Zealand, with much intermarriage, but statistics still show Maori to be disadvantaged: the Maori unemployment rate is almost three times the national average (19 per cent against 7.2 per cent). Average life expectancy is eight to nine years less than that of Europeans. In Australia, the contrasts between the European and indigenous peoples are even greater. Life expectancy for Aborigines is 57 for males, 62 for females – nearly 20 years less than the national average. In 1996, unemployment among Aborigines was at 22.7 per cent, against a national average of 9.2 per cent.

DISTANCES BETWEEN MAJOR AUSTRALIAN CITIES BY ROAD *in miles (km)*

The dynamics of distance touch upon everyday life in Australia, a large country with population centres at its extremities. Internal flights are often fully booked, despite there being two national domestic carriers (QANTAS and Ansett Australia) and many regional airlines. The railway system is disjointed and useful mainly in the east. About two-thirds of the road network consists of dirt or gravel tracks. There are about 11 400 miles (18 400 km) of national highways.

	Adelaide	Brisbane	Canberra	Darwin	Melbourne	Perth
Brisbane	1281 (2062)					
Canberra	738 (1188)	792 (1275)				
Darwin	1880 (3025)	2131 (3429)	2465 (3967)			
Melbourne	455 (732)	1068 (1719)	406 (653)	2336 (3759)		
Perth	1642 (2642)	2665 (4289)	2346 (3775)	2502 (4026)	2097 (3375)	
Sydney	877 (1411)	605 (974)	180 (290)	2470 (3975)	546 (879)	2425 (3903)

Index

The page numbers in *italics* denote illustrations. The letter and number references in brackets are the co-ordinates for places in the maps of the atlas, pp.142-7.

Acknowledgments

Abbreviations: t = top, m = middle, b = bottom, l = left, r = right.

Cover: Phone/Tim Acker-Auscape, front; Phone/Darran Leal-Auscape, back.
Pages 4/5: Phone/Parer & Parer-Cook-Auscape; 7: Ciel et Espace; 8l: Phone/J.-P. Ferrero; 8/9: Phone/J.-M. La Roque-Auscape; 10: Phone/J.-P. Ferrero; 11: Phone/Parer & Parer-Cook-Auscape; 12: Phone/Tim Acker-Auscape; 12/13: Phone/J.-P. Ferrero; 14/15: Phone/Wilby & Ciantar-Auscape; 15t: Phone/J.-P. Ferrero; 15b: Phone/Plaza van Roon-Auscape; 16/17: Phone/J.-P. Ferrero; 17t: Phone/Tim Acker-Auscape; 17b: Phone/Parer & Parer-Cook-Auscape; 18/19: Phone/Darran Leal-Auscape; 19: Phone/Darran Leal-Auscape; 20: Phone/Mike Langford-Auscape; 20/21: Phone/Mike Langford-Auscape; 21b: Phone/De Roy-Auscape; 22t: Roger-Viollet; 22/23b: Phone/J.-P. Ferrero; 23t: Giraudon/Bridgeman. Thomas Baines, *The flight of hostile tribespeople near the river Baines.* London, Royal Geographical Society; 23mt: Kharbine-Tapabor; 23mb: Phone/Mike Jensen-Auscape; 23br: Phone/Mike Gillam-Auscape; 24t: Phone/Mike Jensen-Auscape; 24m: Gamma/Alexis Duclos; 24b: Phone/J.-P. Ferrero; 25t: Giraudon/Bridgeman. Samuel Calvert, *Captain Cook takes possession of Australia on behalf of the Engligh crown.* Canberra, National Gallery of Australia; 25m: Phone/Tim Acker-Auscape; 25b: J.-L. Charmet; 26t: Phone/Courtesy of State Library of NSW-Auscape; 26mt: J.-L. Charmet; 26mb: Collection Viollet; 26b: Phone/Geoffrey Lea-Auscape; 27t: Collection Viollet; 27m: Giraudon/Bridgeman. Thomas Baines, *View of Sydney from St Leonard's Road, 1855.* London, Royal Geographical Society; 27bl: J.-L. Charmet; 27br: Phone/J.-M. La Roque-Auscape; 28t: Giraudon/Archives Larousse; 28m: Phone/J.-P. Ferrero; 28b: Kharbine-Tapabor; 29tl: Collection Viollet; 29tr: Phone/J.-M. La Roque-Auscape; 29bl: Phone/Wilby & Ciantar-Auscape; 29br: Giraudon/Archives Larousse; 30l: Collection Viollet; 30r: Giraudon/Bridgeman. Gustavus Ferdinand von Tempsky, *Reconnaissance in Wanganui Bay in New Zealand, 1865.* Canberra, National Gallery of Australia; 31tl: Giraudon/Bridgeman. Marcus King, *Captain Hobson signs the Treaty of Waitangi with the Maori chiefs of New Zealand 1840,* 1938. London, New Zealand High Commission. © ADAGP, Paris, 1998; 31tr: Urba Images/J.-C. Pattacini; 31bl: Explorer/J.M. Francillon; 31br: Phone/John Cancalosi-Auscape; 32/33t: Rapho/Michel Serraillier; 32m: Phone/Darran Leal-Auscape; 32bl: Collection Viollet; 32br: Giraudon/Bridgeman. Gottfried Lindauer, *Tomika Te Muu, chief of the Ngaiterangi tribe of New Zealand, around 1880.* Canberra, National Gallery of Australia; 33tr: Phone/J.-M. La Roque-Auscape; 33mt: Rapho/Gérard Sioën; 33mb: Rapho/Brian Brake; 33b: Phone/J.-M. La Roque-Auscape; 34/35: Phone/J.-P. Ferrero; 36/37: Phone/J.-P. Ferrero; 38/39t: Phone/J.-P. Ferrero; 38/39b: Phone/J.-M. La Roque-Auscape; 39: Phone/G. de Couet-Auscape; 40m: Phone/Darren Jew-Auscape; 41t: Phone/J.-P. Ferrero; 41m: Phone/Becca Saunders-Auscape; 41b: Phone/K. Deacon-Auscape; 42b: Phone/Kathie Atkinson-Auscape; 42m: Phone/M. Grenet-A. Soumillard; 42t: Phone/Parer & Parer-Cook-Auscape; 43m: Phone/Gregory Brett-Auscape; 43t: Phone/Gary Hansen-Auscape; 43b: David Scott-Macnab; 44/45: Phone/J.-M. La Roque-Auscape; 45t: Phone/J.-P. Ferrero; 46/47: Phone/J.-P. Ferrero; 46m: Phone/J.-P. Ferrero; 47t: Phone/Dennis Harding-Auscape; 47b: Phone/Dennis Harding-Auscape; 48: Phone/Mike Langford-Auscape; 49t: Phone/Tom Till/Auscape; 49m: Phone/J.-P. Ferrero; 49b: Phone/J.-P. Ferrero; 50t: Phone/Dennis Harding-Auscape; 50bl: David Nielson; 50/51: Phone/Geoffrey Lea-Auscape; 51t: Phone/Plaza van Roon-Auscape; 51m: Phone/Plaza van Roon-Auscape; 52t: Phone/Dennis Harding-Auscape; 52m: Phone/Dennis Harding-Auscape; 52b: Phone/Geoffrey Lea-Auscape; 53t: Phone/Reg Morrison-Auscape; 53m: Phone/J.-P. Ferrero; 53b: Phone/Mike Jensen-Auscape; 54/55: Phone/J.-P. Ferrero; 56/57t: Phone/J.-P. Ferrero; 56b: Phone/J.-M. La Roque-Auscape; 57t: Phone/J.-P. Ferrero; 57b: Phone/J.-P. Ferrero; 58l: Phone/J.-P. Ferrero; 58b: Phone/J.-P. Ferrero; 59t: Phone/Mike Gillam-Auscape; 59b: Phone/J.-P. Ferrero; 60t: Stock Image/C. Haase; 60b: Phone/De Roy-Auscape; 61t: Rapho/Gérard Sioën; 61m: Phone/Mike Gillam 62t: Phone/Wayne Lawler-Auscape;

62m: Phone/Reg Morrison-Auscape; 62b: Phone/Reg Morrison-Auscape; 63ml: Phone/J.-M. La Roque-Auscape; 63mr: Phone/Parer & Parer-Cook-Auscape; 63b: Phone/J.-P. Ferrero; 64t: Phone/Mike Leonard-Auscape; 64b: Phone/Mike Jensen-Auscape; 65t: Phone/J.-M. La Roque-Auscape; 65m: Phone/Mike Gillam-Auscape; 65b: Phone/Parer & Parer-Cook-Auscape; 65t: Phone/J.-P. Ferrero; 66/67: Bios/Kein-Hubert; 68/69t: Phone/J.-P. Ferrero; 68tl: Phone/J.-P. Ferrero; 68m: Phone/J.-P. Ferrero; 69t: Phone/J.-P. Ferrero; 69m: Phone/J.-P. Ferrero; 70t: Phone/De Roy-Auscape; 70b: Phone/R. Brown-Auscape; 71tl: Phone/J.-P. Ferrero; 71tr: Sunset/Gérard Lacz; 72ml: Phone/Wilby & Ciantar-Auscape; 72mr: Bios/Seitre; 72b: Phone/Parer & Parer-Cook-Auscape; 73tl: Phone/J.-P. Ferrero; 73tr: Phone/J.-P. Ferrero; 73bl: Phone/Jean-Michel Labat; 73br: Phone/J.-P. Ferrero; 74t: Phone/J.-P. Ferrero; 74b: Phone/J.-P. Ferrero; 75tl: Phone/Mike Langford-Auscape; 75tr: Ask Images/Stanislas Fautré; 75mr: Rapho/Gérard Sioën; 75m: Collection Viollet; 76tl: Phone/Mike Gillam-Auscape; 76m: Phone/Plaza van Roon-Auscape; 76b: Phone/Plaza van Roon-Auscape; 76/77: Phone/J.-P. Ferrero; 77tr: Phone/J.-P. Ferrero; 77b: Phone/J.-P. Ferrero; 78/79: Phone/Mike Jensen-Auscape; 80t: Gamma/David Austen; 80l: Phone/Darren Jew-Auscape; 80/81b: Ask Images/Stanislas Fautré; 81t: Gamma/FSP-Simon; 82t: Phone/J.-M. La Roque-Auscape; 82m: Gamma/Saola-Eric Pasquier; 82b: Phone/J.-P. Ferrero; 83t: Rapho/Michel Baret; 83b: Gamma/J. Guichard; 84/85t: Phone/Reg Morrison-Auscape; 84m: Rapho/Gérard Sioën; 84b: Ask Images/Stanislas Fautré; 85tr: Phone/Richard Smyth-Auscape; 85m: Phone/J.-M. La Roque-Auscape; 86mr: Visa/A. Lorgnier; 86ml: Harlingue-Viollet; 86b: Phone/Christophe Courteau; 87t: Phone/Mike Langford-Auscape; 87b: Phone/Matt Jones-Auscape; 88t: Phone/J.-P. Ferrero; 88m: Gamma/J.-M. Loubat; 88b: Phone/Wilby & Ciantar-Auscape; 88/89: Phone/Mike Jensen-Auscape; 89t: Rapho/Michel Baret; 89m: Phone/J. Cancalotti-Auscape; 89b: Phone/D.D. Parker-Auscape; 90tl: Gamma/Spooner-Grosset. Statue of Jackie Howe at Blackall; 90tr: Phone/Mike Langford-Auscape; 90b: With the authorisation of Woolmark; 90/91t: Phone/Colin Monteath-Auscape; 91t: Rapho/Gérard Sioën; 91m: Phone/J.-M. La Roque-Auscape; 92/93: Ask Images/Stanislas Fautré; 92m: Phone/Reg Morrison-Auscape; 92b: Phone/Mike Jensen-Auscape; 93tr: Phone/J.-M. La Roque-Auscape; 93ml: Explorer/J.-P. Ferrero; 93mr: Sunset/Holt studio; 94t: Rapho/Gerster; 94m: Sygma/John van Hasselt; 94b: Phone/J.-P. Ferrero-Auscape; 95t: Phone/Mike Langford-Auscape; 95m: Phone/Tim Acker-Auscape; 95b: Phone/J.-P. Ferrero-Auscape; 96/97: Hoa Qui/Zefa/Smith; 98t: Stock Image/Ken Stimpson; 98m: Rapho/Gérard Sioën; 99tr: Rapho/Gérard Sioën; 99ml: Phone/Christophe Courteau; 99br: Phone/Christophe Courteau; 100t: Rapho/Mireille Kerdiles; 100m: Explorer/J.M. Francillon; 100b: Trip/Eric Smith; 101tr: Ask Images/Stanislas Fautré; 101m: Phone/M. Freeman-Auscape; 101b: Ask Images/Stanislas Fautré; 102tl: Phone/J.-M. La Roque-Auscape; 102tr: Phone/J.-M. La Roque-Auscape; 102b: Phone/J.-M. La Roque-Auscape; 103t: Diaf/Bernard Régent; 103b: Phone/Dennis Harding-Auscape; 104t: Phone/Mike Jensen-Auscape; 104m: Phone/J.-P. Ferrero. National Gallery of Australia. Architect: Colin Madigan; 104b: Phone/C.A. Henley-Auscape; 105ml: Cosmos/R. Ian Lloyd-Westlight; 105mr: Ask Images/Stanislas Fautré; 106/111: Phone/Gregory Brett-Auscape; 106tl: Phone/Auscape; 106m: Ask Images/T. Nectoux; 106bl: Sydney Freelance/Patrick Rivière; 106bm: Gamma/Jamel Balhi; 106br: Hoa Qui/Gellié-Icone; 107t: The Image Bank/Marcel Isy-Schwart; 107ml: Gamma/Claude Poulet; 107mr: Sydney Freelance/Patrick Rivière; 107b: Visa/Dimitri Cleek; 108t: Phone/J.-P. Ferrero; 108tr: Rapho/J. M. Charles; 108mt: Phone/Tim Acker-Auscape; 108mb: The Image Bank/Marcel Isy-Schwart; 108bl: The Image Bank/John W. Banagan; 108bm: Sipa Image/Color Stock; 108br: Phone/J.-M. La Roque-Auscape; 109t: Phone/J.-P. Ferrero; 109mt: Cosmos/R. Ian Lloyd-Westlight; 109mb: Visa/D. Dutay; 109b: Explorer/G. Boutin; 110t: Cosmos/R. Ian Lloyd-Westlight; 110ml: Cosmos/Satilberger-Anzenberger; 110mm: Hoa Qui/T. Perrin; 110mr: Cosmos/

Mattioli-Anzenberger; 110mbr: Gamma/Patrick Rivière-Sydney Freelance; 110bl: Top/Joël Ducange; 110bm: Cosmos/Satilberger-Anzenberger; 110br: Rapho/Michel Baret; 111tl: Cosmos/P. Quirk-Wildlight; 111tr: Cosmos/Sophie Scaglia; 111m: The Image Bank/John W. Banagan; 111bl: Stock Image/D. Hirsch; 111br: Phone/Rob Walls-Auscape; 112t: Phone/Matt Jones-Auscape; 112m: Rapho/Gérard Sioën; 112b: Sygma/Lionel Cixous; 113t: Phone/Mike Gillam-Auscape; 113m: Gamma/Van der Hilst; 113b: Phone/Mike Jensen-Auscape; 114/115: Vandystadt/J. McDonald-Allsport; 116t: Gamma/Wayne L. Miles-Liaison; 116m: Rapho/Gérard Sioën; 116b: Gamma/S. Grosset-Spooner; 117t: Phone/Mike Gillam; 117mr: Sipa Press/V. Rivière; 117bl: Phone/J.-M. La Roque-Auscape; 117br: Explorer/J.-P. Ferrero; 118t: Ask Images/Stanislas Fautré; 118m: Phone/J.-P. Ferrero; 118bl: Phone/Mike Jensen-Auscape; 118br: Phone/J.-M. La Roque-Auscape; 119t: Ask Images/Stanislas Fautré; 119m: Gamma/David Austen; 119b: Ask Images/Stanislas Fautré; 120t: Gamma/Pozarik-Liaison; 120bl: KR Images presse/Régis Martin; 120br: Gamma/Sydney Freelance; 121t: Gamma/Frank Spooner; 121bl: Sygma/R. Reuter; 121br: Phone/J.-M. La Roque-Auscape; 122t: Phone/J.-P. Ferrero; 122m: Sygma/Rick Smolan; 122b: Phone/Mike Leonard-Auscape; 123t: Explorer/J.-P. Ferrero; 123m: Sygma/J. Guichard; 123b: Rapho/Gérard Sioën; 124/125t: Stock Image; 124t: Vandystadt/Adrien Murrell-Allsport; 124m: Popperfoto; 124b: Vandystadt/B. Martin-Allsport; 125t: Vandystadt/M. Thomson-Allsport; 125m: Vandystadt/S. Munday-Allsport; 125b: Vandystadt/D. Rogers-Allsport; 126t: Phone/J.-M. La Roque-Auscape; 126b: Explorer/J.-P. Ferrero; 127t: Phone/J.-M. La Roque-Auscape; 127bl: Gamma/Wayne Miles-Liaison; 127br: Stock Image/D. Hirsch; 128t: Phone/J.-P. Ferrero; 128bl: Hoa Qui/Martel-Icone; 128/129b: Phone/J.-M. La Roque-Auscape; 129h: Diaf/Giovanni Simeone; 129m: Phone/J.-M. La Roque-Auscape; 129b: Phone/Brett Gregory-Auscape; 130t: Phone/J.-M. La Roque-Auscape; 130mt: Phone/Wilby & Ciantar-Auscape; 130mb: Phone/J.-M. La Roque-Auscape, © Courtesy of Red Ochre Grill, Cairns; 130b: Phone/Mike Leonard-Auscape; 131t: Sipa Press/Acikalin-Live Action; 131m: Phone/C.A. Henley-Auscape; 131b: AP-Boomerang; 132/133: Phone/J.-P. Ferrero; 134t: Polygram film entertainment/Pictorial Press; 134ml: Coll. Prod/DB/Photo X, D.R.; 134b: Coll. Prod/DB. *Mad Max, Beyond Thunderdome,* film by George Miller, 1985; 135tl: Évelyne Brochard/© courtesy of HarperCollins Publishers/Avon Books, Unwin Paperbacks, Vintage, Fremantle Arts Centre Press; 135ml: Gamma/Pozanik-Liaison; 135mr: Gamma/Coltier-Freelance; 135bl: Gamma/Patrick Rivière; 135br: Gamma/ Flavia Perrone; 136tl: Gamma/Romaniello-Olympia; 136tr: Harlingue-Viollet; 136bl: Gamma; 136br: Sygma/Keystone; 137t: Phone/J.-M. La Roque-Auscape; 137ml: courtesy of Indigenous Australia P/L; 137mr: Vandystadt/Joe Mann-Allsport; 137b: Gamma/Noël Quidu; 138t: Explorer/J.-P. Ferrero; 138ml: Phone/Christophe Courteau; 138mr: Ask Images/Stanislas Fautré; 138b: Rapho/Gérard Sioën; 139t: Phone/Mike Jensen-Auscape; 139m: Phone/Mike Jensen-Auscape; 139b: Gamma/Gilles Martin; 140-141: Phone/J.-P. Ferrero; 148l: Phone/J.-P. Ferrero; 148r: Rapho/Gérard Sioën.

Printing and binding: Printer Industria Gráfica S.A., Barcelona
Colour separations: Station Graphique, Ivry-sur-Seine
Paper: Perigord-Condat, France

617-003-1